To understand Jewish law, one needs to know the "legal system" of Rome ...

To really grasp the legal ways of epistles, one needs to know the laws of the day. esp Roman law

Slaves, Citizens, Sons

on Roman slaves
JBL Fall '98
481-495 ; sex —

Be sure to see
Supp. index
for reference
p 285 f

Jewish article
on slave
parneia.

Be sure to see JBL '99 Spring
97 + on vice of slave trade! Kidnapping
in ancient world

also 104 on "educated slave"

Slaves, Citizens, Sons

Legal Metaphors in the Epistles

Francis Lyall

Academie
Books Grand Rapids, Michigan
Zondervan Publishing House

ACADEMIE BOOKS is an imprint of Zondervan Publishing House,
1415 Lake Drive, S.E., Grand Rapids, Michigan 49506.

Library of Congress Cataloging in Publication Data

Lyall, Francis.
  Slaves, citizens, sons.

  Bibliography: p.
  Includes indexes.
  1. Law (Theology)—Biblical teaching. 2. Bible. N.T.
Epistles—Criticism, interpretation, etc. I. Title.
BS2545.L34L92   1984   227'.064   83-21773
ISBN 0-310-45191-4

Edited by Ed van der Maas
Designed by Louise Bauer

Printed in the United States of America

84 85 86 87 88 89   9 8 7 6 5 4 3 2 1

For
Fiona Elizabeth,
Gillian Ann,
and
Francis James

Contents

Appendices

Preface

In autumn 1966, I was asked to give a Bible study at my home church, Gilcomston South Church of Scotland, Aberdeen, Scotland. At the time I was preparing some lectures on the Roman law of persons, and therefore chose to relate the principles of the Roman law of adoption to some passages from Paul. Reading other discussions of these passages thereafter led me to wonder whether the possible Roman content of some of the legal metaphors of the Epistles had been adequately explored. These pages are the result—not that they are adequate, but I hope they will lead others to further investigation.

My own discipline is modern public law. I am a scholar in neither Roman law nor theology and am grateful to those who have helped me in both fields. In that connection, and partially as a result, I have not sought to fully cite the numerous theological treatments of the passages discussed. I have read a great many of these, but most are in a technical sense irrelevant to this book, because they do not take adequate account of the underlying legal ideas.

Be that as it may, I am conscious that I am out of my field. In any discipline the minefields are extensive, and I dare say that I have trodden on a few mines and trampled over several presuppositions and sensibilities. In addition, I have not always sought to be dispassionate, as I believe that the attempt to do so has made much academic theology sterile and useless. My own theological perspective might be summed up as that of C. S. Lewis's *Mere Christianity* with a Calvinistic tinge. Put another way, it is traditional orthodoxy with some emphasis on the sovereignty of God.

My purpose has been to look at the evidence, so far as I know it, that suggests further exploration of the Roman background of some of the legal language of the Epistles, going into more detail with regard to certain words and concepts. (The concept of redemption I have referred to Jewish law.) It follows that I have not been concerned with producing a balanced exposition of the Christian faith, since the legal metaphors in the Bible do not give a rounded picture per se; there are many other works available for that (I recommend *Mere Christianity* and the Bible itself). My hope is that this exploration will both intrigue and help those who have puzzled over some of the passages in the Epistles and want to get further into their meaning.

The enterprise is not wholly novel. Regrettably, the work of my predecessors (see note 10 to chapter 1) seems to have had less effect than it probably should. The reason would appear to be the unfortunate division of disciplines that dogs all inquiry. Lawyers and theologians do not often mix, and different presuppositions and methodologies clearly exist in their disciplines, which can affect the conclusions they draw from the same material, to say nothing of their willingness even to consider such material. Professor Derrett discusses the same point in the introduction to his *Law in the New Testament*.

There are many I would like to thank for their help and encouragement. They include my minister, the Reverend W. Still, for much patient help, going well beyond this inquiry; Professor P. G. Stein, now of Cambridge, for early encouragement to a butterfly mind; and Professors J.D.M. Derrett and F. F. Bruce for their kind interest. Professors Morton B. Enslin, Matthew Black, and F. F. Bruce, the editors respectively of the *Journal of Biblical Literature, New Testament Studies,* and the *Evangelical Quarterly,* gave a different form of encouragement by publishing articles using material that now appears in chapters 4, 2, and 3 respectively.* Some of the material of chapters 2 and 5 and Appendix 2 was used in the "Tyndale New Testament Lecture, 1980,"† and the argument of Appendix 1 has also appeared in print in another connection.‡ I am grateful for the permissions to use these various materials.

My friend Stuart Garver, the editor of *Christian Heritage,* then the journal of Christ's Mission, Hackensack, New Jersey, provided a significant impetus by publishing from December 1975 to June 1976 a series of articles drawing on the ideas of chapters 2-9. I am grateful to him for permission to use that material. Stuart also put me in touch with B. Duncan Boss, without whom I might not have persevered. I would thank both these gentlemen for their invaluable help.

Domestically, I would thank my friends at Gilcomston for listening to, and helping amend, trial runs at different concepts; Professor G. D. MacCormack of the Department of Jurisprudence of the University of Aberdeen; Mr. D. J. Cusine, then of the Department of Private Law; Dr. A.I.L. Campbell and Mrs. A. L. Seager

Journal of Biblical Literature 85 (1969):458-66; *New Testament Studies* 17 (1970):73-79; *Evangelical Quarterly* 48 (1976):3-14.

†*Tyndale Bulletin* 32 (1981):81-95.

‡"Of Metaphors and Analogies: Legal Language and Covenant Theology," *Scottish Journal of Theology* 32 (1979):1-17.

of the Department of Public Law; and my wife, Heather, for comments (mostly useful) on drafts. I would also like to thank an anonymous reader in the United Kingdom, Dr. Stanley N. Gundry of Zondervan Publishing House, and Ed M. van der Maas for their help. The remaining errors, obscurities, and infelicities are all my own. And, very importantly, there has been a succession of typists: Miss E. Carr, Mrs. L. Sutherland (nee Kavanagh), Miss G. Shepherd, Mrs. P. Simpson, Miss B. Gibb, Mrs. F. Chaplain, Mrs. M. Mercer, and Miss A. Diack, and Miss M. Tough to whom I am also grateful.

Finally, I would ask those who discern these things that they would "remember Baruch" (Jer. 45).

Department of Public Law   F. Lyall
University of Aberdeen
Scotland

Abbreviations

JB	Jerusalem Bible
KJV	King James Version
mg.	margin
NASB	New American Standard Bible
NIV	New International Version
RSV	Revised Standard Version

Ball	William E. B. Ball, *St. Paul and the Roman Law* (Edinburgh: T. & T. Clark, 1901) (an expanded version of his article of the same title in *Contemporary Review* 60 [1891]:278-92).
Baron	Salo W. Baron, *A Social and Religious History of the Jews*, 2nd ed., 14 vols. (New York and London: Columbia University Press, 1962); vol. 1, *To the Beginning of the Christian Era*; vol. 2, *Christian Era: The First Five Centuries*.
Beauchet	Ludovic Beauchet, *Histoire du Droit Privé de la République Athénienne*, 3 books in 4 vols. (Paris, 1897; reprint, Amsterdam: Editions Rodopi, 1969).
Bruce, *History*	Frederick F. Bruce, *New Testament History* (New York: Doubleday, 1971) (the British edition [London: Nelson, 1969] is differently paged).
Buckland, *Slavery*	William W. Buckland, *The Roman Law of Slavery* (Cambridge: Cambridge University Press, 1908, 1970).
Buckland, *Textbook*	William W. Buckland, *A Textbook of Roman Law, Augustus to Justinian*, ed. Peter G. Stein, 4th ed. (Cambridge: Cambridge University Press, 1970) (retains pagination of 3rd ed., 1963, and 2nd ed., 1932).
Cohen	Boaz Cohen, *Jewish and Roman Law: A Comparative Study*, 2 vols. (New York: Jewish Theological Seminary of America, 1966).

Cohn   Menachem Cohn, ed., *The Principles of Jewish Law* (Jerusalem: Keter Publishing Co. Jerusalem, Ltd., 1975) (articles on legal topics from the *Encyclopedia Judaica*, 1971).

Crook   John A. Crook, *Law and Life of Rome* (London: Thames and Hudson, 1967).

Davies   William D. Davies, *Paul and Rabbinic Judaism: Some Rabbinic Elements in Pauline Theology*, 3rd ed. (London: S.P.C.K., 1970).

Derrett   John D.M. Derrett, *Law in the New Testament* (London: Darton, Longman and Todd, 1970).

De Vaux   Roland De Vaux, *Ancient Israel: Its Life and Institutions*, trans. John McHugh (London: Darton, Longman and Todd, 1961).

Falk, *Hebrew Law*   Ze'ev W. Falk, *Hebrew Law in Biblical Times: An Introduction* (Jerusalem: Wahrmann Books, 1964).

Falk, *Jewish Law*   Ze'ev W. Falk, *Introduction to Jewish Law of the Second Commonwealth*, 2 vols. (Leiden: E.J. Brill, 1972, 1978).

Finley, *Slavery*   Moses I. Finley, ed., *Slavery in Classical Antiquity* (Cambridge: W. Heffer and Sons, 1960).

Fontes   S. Riccobono, J. Baviera, C. Ferrini, J. Furlani, and V. Arangio-Ruiz, eds., *Fontes Iuris Romani AnteJustiniani*, 2nd ed., 3 vols. (Florence: Barbera, 1968).

Gaius, *Institutes*   Gaius, *Institutes*. In Fontes, 2:3-228 (Latin text only). *The Institutes of Gaius*, ed. and trans. Francis de Zulueta, 2 vols. (Oxford: Clarendon Press, 1946, 1953). *The Institutes of Gaius and Rules of Ulpian*, ed. James Muirhead (Edinburgh: T. & T. Clark, 1880). *The Civil Law*, trans. Samuel P. Scott, 14 vols. (Cincinnati: The Central Trust Co., 1932) 1:81-219.

    Citation of Gaius is by book and paragraph. Thus, Gaius, *Institutes* 1.21 is book 1, paragraph 21.

Harrison   Alick R.W. Harrison, *The Law of Athens*, 2 vols. (Oxford: Clarendon Press, 1968, 1971); vol. 1, *The Family and Property*; vol. 2, *Procedure*.

Herzog	Issac H. Herzog, *The Main Institutions of Jewish Law*, 2nd ed., 2 vols. (London and New York: Soncino Press, 1967); vol. 1, *The Law of Property*; vol. 2, *The Law of Obligations*.
Hester	James D. Hester, *Paul's Concept of Inheritance: A Contribution to the Understanding of Heilsgeschichte*, Scottish Journal of Theology, Occasional Paper no. 14 (Edinburgh: Oliver and Boyd, 1968).
Horowitz	George Horowitz, *The Spirit of Jewish Law* (New York: Central Book Co., 1953, 1963).
JBL	*Journal of Biblical Literature.*
Jolowicz, Introduction	Herbert F. Jolowicz, *Historical Introduction to the Study of Roman Law*, 2nd ed. (Cambridge: Cambridge University Press, 1952).
Jolowicz, Introduction 3	Herbert F. Jolowicz, *Historical Introduction to the Study of Roman Law*, ed. Barry Nicholas, 3rd ed. (Cambridge: Cambridge University Press, 1972).
Jones, Cities	Arnold H. M. Jones, *Cities of the Eastern Roman Provinces*, 2nd ed., revised by Michael Avi-Yonah et al. (Oxford: Clarendon Press, 1971).
Jones, Greek City,	Arnold H. M. Jones, *The Greek City from Alexander to Justinian* (Oxford: Clarendon Press, 1940).
Jones, Greek Law,	John W. Jones, *The Law and Legal Theory of the Greeks: An Introduction* (Oxford: Clarendon Press, 1956).
JRS	*Journal of Roman Studies.*
Juster	Jean Juster, *Les Juifs dans L'Empire Roman: Leur Condition Juridique, Économique et Sociale*, 2 vols. (Paris: Librairie Paul Geunther, 1914).
Lacey	Walter K. Lacey, *The Family in Classical Greece* (London: Thames and Hudson, 1968).
Leggett	Donald A. Leggett, *The Levirate and Goel Institution in the Old Testament, with Special Attention to the Book of Ruth* (Cherry Hill, New Jersey: Mack Publishing Company, 1974).

McDowell   Douglas M. McDowell, *The Law in Classical Athens* (London: Thames and Hudson; Ithaca, New York: Cornell University Press, 1978).

Magie   David Magie, *Roman Rule in Asia Minor to the End of the Third Century After Christ* (Princeton: Princeton University Press, 1950).

Millar   Fergus Millar, *The Emperor in the Roman World, (31 B.C.—A.D. 337)* (London: Duckworth, 1977).

Mishnah   *The Mishnah*, trans. Herbert Danby (Oxford: Clarendon Press, 1933). Citation is by name of tractate and number of paragraph and subdivision.

Muntz   William J. S. Muntz, *Rome, St. Paul and the Early Church* (London: John Murray, 1913).

Ramsay,   William M. Ramsay, *The Church in the Roman
  Church   Empire before A.D. 170*, 5th ed. (London: Hodder and Stoughton, 1897).

Ramsay,   William M. Ramsay, *The Cities of St. Paul: Their
  Cities   Influence on His Life and Thought* (London: Hodder and Stoughton, 1907; reprint, Grand Rapids, Michigan: Baker Book House, 1960).

Ramsay,   William M. Ramsay, *A Historical Commentary
  Commentary   on St. Paul's Epistle to the Galatians* (London: Hodder and Stoughton, 1899; reprint, Grand Rapids, Michigan: Baker Book House, 1965).

Ramsay,   William M. Ramsay, *The Letters to the Seven
  Letters   Churches of Asia* (London: Hodder and Stoughton, 1904; reprint, Grand Rapids, Michigan: Baker Book House, 1963).

Ramsay,   William M. Ramsay, *St. Paul the Traveller and
  St. Paul   the Roman Citizen* (London: Hodder and Stoughton, 1897; reprint, Grand Rapids, Michigan: Baker Book House, 1960).

Ramsay,   William M. Ramsay, *The Teaching of Paul in
  Teaching   Terms of the Present Day*, 2nd ed. (London: Hodder and Stoughton, 1914).

RIDA   *Revue internationale des droits de l'antiquité.*

Sanders   Ed. Parrish Sanders, *Paul and Palestinian Ju-*

	daism: a Comparison of Patterns of Religion (Philadelphia: Fortress Press; London: S.C.M. Press, 1977).
Schulz, Roman Law	Fritz Schulz, Classical Roman Law (Oxford: Clarendon Press, 1951).
Schulz, History	Fritz Schulz, History of Roman Legal Science (Oxford: Clarendon Press, 1946; reprint ed. with addenda, 1953, 1963).
Sherwin-White, Citizenship	Adrian N. Sherwin-White, The Roman Citizenship, 2nd ed. (Oxford: Clarendon Press, 1973).
Sherwin-White, Society	Adrian N. Sherwin-White, Roman Society and Roman Law in the New Testament (Oxford: Clarendon Press, 1963).
Schürer	Emil Schürer, The History of the Jewish People in the Age of Jesus Christ, 175 B.C.-A.D. 135, rev. and ed. Geza Vermes and Fergus Millar, 2 vols. to date (Edinburgh: T. & T. Clark, 1973, 1979).
Smallwood	E. Mary Smallwood, The Jews Under Roman Rule, Studies in Judaism in Late Antiquity, vol. 20 (Leiden: E. J. Brill, 1976).
Thomas	Joseph A.C. Thomas, Textbook of Roman Law (Amsterdam, New York, Oxford: North-Holland Publishing Company, 1973).
Winter	Paul Winter, On the Trial of Jesus, 2nd ed., rev.; ed T. A. Burkill and Geza Vermes (Berlin, New York: Walter de Gruyter, 1974).

1

Introduction

A CHARACTERISTIC OF THE GREAT COMMUNICATOR is the ability to present material in such a way that it is easily grasped by the audience. Often this is done through figures of speech, drawing upon familiar facts and circumstances, shared experiences, and the like. Most of us can do it after a fashion, but by the use of a progression of images the skillful practitioner can transmit a vast quantity of information and feeling by a few well-chosen words. It is akin to the use of jargon in any profession, where particular words carry a wealth of meaning among professionals.

In the New Testament Epistles such skill is at work. Metaphors and analogies abound, to say nothing of more esoteric figures of speech. Some of them are reasonably clear: "Let us run with perseverance the race that is set before us" with its comment about stripping down to essentials (Heb. 12:1), or, "all [run], but only one receives the prize" (1 Cor. 9:24). There is the imagery of the leaven and the dough (1 Cor. 5:6–8), of grafted branches (Rom. 11:16–24), and of planting and watering (1 Cor. 3:6–9), followed immediately by that of buildings and foundations (1 Cor. 3:9–12). These and many others carry their message with telling simplicity and are as readily understood now as in the day they were written.[1]

In other instances there may be more difficulty. Times

have changed, and the world in which we live no longer contains the facts on which some figures of speech draw. An example is the "armor" passage in Ephesians: "The whole armor of God . . . breastplate . . . shield . . . helmet . . . sword" (Eph. 6:13–17). The passage still communicates, but now in a romantic way, and its impact is thereby lessened. It is pleasing to think of oneself as a knight, with all the overtones of chivalry. The reality of which Paul spoke was different. Battle by sword in armor was nasty. The "flaming darts of the evil one" that are to be dealt with by the shield of faith (Eph. 6:16) are, in modern terms, attacks by napalm. We have weakened our appreciation of what Paul is saying and that to our detriment.

I am a long way, however, from arguing for the rewriting or updating of the Epistles. All I want to show by the example of the "armor" passage is first, that it is important properly to understand the content of a figure of speech in order that it may fully do its work, and second, that there are times when we do not notice the diminution of the force of a figure of speech because we do not appreciate that our perception is different from that of the writer.

Some of the figures of speech in the Epistles draw their meaning from the rules and terms of law. We read of "slaves of sin" and "slaves of God," of "freedmen," of "strangers and foreigners," of "aliens" and "citizens of heaven," of "adoption," and of being a "son" with its attendant consequences of "inheritance," of being "heirs of God" and "joint heirs with Christ." We read of "trust" and of "faithfulness," of "partners" and of the "earnest," and so on. These and others are technical legal expressions, shorthand ways in which much information is communicated between lawyers. In their use as figures of speech in the Epistles they can also transmit a great deal to us.

But there is a problem. If we are not simply to gloss over these expressions, we have to understand to some extent what they meant within the society of New Testament times. Figures of speech only help communication when the person using the figure and the person reading or hearing the words give the words the same content. It is not too much to say that if they do not, they might as well be speaking two different languages.[2] There are, of course, gradations from total incomprehension to full understanding, and it is clear that many people get some sort of meaning out of some of the legal metaphors in the Epistles, even though a better understanding of the law involved would communicate more. Adoption is a good example. Now that most legal systems permit adoption, many can to some extent understand Paul's five uses of the term. But, as shown in chapter 4, the Roman notion meant more than we today are accustomed to.

In the case of legal notions, one has to understand law if one is to get the point of their use in figures of speech. This is not to say that it is necessary to have legal training. It is, however, necessary to overcome the various hindrances the modern attitude toward law can raise. Law is not arcane and mysterious. It is a fairly consistent body of rules regulating society, with a mechanism to enforce its application. In New Testament times, when societies were smaller and the whole of a community took an interest in what was going on, there was a greater appreciation of the fewer and simpler rules such societies needed. This is why many Greek and Roman plays turn on legal points, points the audience would be familiar with. And for the Jews, of course, instruction in the law was part of elementary education. The explanation of the very existence of the legal analogies and metaphors in the Epistles is that the writers could be confident that they conveyed a message to their recipients. People did know sufficient law to decode the meaning of the imagery.[3]

But what meaning? Legal terms have meaning within legal systems, and the same word may have a meaning in one system different from its meaning in another. Take the word "moot." In both the U.K. and the U.S., something that is "moot" is unsettled and up for discussion, but the U.S. usage carries with it overtones that the matter is hypothetical and often unimportant or insignificant. In legal terms, if a U.S. court holds a case moot it will strike the case from its roll, since there is no matter disclosed in it requiring judicial decision. In the U.K., a moot case is simply one that is undecided—if it is brought before a court it will be decided. Thus, if I were to say in the following pages that some point or other is "moot," at least some readers would get entirely the wrong message—a difficulty that is compounded by the fact that the problem is quite concealed.

Then again, even where there are similarities there may also be significant differences between the meanings given to the same word in different legal systems. Both Greek and Roman law had a notion of Adoption, but as mentioned above, chapter 4 shows that the contents of these notions were dissimilar. For a writer to communicate by using the language of adoption, he and his audience must refer the notion to its meaning in the same legal system.

If then for these reasons we have to select a legal system to give meaning to the legal figures of speech in the Epistles, how shall we make a choice? Further difficulties face us.[4] The evidence of Jewish law is rather mixed; our knowledge of it is largely dependent upon the Mishnah, compiled in Babylon around A.D. 200 by Pharisees, whose approach was idealistic and who largely ignored Sadducean opinion. The Sadducees were in the ascendancy in New Testament times until the destruction of Jerusalem in A.D. 70 brought about their eclipse. It is likely that Jewish law in New Testament times reflected their opinions, but we have very little evidence of their views or of the actual law of the time.

The evidence as to Greek law is equally problematic, but for different reasons. Despite the neatness of the phrase, there was no such thing as Greek law, but only the laws of the separate Greek city-states of the eastern Mediterranean. While there were similarities among them, each state had its own laws, and the result can be classified only generically as Greek law. We do not know completely the law of any of these states, and the evidence for those we know best is patchy, extending over many centuries.

By contrast, Roman law is well evidenced to a degree that allows us to be certain as to its broad lines and most of its fine detail in New Testament times. Of itself that is not a sufficient argument for referring the legal metaphors in the Epistles to Roman law, but there are other matters to be considered. The most important of these is that, as will be shown in the succeeding chapters, it is often the Roman notion that provides the fullest meaning for a legal metaphor or analogy. That, of course, is a circular argument, but sometimes the notion used has meaning only in Roman law.[5] In that case the argument for a Roman referent is strong.

The situation is made even more complicated by the three legal systems existing, not only simultaneously, but intermixedly.[6] In New Testament times, the Roman Empire was an example of what scholars call "legal pluralism." The individual was subject to the law of his home city-state or of his nationality. Arrangements were sometimes made for substantial minorities in a given city to be given justice according to that of their own citizenship, but of course, such arrangements worked erratically. If a person did not have access to his "own" justice, then he had to make do with the local brand, which might well not be too favorably inclined to aliens. (It was always best to possess Roman citizenship, because Rome was the dominant power.)

In short, it is wrong to think of the Roman Empire as a state throughout which a single law applied. It was a legal conglomeration, for the Romans did not necessarily apply their law in, or displace the indigenous legal systems of, the territories they took over during their expansion. Outside Italy, Roman law was applied only in the Roman colony cities, and in other places only when the governor's court went on circuit. Then Romans could appeal for justice if they felt that they had not received justice in some local tribunal (or even if they felt they could get a more favorable decision irrespective of justice).

Mention of the colonies brings us to another important matter: the churches that were the first recipients of the Epistles.[7] The church in Rome was in the capital of the empire, where Roman law held sway. The Epistle to the Romans contains blocks of continuous legal metaphor, particularly in chapter 6. Corinth, Phillipi, and the cities of the churches of Galatia were all Roman colony cities where Roman law was the local law. Thessalonica was a free city, but it was the seat of the Roman governor. Ephesus also was not a colony, but it was the major city of Asia (although the governor resided at Pergamum), and it was the terminus of the major trade route from the east. As such Roman law was well known there. In each of these cases, therefore, the law of the locality of the church was Roman law.

Another strand of evidence is the composition of these various churches. Again and again we read of some upper-class persons being involved in the churches, persons whom Paul knew. Such persons would either be of Roman citizenship and subject to her laws, or (and there is clear evidence for such in secular records), being non-Roman, they would aspire to her citizenship.

In short, it would seem that in most of the churches the audience would be familiar with Roman law and would interpret the legal images in the Epistles by that law. The writers could rely on that common knowledge.

But did the writers of the epistles know Roman Law? We must remember that Paul, the writer of most of the Epistles that have come down to us, was himself a Roman citizen.[8] He made good use of that citizenship on various occasions—at Philippi (Acts 16:16–40), in the temple incident (Acts 22), and in the appeal to Rome (Acts 25).[9] He was also a trained lawyer. True, he was a lawyer trained in Jewish law, but that does not rule out a Roman reference—indeed, rather the contrary. Once one is trained in one legal system, getting to know another is not very difficult. In Paul's case there were twin stimuli at work. First, being a Roman citizen, Roman law was his "national" law. Second, Roman law was the law of the empire, the ruling law of the Gentiles to whom he was the commissioned apostle. He would need to know this law for his travels. He would also swiftly realize that that law provided a ready stock of images in which to present the gospel. He was to speak and write to Jews and Greeks, to Romans and Scythians, to all the various nationalities within a very heterogenous empire. Roman law was one of the few common and binding elements of that empire. And we find that he used many legal figures of speech that make best sense in the light of Roman law. He must have consciously intended that result; the skill with which these images are deployed is not otherwise explicable. The brilliant use he makes of legal images in his epistle to the Roman church, a church he had not visited and the one church above all where Roman law was the local law, seems to me to clinch the argument.

Accordingly, most of the discussion in the following chapters refers each set of images to Roman law for its content. In the case of redemption, however, the explanation is given mostly in terms of Jewish law for the reasons set out in chapter 9; there are special factors at work that make Jewish law the best place to look for a full meaning for the various concepts of redemption. Also on other occasions Greek and Jewish laws may provide some light; where this is the case I have included such information.

As indicated, the reasons why we should turn to Roman law to explain words and phrases used by Jewish writers are bound up with the very nature and usefulness of figures of speech, with the social and legal context in which the infant church was placed, and in the case of Paul, with his own legal status and training. These different elements are discussed at greater length in appendices 1–5 for those who would require a more detailed argument.

Finally I would acknowledge that to use Roman law to explore the legal imagery in the Epistles is not an original step. I have predecessors.[10] But their discussions seem not to have been taken up when they were published, and more recent explorations seem to be a separate development.[11] It is a pity that the suggestions of our forebears were not given more attention, for I have found the appreciation of these facets of the Epistles and the truths they present enriching (even if, on occasion, challenging and painful).

2

The Slave and the Freedman

IN NEW TESTAMENT TIMES slavery was widespread. Indeed, the social structure and whole economy of the Roman Empire were dependent upon the pool of slave labor, skilled and unskilled.[1] Work done by slaves ranged the gamut of occupations from factory work and mining to medicine, from farming to business management, from cooking to teaching. Some slaves even acted as secretaries to the administrators of the empire, rising to important positions of high responsibility before being freed to become useful additions to the higher echelons of the citizenry. One New Testament character who had such a career was Felix the procurator of Judea, who was a freedman of the emperor Claudius (Acts 23:24—24:27). His success, however, was exceptional. The bulk of the slave population was occupied in the more menial tasks, laboring in mines or factories or in the day-to-day running of the households, estates, and businesses of their owners. To put it crudely, but not inaccurately, slaves were the machines of their day.[2]

The economic and social dependence of the Roman Empire upon the institution of slavery at the time of the Epistles was a relatively recent development. Although the specific rules of law relating to slavery were well developed before then, it was the more rapid growth of the Roman Empire that began with the conquest of Gaul that

27

produced dependence. The increase in the slave-labor force was both an effect and a cause of the expansion of the empire, as it enabled men to devote themselves more to matters of state and public service rather than to running their own estates and businesses. The conquest of successive territories and the subjugation of their peoples brought into the slave market larger numbers than before, partially as a matter of policy. Also, the sale as slaves of prisoners of war and of captured populations was one of the ways in which the army was financed. More personal considerations, such as captives as booty or reward for the troops and as glorifying the conqueror, also played their part. Lastly, once the slave market had established itself, slave traders emerged, acquiring their goods in a variety of ways.

It is against this background that we must consider the use of the idea of slavery and its allied concepts in the New Testament. We are not here concerned with "Christian" attitudes toward slavery. The facts are that the institution of slavery existed; that its legal incidents had been thoroughly worked out, particularly in Roman law, and were well known to all; and that it is evident from the Epistles that it was a fruitful source of metaphors for the New Testament writers. Even today the word "slave" is not without meaning when we read it in the Epistles, but the usual meaning we give to the word is significantly weaker than the reality known to the writers. Their concept, particularly if referred to Roman law, is richer than ours. The relationship of a slave to his owner, and of a freed slave to his former owner (his patron), had aspects and overtones, that are not present to our minds today. For us the concept of the slave has been attenuated by nonexistence in our day-to-day world. Most think rather romantically of slavery as they read about it in the Epistles. There is a certain quaint charm in being "a slave of Christ" because we are accustomed to speak of ourselves as "slaves" only metaphorically. The reality was rather different.

Of course, in New Testament times it was possible to be a slave under Greek law, Jewish law, or Roman law,

apart from any local laws the Romans might have left un-
touched. Indeed, legal systems other than the Roman do
present possible sources for the metaphor of slavery in the
Epistles, and in broad outline the different systems would
provide the same interpretation of the language involved.
However, I intend to discuss the language of slavery from
the point of view of Roman law, not only because it provides a richer meaning, but particularly because there is
one passage, 1 Corinthians 7:21–22, where Paul contrasts
slave status and freed status in a way that is meaningful
only in Roman law. We will go into the details of this
verse later, when dealing with termination of slavery, but
for me it provides adequate grounds to interpret other uses
of slavery also in the Roman context. In any event, the
general similarity of the Roman provisions with those of
the other legal systems is such as to justify this way of
proceeding.

Entry into Slavery

A person could enter into slavery in three principal
ways, examples of which can be found in the New Testament. These were (1) by capture, (2) by birth to a slave
mother, and (3) by self-sale or submission to slavery.

1. Capture

Many persons became slaves through capture in war.[3]
Thus Peter points out that "whatever overcomes a man, to
that he is enslaved" (2 Peter 2:19), but although Paul makes
extensive use of the other metaphors of slavery, he does
not make the same use of the idea of capture. It is found
explicitly only in Romans 7:23: "I see in my members
another law at war with the law of my mind and making
me captive to the law of sin which dwells in my members." However, Paul does occasionally use expressions
that echo capture and the ceremony of reduction to slavery: being a "prisoner" and the "yoke."

In two instances Paul speaks of himself as a prisoner
of Christ (Eph. 3:1; 4:1 KJV). In both instances the RSV

This is does speak hear "apprehended"

translates the phrase as "a prisoner *for*" Christ, but this seems to be an unnecessary interpretation of the Greek text based on the fact that at the time of writing Paul was in prison in Rome (cf. Col. 4:3, 10). The text can easily have the dual reference: to being a prisoner *for* Christ and to being a prisoner, that is a slave, *of* Christ. In either case the reference to "capture" is not clear-cut. *not captured.*

One instance in the Epistles where Paul may speak of reduction to slavery through capture by the Devil is 2 Timothy 2:26. The servants of the Lord are told to be gentle and apt to teach in the hope that those who oppose themselves to God will be given repentance and "may escape from the snare of the devil, after being captured by him to do his will." One interpretation of this language could be that the persons captured are snared like animals or birds and thereafter trained—a stark image in itself. It is possible also to interpret this passage as a reference to enslavement through capture, but there is a difficulty with such an interpretation. The doctrine of original sin means that people do not have to be captured in battle by the Devil in order to remove them from freedom under God. I prefer to take the quotation from 2 Timothy to cover the case of the person who is more particularly used by the Devil in order to lead others astray. This capture would therefore be a selection within slavery to do a particular task, rather than an entry into slavery, and I think this reading of the verse is supported by Paul's later comment in 2 Timothy 3:6, where dishonest teachers are said to "make their way into households and capture weak women."

A clear reference to enslavement by capture is implicit in Colossians 1:13. "He has delivered us from the dominion of darkness and transferred us to the kingdom of his beloved Son." Here the transference of the Christian to the kingdom of the Son operates to recover the Christian's citizenship of heaven by *postliminium.* That citizenship was lost by the Christian's being reduced to the dominion of darkness by capture in war; it is recovered when he is brought back or escapes to the territory of his true sovereign.[4]

The other metaphor that may possibly have him drawn from the technicalities of reduction to slavery by capture is the metaphor of the yoke. Entry into slavery as a result of capture was symbolized by requiring captives to pass underneath three spears lashed together to form an outline doorway. This required them to bow their heads and was called "passing under the yoke." "The yoke" was therefore an accepted way of referring to slavery and is found as such in 1 Timothy 6:1, where Paul is addressing those who are "slaves under the yoke' " (JB).

It is possible to use this idea to interpret Christ's words in Matthew 11:29–30, "Take my yoke upon you, and learn from me; for I am gentle and lowly in heart, and you will find rest for your souls. For my yoke is easy, and my burden is light." The metaphor would then mean either that one should be enslaved to Christ, as various of the writers of the Epistles speak of themselves (Rom. 1:1 mg.; Phil. 1:1 mg.), or that one should become a slave of God like Jesus Himself (Titus 1:1). But in other references, such as to "yoke-fellow" in Philippians 4:3 and to the impropriety of being "unequally yoked" in 2 Corinthians 6:14 the "yoke" can easily be construed as the ordinary ox yoke, and to interpret Christ's words in that way is not wrong. His burden is light, whether we think of taking His yoke upon us as slavery or as assuming a load. Either way an ambiguity remains. Do we assume the same burden as Christ, or a burden He puts on us? I think both ideas are right.

Another use of the language of the yoke is found in the discussions of the Jerusalem Council about the obligations that should be laid upon the Gentile believers. Peter argued strongly that the Gentiles should not be so subjected to the law: God has "cleansed their hearts by faith. Now therefore why do you make trial of God by putting a yoke upon the neck of the disciples which neither our fathers nor we have been able to bear?" (Acts 15:9–10). These words also could be simply a metaphor

of oxen dragging a heavy burden, though to a lawyer it
has other overtones. However, when Paul has occasion to
deal with the same point, arguing against "enslavement"
to the law, he clearly makes use of slavery metaphors. In
Galatians 5:1 he concludes an extended metaphoric use of
slavery by reference to the yoke: "For freedom Christ has
set us free; stand fast therefore, and do not submit again
to a yoke of slavery." In this context the yoke is clearly a
reference to a reduction to slave status rather than a reference to the plow, for it sums up an argument that
begins with the second way in which a person might become a slave: by being born to a slave mother.

2. Birth to a Slave Mother

As a general proposition, a child born to a slave mother
acquired the mother's status at the time of its birth.[5] There
was discussion in Roman law as to the effect of a mother
changing her legal status during pregnancy, but this need
not concern us for our present purposes.

Paul makes use of this legal principle in Galatians
4:21–31. He wrote the Galatian letter to warn the young
church in Galatia against the activities of some mission-
aries who had followed him into the area. These apparently were insisting that before a person could become a
Christian he had to become a Jew and had to observe the
full formal Judaic law as it stood at the time, including the
rite of circumcision (cf. Acts 15:1 and Gal. 5:2–12). Paul,
seeking to point out (as he does in other epistles) that
bondage to the law is not faith in Christ (cf. Rom. 2–8),
underscores the difference between bondage to the law
and freedom in Christ by the story of Abraham and his
two sons: Ishmael, the son of Hagar, and Isaac, the son of
Sarah. The child born to Hagar, being the son of a slave,
was born into slavery. Isaac, the son of Sarah the free
woman, was born into freedom. In Galatians 4:21–31 Paul
allegorizes that story by saying that the two women represent the two covenants. Hagar represents Mount Sinai,
symbolic of the law, "bearing children for slavery" (v. 24).
This corresponds to the present Jerusalem, which is still

in slavery with all her children (v. 25). There is therefore a contrast with the child of Sarah the free woman, who is "the Jerusalem above, which is free, and she is our mother" (v. 26). She bears children who are free by virtue of their birth to her in her free status—children who are free and who will not be cast out, but who will inherit with the other sons of the free woman (vv. 30–31). In short, Christians as children of freedom are not enslaved to the law by reason of their birth and must not behave as though they were. The imagery is exact—a beautiful use of legal ideas to teach spiritual truth.

The same idea of acquiring a status at birth may lie behind the curious language of 1 Corinthians 7:14. The passage runs from verse 12 through verse 16 and is mainly concerned with the Christian married to a non-Christian.[6] Verse 14 affirms that the believing partner "consecrates" the unbelieving spouse: "Otherwise, your children would be unclean, but as it is they are holy." Such language lends support to the view that believing parents can be assured of the salvation of their children, and it does so by an allusion to a legal commonplace of New Testament times—one takes the status of one's mother at birth.

3. Sale, Self-Sale, or Yielding Oneself as a Slave

The third method by which a person might become a slave was simply by sale—by being sold, selling himself, or yielding himself into slavery. We have examples of the sale of a person in both the Old and New Testaments. By Old Testament law a thief could be sold into slavery (Exod. 22:3), and there were regulations dealing with the sale of children (Exod. 21:7–11). In 2 Kings 4:1–7, Elisha by a miracle prevented the widow's sons being enslaved for the debt of their father, and in the parable of the wicked servant (Matt. 18:23–35) the servant was to be sold with his family to meet his debt. Further, in Nehemiah 5:1–5 the people complain that they have had to sell their children to buy food.

In these instances the sale was involuntary on the part of the person sold, but this was not always the case.

In a sense, a person surrendering in war yielded himself into slavery by capture. But other voluntary self-sale was possible. The Egyptians sold themselves to Joseph, Pharaoh's representative during the famine (Gen. 47:18–19, 21). Self-sale in time of famine did occur in the Land also (1 Sam. 2:5). Leviticus 25:47–55 deals with the redemption of an Israelite who had sold himself into slavery on account of poverty. It was a normal matter requiring legal regulation. We have already seen one New Testament example, Galatians 5:1, where Paul instructs his readers not to "submit again to a yoke of slavery," but to behave as the free people they are.

The clearest and most telling use of the metaphor of yielding or self-sale is found in Romans 6:16–22: "Do you not know that if you yield yourselves to anyone as obedient slaves, you are slaves of the one whom you obey, either of sin, which leads to death, or of obedience, which leads to righteousness? . . . You who were once slaves of sin . . . have become slaves of righteousness . . . you were slaves of sin . . . and have become slaves of God." Here entry into slave status by yielding oneself to another as his slave is clearly indicated.

Yielding oneself into slavery was not necessarily a formal transaction. It was possible for a free person to behave as a slave and as a result to find it impossible to assert his freedom. In Roman law one was barred from claiming to be free if one had fraudulently pretended to be a slave, but there would clearly be difficulties in proving that one had not acted fraudulently, and in practice the position would be that if one behaved as a slave, one was a slave.[8] This is the kind of reasoning one finds in Jesus' words in John 8:34, "Everyone who commits sin is a slave to sin" (cf. 1 John 3:8).

"If you yield yourselves to any one as obedient slaves, you are slaves of the one whom you obey." The propositions of Romans 6:16–22 are as stark as any of those we have looked at—but only if we realize what slavery entailed. As indicated earlier, there is a danger that the imagery of slavery is taken too lightly, as quaint, intriguing,

and romantic. Slavery was not. Self-sale was not a quid
pro quo contract enforceable as such. It was slavery.

The Slave Life

The passage from Romans 6 just quoted not only deals
with the question of entry into the slave status but carries
over into the state of slavery itself. The contrast is made
between being a slave of sin and being a slave of righteousness. In other places Paul speaks of himself as "a
slave of Jesus Christ" (Rom. 1:1 mg.; Phil. 1:1 mg.) and as
"a slave of God" (Titus 1:1 mg.; cf. James 1:1). In two
places he speaks to slave-owning Christians, instructing
them to be good masters as they have a Master in heaven
(Eph. 6:9; Col. 4:1), and at least once he indicates that
Christian slaves should consider themselves slaves of
Christ, not just slaves of their earthly masters (Eph. 6:5–8).
What does this mean?

Gaius, the Roman jurist whose *Institutes* are the most
complete Roman law book that has come down to us from
near the time of Paul, states that the basic distinction in
the law of persons is that all men are either free or slaves
(Gaius, *Institutes* 1.9). Later he informs us that slaves are
in the *potestas*, the power, of their masters, and it is in the
detail of this power that the fullness of Paul's analogy is
to be seen (cf. Gaius, *Institutes* 1.52ff.). Gaius takes slavery
for granted, as Paul does. For both, slavery existed as a
common phenomenon requiring no special explanation.
In the street there was no way of telling who was a slave
and who was not. Upper-class citizens might dress in a
toga, but apart from these social indications a person in
the street was simply another human being. That did not
necessarily mean, however, that the other human being
was legally a *persona*, "a person": in law slaves were not
people. A slave was a human being, and by Gaius's time
that fact had resulted in certain protective legislation, yet
even that legislation was more akin to our present laws
protecting animals than human rights. In law the slave
was a thing, a *res*, a commercial asset that could be owned.

The slave differed from other physical assets only in that
he could become free and in that, under certain circumstances, his master could acquire rights through him or
even be laid under an obligation by reason of his acts.

The slave was a chattel, a thing that could be bought
and sold. "You were bought with a price; do not become
slaves of men" (1 Cor. 7:23); "I am carnal, sold under sin"
(Rom. 7:14). The slave belonged wholly to his master. A
repeated element of Romans 6:12–23 is the concept of
dominion, which means ownership, not mere domination.
The slave was therefore required to do his master's will to
the fullest extent of his abilities and wholly to serve his
master's interests. Bearing this in mind we can return to
Romans 6:16–22, already quoted: "You who were once
slaves of sin . . . have become slaves of righteousness."
The utter division between a Christian life and any other
is made quite plain.

Of course, this was the ideal legal position, and Paul
did find it necessary to remind Christian slaves of their
duties towards their masters, and he specifically tells both
Timothy and Titus about the duty of preaching this:

> Bid slaves to be submissive to their masters and to
> give satisfaction in every respect; they are not to be
> refractory, nor to pilfer, but to show entire and true
> fidelity, so that in everything they may adorn the doc-
> trine of God our Savior (Titus 2:9–10).

> Let all who are under the yoke of slavery regard their
> masters as worthy of all honor, so that the name of
> God and the teaching may not be defamed. Those who
> have believing masters must not be disrespectful on
> the ground that they are brethren; rather they must
> serve all the better since those who benefit by their
> service are believers and beloved (1 Tim. 6:1–2).

> Slaves, be obedient to those who are your earthly mas-
> ters, with fear and trembling, in singleness of heart, as
> to Christ; not in the way of eyeservice, as men-pleasers,
> but as slaves [mg.] of Christ, doing the will of God
> from the heart, rendering service with a good will as

to the Lord and not to men, knowing that whatever good any one does, he will receive the same again from the Lord, whether he is a slave or free (Eph. 6:5–8).

Slaves, obey in everything those who are your earthly masters, not with eyeservice, as men-pleasers, but in singleness of heart, fearing the Lord. Whatever your task, work heartily as serving the Lord and not men, knowing that from the Lord you will receive the inheritance as your reward; you are serving the Lord Christ. For the wrongdoer will be paid back for the wrong he has done, and there is no partiality (Col. 3:22–25).

Paul was not being idiosyncratic in such passages. The problem seems to have been general. Peter also has to warn: "Servants, be submissive to your masters with all respect, not only to the kind and gentle but also to the overbearing" (1 Peter 2:18; cf. 2:19–25).

It is clear from these admonitions that there was often something of a gulf between the actual conduct of slaves and the legal norm, but this does not destroy Paul's use of the metaphor of being a "slave of sin" or a "slave of Christ." I must confess, however, that I consider the possibility of being a half-hearted, idle, refractory, and thieving slave of sin with a certain amount of amusement. (Many of the plays of Plautus contain such a slave character.) But the errant slave was not safe. He was at the disposal of his master in all respects and this included matters of discipline. Well past the time of Paul, the master had the *ius vitae necisque*, the power of life and death over his slaves, and he always had the power of reasonable chastisement. This certainly lies behind Paul's warnings to slave masters to be just and fair, impartial and not threatening, because they have a Master in heaven (Col. 4:1; Eph. 6:9).

An interesting use of the slave analogy occurs when Paul speaks of himself as the slave of Christ (Rom. 1:1 mg.; Phil. 1:1 mg.; cf. Titus 1:1 mg.). Naturally, since the slave was not legally a person, he could own no property and he did not even have power over himself. He only did what he was told to do. This in measure indicates the extent of Paul's self-surrender to his Master. It was, however, usual for the slave to be given a fund, the *peculium*, which he was at liberty to use.[10] Though in practice in many cases the profit would be left in the hands of the slave and would on many occasions be used by the slave in buying his freedom, in law the *peculium*, together with all profits and all acquisitions made by using the *peculium*, belonged to the Master. It is tempting therefore to link the idea that all one's goods are in fact God's with other instances where Paul indicates that Christians are given gifts from God to use—the *peculium* capital perhaps? We, the slaves of God, are given talents to trade with. At the end of the day the capital and the resulting profits are our Master's (1 Cor. 14; cf. the parable of the talents, Matt. 25:14–30). I cannot prove that such an idea was ever present in Paul's mind, but it is an interesting and thought-provoking speculation. Be that as it may, it is nonetheless clear that for Paul, "the slave of Christ," all his goods, time, ambitions, and purposes were subject to the determination of Christ. Paul was no different from the ordinary slave: he was at his Master's disposal. He was also *only* at his Master's disposal. Just as a man can serve only one master (Matt. 6:24; Luke 16:13), so he was responsible only to his Master (Rom. 14:4)—a liberating thought for those dogged by the opinions of others.

One final point should be made from the data we have on the slave life. The slave was an asset for his owner, to be looked after and cared for as such, but for the good owner such responsibilities went much further than the simple care one might give, e.g., a race-horse. The good owner looked after and cared for his slaves throughout their lives, into retirement. He would not seek to rid himself of the slave that was no longer "useful" by reason of age or infirmity. That God is a good "owner" of his "slaves" seems both axiomatic and reassuring.

Transfer

As slaves were things, mere commercial assets, they might be bought and sold or their ownership otherwise

transferred without any say on their part.[11] The transfer
of a slave was a technical matter, but it would often be
occasioned by a purchase. It is interesting therefore to find
two instances of such imagery in 1 Corinthians, a letter
addressed to the church in a city that housed an important
slave market. In 1 Corinthians 6:20 and 7:23 we learn that
we are "bought with a price." As a Calvinist I find it interesting that, in a question of sale and purchase, the will
of the slave was totally unimportant, but to explore that
line of argument would take us beyond our present
interests.

Of course, most of the references in the Epistles to
purchase definitely include the concept of redemption,
but this is quite a different legal notion from the idea of
the purchase of a slave. Unfortunately, many modern commentators fail to distinguish between the two metaphors.
The redemption of an individual who was up for sale in
a slave market was quite possible, but that does not mean
that the person involved was a slave. Indeed, from the
discussions in the Roman law texts we know that it was
not unknown for a free person to find himself, for one
reason or another, in the slave market. That is a different
matter, and we ought to keep redemption and the transfer
of a slave following a sale quite separate.

Termination of Slavery

A slave could pass out of slavery in two ways. First,
he might die. In Romans 6 Paul puts together many metaphors, some of which are based upon a concept of slavery. In the middle of the chapter (vv. 6–7) Paul indicates
that through Christ's death "our old self was crucified with
him so that the sinful body might be destroyed, and we
might no longer be enslaved to sin. For he who has died
is freed from sin." Death ends slavery, and we need to be
resurrected to life with Christ (v. 8).
Second, a slave might be freed.[12] As stated before, the
main characteristic separating the slave from other assets
the master might own was that it was possible for the slave
to be freed. By going through the appropriate ceremony

of manumission a slave could be given his freedom, and provided that the ceremony was appropriately performed, he was thereby given both his freedom and also citizenship. He became a freedman, his former owner becoming his patron, and a relationship continued between these two, a relationship that was terminated only in exceptional circumstances by the civil authorities intervening on their own account with good reason. Neither patron nor freedman could destroy the legal relationship himself.

The twin statuses of freedman and patron were unique to Roman law, and it is clear therefore that in at least one instance Paul uses this very particular and special legal concept as the basis of one of his explanations of the Christian life. In 1 Corinthians 7:21-22 Paul says, "Were you a slave when called? Never mind. But if you can gain your freedom, avail yourself of the opportunity. For he who was called in the Lord as a slave is a freedman of the Lord. Likewise he who was free when called is a slave of Christ." Paul here makes a fascinating contrast between the position of the slave and that of the freedman, yet uses the contrast to show that the two men involved are fundamentally in the same position in relation to Christ. There is a possible variant reading in verse 21b that would replace "avail yourself of the opportunity" with "make use of your present condition instead," but this detail does not affect the matter we are considering. Verse 21b is really an interjection; the line of thought runs, "Are you a slave? Never mind. You are a freedman of the Lord. Are you a free man? You are really a slave of Christ." Interesting words, but what do they mean?

The impact of the second sentence of verse 22 would be more or less the same whatever legal system one had in mind. A free man is to consider himself to be the *slave* of Christ—a metaphor that would strike home to all free men in the slave-tolerating society of the New Testament age. Total subjection to the Master was required. But the slave is not to consider himself a free man. That would have had little force. Indeed, it would be a rather appalling thought to a slave, involving his being cast off from the care and attention of his former owner. This is not what is involved here. The slave is to consider himself as the *freedman* of Christ—quite a different matter; but only if we read the word in the light of Roman law, for only it had a concept of freedman that will highlight the metaphor involved.

There was nothing to correspond to the Roman status of freedman in Jewish law.[13] A Hebrew slave in most cases would go free in the seventh year, the Year of Jubilee (Exod. 21:2–11, esp. v. 2; Lev. 25:39–41; Deut. 15:12), unless he chose permanent slavery (Exod. 21:5–6; Deut. 15:16–17). The rules of Jubilee apparently did not apply to the gentile slave. In any event, there were not many Hebrew slaves,[14] and the rabbis discouraged slavery and manumission lest the number of freed slaves cause the dilution of the Jewish race,[15] a point they could certainly establish by the Roman experience. Manumission of either the Hebrew or gentile slave was possible and could occur either in consideration of payment of a redemption price or for any other reason satisfactory to the master. However, when manumission occurred it was normally final, and any attempt to reserve any rights to the master invalidated the transaction. The only situation in which something like the Roman status of freedman was achieved occurred when the full redemption price was not paid. Then the slave was considered in some sense half free and worked for his master on alternate days.[16] I cannot think that this is what Paul had in mind when he suggested that a person might consider himself as the freedman of Christ. Paul would not be in favor of part-time Christians. In any event, this duty arose only when a full redemption price had not been paid—again an inapplicable idea. Christ's death is a full redemption. In Jewish law, therefore, there was not the automatic continuing link between former slaves and their masters, which clearly contrasts with the Roman position. It is the existence of that link between the freedman and the patron that is one focus of Paul's figure.

All this is not to say that there was not a status of

"freed slave" in Israel—there was. We read in Acts 6:9 of the "Synagogue of the Freedmen"[17] and freedmen did suffer from certain legal disabilities in both private and public life. This is not, however, the point. Such freedmen were no longer linked in law to their patrons, and it is that link that Paul is referring to.

The law of the freedman in Greek law also does not provide a satisfactory basis for Paul's illustration.[18] It was possible in Greek law for the master upon manumission to reserve what was known as the *paramone*.[19] Under this device the freedman was bound to reside in the master's house and obey his master's orders, in effect working off his redemption price. However, the *paramone* extended only for a definite period of time, at the end of which the former slave became fully free.[20] He was subjected to certain disabilities relating to his rights and duties in the state, but not in relation to his former owner. Once the *paramone* period had expired, or in the case where a *paramone* was not reserved, the slave was totally free of obligations and duties to his former owner and vice versa. It follows that the freedman in Greek law was not a satisfactory basis for Paul's illustration. The continuing link between slave and former owner was not automatic and in any event terminated after a period of time. Being a "freedman of Christ" under these circumstances is meaningless.

While there is, therefore, an interesting contrast in 1 Corinthians 7:22 between being free and being a slave under both Jewish law and Greek law, the metaphor breaks down when it contrasts the status of freedman and of slave using these legal systems. However, the primary law in Corinth was neither Greek nor Jewish, for Corinth was a Roman colony: its markets operated under Roman law, its courts enforced Roman law, and it is Roman law that provides a fruitful metaphor in its concept of freedman.[21]

Under Roman law, the manumission of a slave gave him his freedom and, if properly done, his citizenship— he became a Roman citizen, a citizen of the empire. I do not wish to go into the metaphor of citizenship for the freedman at this point. That will be dealt with in the next chapter,[22] but we can note here that, interpreting 1 Corinthians 7:22 by Roman law, the freedman of Christ has gained the citizenship Christ Himself has, the citizenship of heaven (Eph. 2:19; Phil. 3:20).

The freedom a slave acquired on manumission was for most purposes exactly the same as the freedom possessed by the freeborn.[23] However, a fundamental difference existed between the freed and the freeborn. The former was still to a degree subject to his former owner—his patron. He was also, like his Greek and Jewish counterparts, subject to certain disabilities under public law, but these need not concern us here.

One of the remaining ties with the patron was that it was usual for the *libertinus*, the freedman, to agree to render certain services to his master (*operae*). These, enforceable by civil action, normally consisted of a certain number of days of work per week, month, or year, geared to his abilities and former employment in the household of the master. Another tie was the right of the patron to succeed to the estate of the freedman under certain circumstances, the patron being seen in some sense as the general heir of his freedman. The patron might also require gifts to be given to him (*munera*). But the most general tie between patron and freedman is found in the concept of *obsequium*. *Obsequium* may be roughly translated as "respect," but it is not easy to define; it consists of a variety of elements, and the duty of respectful conduct on the part of the freedman towards his patron showed itself in many specific rules. For example, the freedman might sue his patron only with the consent of a magistrate and was totally debarred from raising an action involving *infamia*, such as an action for theft. *Infamia* was a concept similar to loss of prestige or loss of face, which meant much more to the Romans than it does to us. Indeed, the comparison lies with the concept of loss of face for the Japanese or Chinese rather than the average Westerner. *Obsequium* even went to the extent of obliging the freedman to care financially or otherwise for his patron if the patron fell into

need. This would be entirely apart from the specific obligations of *operae* and *munera*. There were, therefore,
considerable duties owed by the freedman to his patron.
He was not entirely free of his former owner.

The obligations of the status did not lie solely with
the freedman. The patron was under a duty to look after
a needy freedman (a far more real obligation in many cases
than the reverse), for otherwise freedom might be a disaster for the ex-slave. Freeing a slave would have been an
easy way for a master to get rid of one who had become
a burden and whose days of usefulness were past. As a
slave a man did have security: his master would feed him
and look after his health and other needs as he would take
care of any valuable asset. Freed, apart from the patron's
obligation to care for him, he would have had no security.
Thus it was important that in law the patron was bound
to feed a starving freedman, to care for a sick one, or simply
to give him a roof over his head. Another interesting point
is that the patron could not be a witness against his freedman in criminal matters. In other words, Christ will never
be a witness against a Christian.

The various obligations between patron and freedman
could be annulled under certain circumstances, or they
might never exist, for example, when the slave was freed
by the state due to the misconduct of his owner. But in
the majority of cases they did apply. So, if we return to
1 Corinthians 7 and look again at the meaning of verse 22,
we see that the point Paul is making is clearly the fundamental equality and worth of all believers. The free
Christian is to consider himself the slave of Christ, subject
to the full control and care of his Master. The Christian
slave is to consider himself Christ's freedman, a full human being, yet not detached from his patron. Christ has
freed him and will perform the duties of a patron towards
him, summed up in caring for him. The freedman owes
reciprocal duties to Christ to the fullest extent. There is a
continuing, living relationship between the two. We have,
therefore, in this verse a beautifully balanced exposition
of the relationship between the believer and his Lord, ap-

plicable both to the slave and to the free man. This balance exists only if we interpret the language by reference to Roman law. I find it impossible to believe that this beautiful illustration is purely accidental; that Paul did not know what he was saying; that he was not deliberately constructing this little metaphor from Roman law for our instruction. Accordingly, I would interpret most of the uses of the metaphors of slavery in other parts of the Epistles by reference to Roman law, although I concede that the teaching contained in some of the "slave" metaphors would not be significantly altered were they to be interpreted by Jewish or Greek law.

There are certainly examples of the metaphorical use of slavery in the New Testament that may be interpreted by Greek usage. In particular Professor Deissman gathered together examples of manumission under Greek law occurring through the medium of the temple.[24] The slave paid to the temple officials out of his savings (saved presumably by informal permission) the price to which his owner had agreed. The owner received this price from the temple officials and transferred the slave to the temple god. The transfer or sale was not for the purpose of serving the temple deity but for the purpose of manumission. It was customary in the documents of such sale to specify that the slave was sold either "for freedom" or "on condition that he shall be free." Such background information could be used to interpret such passages as Galatians 5:1: "Stand fast, therefore, in the liberty wherewith Christ hath made us free, and be not entangled again with the yoke of bondage" (KJV). The NIV begins this verse: "It is for freedom that Christ has set us free." It is arguable in that instance that the god (Christ) has bought us and liberated us and that we must therefore not become slaves again. A similar argument, perhaps even stronger, may be made in relation to 1 Corinthians 6:19–20: "You are not your own; you were bought with a price" and 1 Corinthians 7:23: "You were bought with a price; do not become slaves of men." These instances, however, are not necessarily references to sacral manumission. In Galatians, Christ has freed us; we must therefore not again become slaves to the law. In the Corinthian passages, which should be referred to Roman law as the local law, we have been bought with a price; we are therefore the slaves of Christ and it is not possible for us lawfully to become the slaves of men. In neither instance need the pagan cultic practice be invoked.

In short, reference to Greek practice, though interesting, does not really add to the richness of the Roman reference, and particularly in the case of freedmen, does not even approximate it. To conclude this chapter, therefore, I will list some of the main slavery metaphors. If they are considered in the light of Roman law, the teaching they hold is clear.

> Every one who commits sin is a slave to sin (John 8:34).
>
> Paul, a slave of Jesus Christ (Rom. 1:1 mg.; Phil. 1:1 mg.).
>
> You were bought with a price; do not become slaves of men (1 Cor. 7:23).
>
> You also have a Master in heaven (Col. 4:1; cf. Eph. 6:9).
>
> He who was called in the Lord as a slave is a freedman of the Lord. Likewise he who was free when called is a slave of Christ (1 Cor. 7:22).
>
> For freedom Christ has set us free; stand fast therefore, and do not submit again to a yoke of slavery (Gal. 5:1).
>
> Do you not know that if you yield yourselves to any one as obedient slaves, you are slaves of the one whom you obey, either of sin, which leads to death, or of obedience, which leads to righteousness? . . . you who were once slaves of sin . . . have become slaves of righteousness . . . you were slaves of sin . . . and have become slaves of God (Rom. 6:16–22).

3

Aliens and Citizens

IDEAS DRAWN FROM THE LAWS OF CITIZENSHIP, of aliens and alienage, and of sojourners are found not only in the Pauline epistles but also in 1 Peter and in Hebrews. The words reflect the conditions of that time, when to be a Roman citizen made one a member of the elite of the earth, no matter how sorry one's actual condition might be. Paul, the citizen, speaks of citizenship. The other writers, aliens, speak of alienage.

Such images express and elaborate the thought of Jesus that the Christian is in the world but not of the world (John 15:16–20 and 17:6–16). In Philippians 3:20 Paul exhorts the recipients of his letter to imitate his walk with Christ "for our citizenship is in heaven" (NASB). In Ephesians 2:19 they, through the death of Christ, are "fellow citizens with the saints." The corollary is that they are now "no longer strangers and foreigners" in relation to heaven. In their former state they had been "aliens from the commonwealth of Israel, and strangers from the covenants of promise" (Eph. 2:12 KJV) and "alienated from the life of God" (Eph. 4:18; cf. Col. 1:21).

Peter addresses his first epistle "to the strangers scattered throughout" Asia Minor (KJV), or in some translations, to "the sojourners of the Dispersion" in that area (1 Peter 1:1 ASV). Later he takes up the idea of alienage inherent in these expressions, speaking to them as "aliens

47

and exiles" ("strangers and pilgrims," KJV), asking them
to abstain from fleshly lusts (1 Peter 2:11) because they are
now "God's own people" (1 Peter 2:9–10, echoing Deut.
14:2; 26:18).

The writer to the Hebrews makes it quite clear that
Christians are not (or should not be) really at home in this
world, for they look for another. Abraham by faith "so-
journed in the land of promise, as in a foreign land . . . for
he looked forward to the city which has foundations, whose
builder and maker is God" (Heb. 11:9–10). Unlike the Is-
raelites, Christians now have "come to Mount Zion and to
the city of the living God" (Heb. 12:22). This is not, however, the earthly Zion, but "the Jerusalem above . . . [which]
is our mother," as Paul puts it in Galatians 4:26, "for here
we have no lasting city, but we seek the city which is to
come" (Heb. 13:14). In particular, all the heroes of faith
listed in Hebrews 11

> died in faith, not having received what was promised,
> but having seen it and greeted it from afar, and having
> acknowledged that they were strangers and exiles on
> the earth. For people who speak thus make it clear
> that they are seeking a homeland. If they had been
> thinking of that land from which they had gone out,
> they would have had opportunity to return. But as it
> is, they desire a better country, that is, a heavenly one.
> Therefore God is not ashamed to be called their God,
> for he has prepared for them a city (Heb. 11:13–16).

The propositions of such imagery may be summarized
as follows: (a) if we are Christians, our citizenship is in
heaven; (b) accordingly, here in this world our status is
that of stranger and foreigner—the resident alien; and
(c) prior to our conversion these statuses and conditions
were the reverse of what they are now. Inherent in such
expressions and ideas is the notion of the "two cities,"
later to be expounded by St. Augustine and other writers
with important effects in political theory as well as in
theological enquiry,[1] but for the present purposes we need

only consider the content that could have been read into the metaphors at the time the Epistles were written and the truths the authors intended to communicate.

We can refer to three possible sources for the ideas of citizens and aliens in the Epistles. There may be a reference to Jewish law, to Roman law, or to principles common to the different legal systems of the day. In this instance it is important to remember that the several jurisdictions and civic communities considered outsiders as foreigners. Even the Greek cities treated a citizen of another Greek city as an alien, unless there was an appropriate treaty.[2] As with the other legal metaphors it is, of course, further possible that the readers of the Epistles would or could read into the imagery whatever legal system was familiar to them, and that the ideas of the writers were grounded in more than one legal system; but these are questions we cannot decide. However, we can be certain that some role is played by Jewish law and some by Roman law in the selection and interpretation of these metaphors. We will first consider the idea of strangers and foreigners (aliens) and then deal with citizenship.

Aliens—The Jewish View

The Jewish reader of the Epistles would find the idea of the stranger and foreigner familiar. It had been burned into his thought patterns by history and was present with him in his everyday life. It was enshrined in the Law, and in practice the alien, the foreigner, the Gentile, was for the majority of Jews a known and detested object. There were many Gentiles in the Land and its environs. One large foreign group were the Samaritans, descendants of those settled in the Land by the Assyrian king Shalmaneser in place of the Ten Tribes (2 Kings 17:24–41). Another group was of Greek origin and culture. They were particularly to be found in the Decapolis region, the "Ten Cities" east of the Sea of Galilee, which had been settled as a result of the conquests of Alexander the Great and his successors; the Seleucid Antiochus Epiphanes IV deliberately sought to Hellenize his domains (1 Macc. 1:41), an effort the Jews resisted. Even so, the Books of the Maccabees and Josephus make plain the presence of many aliens in the Jewish environment, who formed a substantial and politically important element.[3]

References to such aliens, whether to the resident alien, the ger, or to the nonresident transient foreigner, the nokri, certainly carried meaning, though different from that reflected in the Old Testament. In the Jewish law itself there was tension over the question of aliens. The Pentateuch insisted on fair dealing, indeed generous dealing, with foreigners, in a way not found in other legal systems of its time. To wrong the stranger or to oppress him (Exod. 22:21; 23:9; Lev. 19:33–34; Deut. 24:14), to pass by his need (Deut. 10:18–19), or to fail to give him justice (Deut. 24:17–18) was forbidden on the simple ground that "you were sojourners in the land of Egypt." It is true that these passages were later interpreted to refer only to the ger toshav, the resident (and one assumes friendly) alien, the proselyte. However, so to interpret them is to wrest their sense, for the Jews as strangers in Egypt were hardly to be equated with resident converts. In Egypt the Jews were slaves, despised, hated, and overworked (Exod. 1:8–22). To hold that the stranger of the Pentateuch is to be restricted to a favored group of aliens is to confuse the language. The passages attain their full meaning only if it is recognized that the legislation assumes that in the ordinary event all aliens were without rights and that this general position was being altered by the edicts of the Law.[4] Other passages seem to make this clear. Every stranger, whether resident or transient, was to be subject to the same general civil and criminal law as the native Jew (Lev. 24:22). He enjoyed the benefits of the law concerning the poor (Lev. 25:35; Deut. 14:29; 24:19; 26:11–15), could own slaves, even Jewish slaves (Lev. 25:47), and in trouble could flee, like a Jew, to the cities of refuge (Num. 35 passim; v. 15 refers to the stranger). On the other hand, the alien was subject to certain of the external observances and religious practices of the Jews, whether or not he was a proselyte. Thus, he was bound to keep the Sabbath (Exod. 20:10), had to refrain from worshiping idols (Lev. 20:2), from blasphemy (Lev. 24:16), and from sexual offenses (Lev. 18:26), and had to observe the basic dietary laws (Lev. 17:8–16). However, only the resident alien, the ger, had recourse to the ceremonial law, and then only if he became a proselyte (Num. 9:14; 15:14–16).

During what may be termed the initial period of the laws of Moses, there were also other population elements in the Land contributing to the vitality of the idea of strangers and foreigners. These were groups of inhabitants who were not displaced by the incoming tribes, either because they had come to an arrangement with the Jews by way of treaty, as in the case of the Gibeonites (Josh. 9:3–27), or by tacit agreement, in some cases following a struggle. The opening chapters of the Book of Judges list many examples of such communities and enclaves that were tolerated (Judg. 1:19, 21, 27–36; 2:20–23; 3:1–7). In many cases these groups were assigned inferior status: the Gibeonites were made hewers of wood and drawers of water (Josh. 9:27), the Canaanites and Amorites were made tributaries (Judg. 1:28–36). Yet the Jews did protect such peoples against their enemies once they had been accepted (Josh. 10:1–43).

With the development of the kingdom and over the years, the rules for the treatment of strangers changed, and we have hints of this in the Bible. Some of the changes may have been appreciated by the aliens. In particular a tolerance for their religions emerged, contrary to the Levitical prescription, early in the history of the Land. Judges 2:1–3, 8–19 narrates how the second generation in the Land went astray in this respect and describes the consequences. One high spot (from the alien's perspective) occurred when Solomon, in his dotage and under the influence of his foreign wives, worshiped Ashtoreth and Milcom and built altars for the gods of all his wives, including an altar for Molech, expressly forbidden in Leviticus 20:2–5 (1 Kings 11:1–10).

On the other hand, some of the changes introduced

in practice, if not in law, were unfavorable to the alien. The remnants of the older inhabitants of the Land were conscripted for his slave labor force by Solomon (1 Kings 9:20–21), and all strangers were liable to be called upon for forced labor (1 Chron. 22:2; 2 Chron. 2:17–18). Indeed, even before the kingdom it would seem that the stranger could not expect reasonable treatment from the average Jew. Ruth, for example, is amazed that she, a stranger, should be helped in her gleaning by Boaz (Ruth 2:10).

Naturally, all these rules and practices underwent further change when the Jews ceased to be a free people. In theory the rules became broad, generous, and tolerant again. The rules of the Talmud show this particularly, but there are also traces in the Bible. Thus Ezekiel, in outlining the future constitution of the nation, gives strangers an equal share in the Land (Ezek. 47:22–23; cf. Isa. 14:1). However, such glimmers of light envisaged, and the Talmudic rules were designed for, the day of Messiah's reign. The actual law applied within the Jewish boundaries seems to have been different. We can adduce evidence from the Old Testament itself. Before, during, and after the Captivity, recurrent complaints were made by the prophets about the oppression of strangers (normally coupled with the fatherless and widows). It is made quite clear that such conduct was one reason for judgment coming on the people (e.g., Jer. 7:6; 22:3; Ezek. 22:7, 29; Zech. 7:10; Mal. 3:5). Later, even in New Testament times, the problem of the right treatment of strangers was still present, and faulty conduct implies faulty law. One of the well-known passages in Matthew's Gospel is concerned with the topic; Jesus said, "I was a stranger and you welcomed me . . . I was a stranger and you did not welcome me" (Matt. 25:35, 43). We may also cite the surprise of the woman at the well, a Samaritan, that Jesus, a Jew, would even talk to her (John 4:4–26), and the determination of the Syro-Phoenician woman that Jesus would meet her need, even though Jews did not normally have anything to do with aliens if they could help it (Matt. 15:21–28; Mark 7:24–30). In fact, by that time it was for religious reasons unlawful for a Jew to associate with a non-Jew on terms of equality, as Peter explained to Cornelius and his colleagues in Caesarea (Acts 10:28). Indeed, Peter had to defend his actions (Acts 11:2–3), and Paul later had to challenge Peter when he withdrew from the gentile Christians in Antioch (Gal. 2:11–14).

This hostility to aliens underlines and reinforces Jesus' remark that it was only the Samaritan leper who thanked Him for his cure (Luke 17:17), and makes the effect of the parable of the Good Samaritan (Luke 10:25–37) even more striking. A final piece of evidence can be taken from the Mishnah tractate *Abodah Zarah* ("On Idolatry"), which contains a discussion as to the purity of materials touched or even seen by Gentiles, indicating the attitudes and concerns of the leaders of the nation.

Such attitudes were instrumental in the development of the discriminatory laws of the Talmud, which were in practice more important than the more generous principles it also enunciated. In day-to-day business, strangers were not as well treated under the developed law as they might have been. George Horowitz gives numerous examples, quoting both from the Talmud and the Mishnah.[5] For example, in strict law it was necessary for lost property to be returned only between Jews, since Gentiles might be assumed not to be honest and therefore not to reciprocate. Also, the laws against overcharging for goods or overreaching in bargains did not apply in dealings with Gentiles, since they were considered not to recognize such principles themselves, preferring the precept "a bargain is a bargain." Such ideas are even to be found in the Pentateuch: the well-known prohibition on usury (Deut. 23:19–20) expressly exempts loans to foreigners from its operation.

In practice the Gentile was at a disadvantage before the Jewish courts. Despite rules in Exodus 12:49, Leviticus 24:22, and Numbers 15:16, framed broadly enough to forbid such a development, Talmudic opinion was that in a situation involving a choice of law, the court should apply either the Jewish law or the law of the Gentile's country

of origin; where it was clear the Gentile had resorted to
the Jewish courts and their rules because these might be
more favorable to his case, the court should apply whichever law was less favorable to the Gentile.[6] The Talmud
itself preserves criticism of the Jewish law expressed by
Roman officials, on precisely these grounds: they objected
to the fact that a Gentile could not sue the Jewish owner
of an animal that had done him damage, while the Jew in
reverse situation could bring a noxal action against the
Gentile (i.e., an action for money damages or for the sur-
render of the offending beast).[7]

Apart from such legal applications of the idea of
strangers and foreigners, there was within the religious
tradition of the Jews an ingrained concept of the otherness
of the stranger, of the fact that he did not belong, which
could give some meaning to the New Testament imagery.
Reference has already been made to the justification of the
Mosaic rules concerning strangers on the grounds that
"you were sojourners in the land of Egypt," and the Jews
would have been reminded of this by the annual Passover
ceremonies. Furthermore, the idea of the stranger recurs
in the Bible as connoting an unwelcome status. For example, God, through Isaiah, has to reassure the resident
stranger (Isa. 56:3, 6–8), and both Job (Job 19:15) and David
(Ps. 69:8) have cause to lament that they have become
strangers in the sight of their households, indicating the
depth of the dissociation that had arisen between them.
But it is perhaps the use that is made of the idea of strangers
and foreigners to indicate the impermanence of the present world that most clearly can contribute to some of the
New Testament imagery.

Impermanence is a recurrent theme of the Old Testament. Jacob before Pharoah talks of his life as having been
a sojourning (KJV, "pilgrimage") and indicates that it has
not all been pleasant (Gen. 47:9). The justification given
for the institution of redemption of land in Leviticus 25:23
is that in the last analysis the Land belongs to God, and
the Jews are merely strangers and sojourners in it from
God's perspective. This idea finds echoes in David's great

hymn of praise to God at the installation of Solomon as king. He stresses the impermanence of all things before God, and God's control of all things—how marvelous it is that God accepts such praise and sacrifice from people who "are strangers before thee, and sojourners, as all our fathers were" (1 Chron. 29:15). Inconsistently, David also uses his status as a stranger as a reason why God should hear his prayers (Ps. 39:12), but in both instances it is the presence of the concept that is important for us. This same concept even formed the basis of a religious movement: "sojourning" was the basis of the way of life of the Rechabites (Jer. 35:1–11, esp. 6–9), who date from the time of Ahab (2 Kings 10:15).

All such ideas of strangers, of impermanence, and of a future "real" homeland would naturally be taken up by the Jews under military occupation, when the temporary nature of their status in the Land as a subject people became an article of faith. Thus, around the time of Christ there was an upsurge in Messianic interest and a looking forward to a permanent kingdom, a lasting city, compared with which their existing state was that of strangers.[8]

To these legal and religious ideas of aliens we must, as indicated earlier, add the political fact that in New Testament times the Land had been invaded and infiltrated by a variety of non-Jewish peoples. There were Samaritans, Greeks, Syrians, and Romans, whose presence fed a hostility to aliens that amounted on occasion to xenophobia. The Zealots favored armed resistance. The Sicarii ("dagger carriers") practiced selective assassination. Uprisings were common (cf. Acts 5:34–37), until eventually the situation erupted in the general rebellion of A.D. 66, crushed by Titus in A.D. 70 with the destruction of the temple. The later rebellion led by Bar Kochba in A.D. 132–135 led to the final dispersion of the Jews and their removal from the Land for almost nineteen hundred years. Jewish hostility to aliens was a strong, self-destructive force.

From all this it appears to me that in using the imagery of aliens and strangers the New Testament writers were using a language that would not have been seriously misunderstood by their Jewish readers or by reasonably knowledgeable and interested Gentiles. There was a conceptual background in the Jewish law, history, and climate of ideas that would in measure fill out the metaphors employed. However, a Jewish reference does not constitute a complete explanation of the metaphors of alienage we are considering. A fuller, more adequate explanation can be found if we look at Roman law.

Aliens—the Roman View

Of the New Testament writers only Paul, the Roman citizen, uses ideas both of citizenship and of alienage. Certainly Peter, and perhaps the writer to the Hebrews, did not have Roman citizenship, and they, by contrast, talk only in terms of aliens, strangers, and sojourners. These images are obviously drawn in part from their own experience, although the Jewish background of such language could well be present. In the case of Paul, the Roman reference starts as favorite, especially because Roman law provides a satisfactory content for these images as well. The alien, stranger, and foreigner held a known status in Roman law—they were by and large outside the formal law.

Roman citizenship was not held automatically by all persons born and resident within the boundaries of the Roman Empire until the *Constitutio Antoniniana* (the Edict of Caracalla) of A.D. 212. The bulk of the inhabitants of the empire were classed from the point of view of Roman law as *peregrini,* aliens. It is interesting therefore to see that the Roman technical term *peregrinus* originally meant simply "wanderer"—a stranger and foreigner. Peregrines might be of two kinds: those whose territories were part of the empire and those whose territories were allied to Rome. Complete outsiders, with whose native land there was no treaty or alliance, were treated as hostile and were liable to be enslaved.

In practice, their origin made little difference to the

aliens within the empire. Those whose territories were part of the empire retained their own forms of government and their own domestic laws insofar as these did not directly run counter to Roman ideas and interests or to the local peace.[9] These *peregrini* were "subjects" of Rome, but not Romans, because they were not citizens. They were not liable to military service, but they were subject to supervision and to the heavy burden of imperial taxation. In terms of strict Roman law they were without rights, existing as objects and not as subjects of law. This pattern also effectively held good in the case of territories allied to Rome: the rights of their inhabitants, who were permitted to travel within the empire, depended upon treaty.

Both kinds of arrangement can be illustrated from the case of the Jews themselves. Part of the Jewish territory was placed by Rome under members of the Herodian dynasty and existed as "allied" states, and part was made into the province of Judea. Both areas continued to be governed by the old laws and institutions, including the Sanhedrin, save only insofar as the Romans considered it necessary to interfere. The Romans did, for example, reserve the right to impose capital punishment, as seen in the case of Christ, but the day-to-day administration was none of their concern. The attitudes of Festus to Agrippa (Acts 25:13–26:32) and of Pilate (John 18:31) show this. Jews resident in the kingdoms or in the province continued to hold their earlier citizenship, becoming Romans only if Roman citizenship was expressly granted them, usually for services rendered, as in the case of Josephus. In terms of Roman law the ordinary Jew was an alien, a *peregrinus*.

The distinction between a Roman and a peregrine was fundamental. As we shall see in the case of Paul, the Roman citizen was entitled to a certain standard of treatment well above the minimum accorded the peregrine. There were also gradations of treatment according to one's social class, which became increasingly important,[10] but that is not the point here. The basic distinction was between the citizen and the alien. The disadvantages of being an alien compared with the advantages of Roman citizenship were many, as we shall shortly see in more detail, but certain aspects of the peregrine status are very informative when considered on their own.

Contemporary legal theory held that a person was subject to the law of his citizenship, of his native city or land. When he went elsewhere he was not entitled to make full use of the laws of his new territory. He was still subject to his old law, carrying it with him as a snail does its shell.[11] Vis-à-vis the law of the new abode the alien was at a disadvantage. He had no right of access to the local courts, and his "rights" might well receive no legal recognition. On the other hand, the local authorities were quite liable to enforce what they considered to be the alien's duties. The analogy with the way the Christian should consider his place in the world is clear.

In a few instances, however, the alien's position was ameliorated. In Rome, for example, there were so many aliens that the office of *praetor peregrinus* was created to cope with their legal problems.[12] Sometimes, where there was a sufficiently large group of aliens of common origin in another territory, the local authority might allow them to form a *politeuma*, a self-sufficient and to a degree self-governing subcommunity within the new jurisdiction. They were resident aliens with their own rules and practices, though mixing to some extent with the life of the rest of the community. The Jews in Rome, Alexandria, Tarsus, and some other cities in Asia Minor formed such groups.[13] Romans in non-Roman cities would do so as well. It is to such groups that Paul refers in Philippians 3:20. He is saying to Christians that their citizenship (NASB; RSV, "commonwealth"; KJV, "conversation") is in heaven and that hence in the cities of this world they are resident aliens, a subcommunity with their own rules. They are not fully integrated into the community at large and are not at home there. Their colony in the midst of the world community has its own rules. They cannot use the "local law" but must follow their own.

Aliens—a General Referent?

But need we refer "aliens" and the correlative "citizenship" to the Roman view for their interpretation? As in the case of the ideas dealt with in other chapters, could these metaphors not be merely simple references to the common ideas of the time? There is no final answer to this question, and it must be conceded that the language used was not meaningless under any legal system of New Testament times. Citizenship and the consequent access to civic rights, alienage and exclusion from those rights, and in some cases also the concept of "resident alien" (metic in Greek law), were ideas present throughout the Mediterranean world of Paul's day.[14] We even know of an interest in the "citizenship" of certain cities.[15]

However, four points weight the probabilities in favor of the Roman connotation, particularly in Paul's letters. The first is that Paul was himself a Roman citizen who had cause to know the importance of his status and the difference it made not to be an alien, a stranger. Second, these "other" citizenships were geographically localized, being effective and of benefit only within the jurisdiction of the city concerned. Third, the Roman citizen was one of the privileged class. It is a curious but well-attested fact that although the privileges of citizenship diminished over the years, yet Roman citizenship was an object of interest and greatly desired by the non-Romans of the empire. Other "citizenships" fell into disfavor, and the urge was not to be alien from the Roman commonwealth.[16] Fourth, there was at the time an upsurge of ideas of patriotism and of national identity (patriality).[17] Under these circumstances a reference to this "superior" citizenship may be implied, and if we so interpret "citizenship" it is reasonable to interpret "aliens" in this context as well.

To summarize at this point, the metaphors of aliens, strangers, and foreigners in the New Testament Epistles are used in two different ways. The non-Christian is pictured as a stranger and foreigner in relation to heaven—

he has no part in God's community (Eph. 2:12, 19; 4:18; Col. 1:21). The Christian on the other hand, is an alien in relation to this world (Phil. 3:20; Eph. 2:19; 1 Peter 2:9–11). These ideas are fruitful for the Christian. But alienage is only half the metaphor, the negative element of these figures of speech. Alienage is further defined by the concept of citizenship, to which we can now properly turn.

Citizenship

It seems obvious and natural that it is Paul, the Roman citizen, who makes the plainest use of the citizenship metaphor, while his fellow writers, aliens, speak of alienage. Paul the citizen tells Christians that they are "fellow citizens with the saints" (Eph. 2:19) and that their "citizenship is in heaven" (Phil. 3:20 NASB). In both these instances Paul was addressing people to whom the idea of Roman citizenship was important. In Ephesians he was writing to a church situated in the commercial capital of the province of Asia, the seat of imperial control in that territory, and also the main entry point for the Roman presence in what is now Asia Minor. Philippians was written to the church in a Roman colony (Acts 16:12), a place where there was a settlement of persons who were technically citizens of Rome, actually the descendants of veterans of Octavian and Anthony's armies who were given citizenship and were settled there on reaching retirement age. Such a colony was in law a "little Rome," and only Roman law held sway there. In both instances, therefore, Paul's readers might be expected to interpret his metaphor in the light of local facts.

Roman citizenship was obtained by birth to a Roman citizen (e.g., Paul, Acts 22:28; cf. the analogy in Philem. 10, "begotten in my bonds") or by other means that provide instructive metaphors. Citizenship might be given to an individual or a group as an act of grace, or more often for services rendered (e.g., Josephus; the veterans of Philippi). Citizenship could also be bought (Acts 22:28). A freedman, if properly emancipated by a citizen patron,

obtained Roman citizenship with his freedom. Christians
can therefore think of themselves as being made citizens
as an act of grace, or perhaps more fruitfully in the light
of chapter 2, as having been freed by Christ into the citizenship of heaven (Gal. 5:1).[18] Indeed, to carry the metaphor further, it may be noted that manumission of a slave
by having him registered in the census lists of the citizenry
was an ancient republican Roman form, not quite dead in
New Testament times. Christians have been registered as
citizens in the official lists of the citizenry of Zion (Ps.
87:5–6). Their names are entered in the Lamb's Book of
Life (Phil. 4:3).[19] *Rev.*

Of course there was the darker side. Citizenship was
lost if one was captured in war by an enemy. This
amounted to civil death. I would not, for theological reasons, press that analogy, but would draw attention to a
further element here. By the *ius postliminii* a former citizen recovered his citizenship on return to Roman territory,
when he crossed the "threshold" (the *limen*): "He has delivered us from the dominion of darkness and transferred
us to the kingdom of his beloved Son" (Col. 1:13).[20]

The importance of being a Roman citizen in New Testament times was that one was, to a degree at any rate, a
member of the governing community—in many ways occupying a position analogous to that of the British citizen
during the heyday of the raj. The Roman citizen was privileged. Citizenship carried with it the right to hold political office and responsibility in the Roman state. It gave
the right to participate in the deliberations of Roman assemblies. It gave the right to inherit Roman property and
the right to contract a marriage valid under Roman law,
with all its attendant rights and duties. More importantly,
in day-to-day life it gave access to the Roman law, especially in regard to commerce and property (the *ius com-
mercii*, the right to hold, buy, and sell). In contrast to the
peregrine the citizen was subject to, and could use, a more
universal and a more effective law than the alien. In theory
the Roman citizen could travel anywhere without problems, being everywhere protected by the Roman law. In

Privileges of Roman citizenship

the territories of the Empire where Roman law did not hold immediate sway he was not subject to the local law unless he consented (though such consent would be usual in business), and he could take matters into his own courts when these were sitting. He owed allegiance to Rome, and Rome would protect him.[21]

Paul's own life illustrates some of these aspects of citizenship. The first time we hear of him making use of his rights as a Roman citizen is in Philippi, the Roman colony (Acts 16:16–40). After Paul and Silas had been beaten and jailed, the city magistrates sent them a message asking them to leave the city quietly. Not so, said Paul. The magistrates would have to come and escort them out of the city with dignity, for to beat and imprison a Roman without trial was a serious offense. In doing this, Paul undoubtedly intended that the new church in Lydia's house would receive some protection and official standing, but for our purposes it is enough to note that the magistrates did as they were required. They had been guilty of a serious offense, and there are instances on record where cities were punished for such crimes, even to the extent of losing their Roman privileges.[22] Paul therefore had the magistrates at a complete disadvantage, and they had to comply with his demand.

In the temple incident (Acts 22) Paul claimed his citizenship status before anything untoward occurred, thus avoiding being scourged. Again the volte-face of the authorities, once convinced of the accuracy of Paul's claim, is to be noted. This incident also illustrates one major difference between the treatment meted out to a non-Roman and that appropriate for a citizen. It was general practice to examine probable offenders under torture, particularly if they were slaves, but also if they were not Roman citizens. This happened to Jesus and perhaps to Paul and Silas at Philippi, though in the latter case we should note that a beating is not necessarily a scourging (Acts 16:22–23).

The last instance is the referral of Paul's case to the emperor at Rome (Acts 25ff.). The example of Paul is the best one we have of the operation of this appellate procedure. A Roman citizen dissatisfied with proceedings taken against him had the right of provocatio, by this time the right of appeal to Caesar, though originally an appeal to the people. In Paul's case the appeal was really irregular in that Festus had not disposed of his case, but it did provide the proconsul with a means of passing this contentious case on to higher authority. Such a procedure was not available to the non-Roman.[23]

In speaking of our citizenship being in heaven, and in using the correlative metaphors of alienage, Paul and the other New Testament writers, therefore, indicate that the Christian is subject to the jurisdiction of heaven and possesses the privileges of that citizenship. His home state will protect him and his interests, will intervene on his behalf, and will itself determine his rights and duties. The Christian is therefore in one sense to a degree, in another sense completely, free from duties imposed by the local law of the world, his temporary residence, which, after all, exists only by the permission of the dominant power, Heaven.

From our standpoint in legal development, the question arises whether dual citizenship or dual nationality was possible in New Testament times (although the concept of the subcommunity, the politeuma, would lessen the need for dual citizenship). Unfortunately, the answer to this question is not clear. On the basis of certain comments by Cicero and others, it was once thought that the Romans did not permit dual citizenship—one was either a Roman or one was not.[24] If this was the position at the time Paul was writing, then the application of the metaphor is clear: one is either a citizen of heaven, or one is not. However, Paul himself was a citizen both of the empire and of Tarsus (Acts 21:39). In any event, more recent academic discussion has suggested that the Romans were not wholly consistent in their attitude toward citizenship. It does appear that by the time of Augustus the Romans were moving to a position where citizens who had been granted Roman citizenship might retain some duties under

the law of their previous citizenship. At first, such a retention of duties was a privilege extended to certain new
citizens, allowing them still to hold civic office and participate in the local government of their area. However,
one corollary of office was liability for the financial obligations of the local authority. As time went on, and econ-
omies deteriorated, this burden increased. At the same
time it became easier to become a Roman, and so it also
became easier to escape civic obligations by doing so. The
government and financial administration of the non-
Roman cities therefore became difficult. To deal with this
problem, "new" Romans were later required to retain some
of the duties of local citizenship.[25] Where such duties were
imposed on new citizens, these new citizens would form
a subcommunity within their local community; then they
were Roman citizens, yet with duties in the community in
which they were placed (this could clearly tie in with the
subcommunity of Philippians 3:20, mentioned earlier,
p. 58). If this was indeed the situation, then perhaps an
argument may be drawn from it. In such cases of "dual
citizenship" the balance between the two citizenships was
not equal. The primary citizenship was Roman, though
certain duties were added with respect to the other citizenship. Christians should be detached, but not uncon-
cerned. Their primary citizenship does not obliterate their
obligations to the society in which they live. Sent into the
world (John 17:18), Christians cannot retire from it unless
they retire from it altogether (1 Cor. 5:9–10). Such a thought
harmonizes with Jesus' prayer, not that his followers be
taken from the world, but that they be protected in it (John
17:15).

Connected with this is the analogy of ambassadorship
Paul uses in 2 Corinthians 5:18–21 and Ephesians 6:19–20.
The Christian is an ambassador for Christ, not a national
of the country to which he is appointed, bearing the mo-
mentous message of the gospel: "God was in Christ reconciling the world to himself" (2 Cor. 5:19).

The contrast between citizenship and alienage has
therefore a considerable content when interpreted legally.

Here Christians are strangers and foreigners, without free
and easy access to the world and its ways. They are not
citizens of the world, subject to its laws, fashions, and
dictates. Indeed, as far as this world is concerned they are
not fully persons and cannot lawfully make full use of its
customs.

On the other side, Christians are presented as possessing a different and lasting citizenship, which they carry
wherever they go and which occasionally allows the for-
mation of subcommunities of their own where they are
numerous. As citizens of heaven they have access to its
councils, and the possibility of being called on to hold
positions of responsibility (cf. Luke 19:11–27). Their Sovereign is of greater authority and power than those of this
world, which exists only by His permission. He can intervene in its affairs to protect His nationals and will ulti-
mately punish those who wrong them (cf. Acts 16:37–38
above). Christians obey and are bound by heaven's laws.
However, this does not justify facile "rebellion" against
the society in which the Christian is placed, nor the easy
use of a "higher law" to evade responsibilities. Christians
are also resident aliens. They should play their part actively in the world and equally actively in the prayer room,
but as aliens they must be detached. Doubtless there will
be occasions on which they must disregard the ephemeral
dictates of the world and put up with the consequences,
which may be serious—see Hebrews 11:32–38 and John
17:14—but to do otherwise is to betray one's real citizenship and to forget the realities of eternity. We are in the
world but not of the world.

In the world and yet not of the world: in that connection one other point can be made, drawing from the
Greek language although the same basic facts hold true for
the Roman communities, as we have seen. Only part of
the total population of a community was the citizenry of
that community. The rest, and often the largest in number,
would be composed of aliens and the slaves of the citizens.

In the Epistles the Greek word ekklesia is translated
as "church." We think of the word in theological, indeed

Ekklesia

"ecclesiastical" terms. However in its original context the ekklesia meant those who were called out, citizens required for the business of the city. At first it seems to have meant particularly the citizens called out to do battle for the protection of the community, and from that meaning it came also to be used to mean the assembly of the citizens met to transact the affairs of the community.

Read that element of meaning into the New Testament uses of the word and it adds light and flavor to many passages. The church is not the dully familiar group of persons who meet every Sunday. The church is the assembly of the citizens of heaven, met according to the summons of the chief citizen, and met to do business either by way of government of the affairs of the community, or to defend its interests. It also means that we can balance the idea that we are resident aliens, discussed above, with the notion that we are the true citizens. That should not be dwelled on to the point of megalomania, but it does get things into a true perspective, which can be useful and a comfort to many who suffer or who are oppressed. Their "real" citizenship is secure and supreme.

4

Adoption

THE CONCEPT OF ADOPTION is found in both ancient and modern legal systems. At the time the New Testament Epistles were being written, Roman law contained far and away the most fully developed adoption procedures and devices, though a variety of adoption procedures was probably also available in the legal systems of the Grecian cities. Interestingly, however, it was not a concept of the Jewish law of the time, though the Jews may well have been aware of the idea from other legal systems.

In law, adoption is a legal act that changes the personal status of a child in relation to his natural parent(s) and constitutes the relationship of parent and child between him and some other person or persons. Though it is, therefore, technically a legal *act*, it is also spoken of as a *device*, and is to be thought of as having a continuing effect in the changes it brings about in the statuses of several persons: the natural parent(s), the child, and the "new" parent(s).

In the New Testament Epistles the language of adoption is used in five places. From there it has passed into theology, for example, as chapter 12 of the Westminster Confession of Faith of 1646. This transition from law into theology is one that does not appear to have been recognized as odd, but odd it is, for adoption was not a legal device found in any of the legal systems of the United

67

Kingdom until the passing of the Adoption Acts earlier in this century. Nonetheless chapter 12 of the Confession fairly expresses the theological implications of the concept:

> All those that are justified, God vouchsafeth, in and for His only Son Jesus Christ, to make partakers of the grace of adoption: by which they are taken into the number, and enjoy the liberties and privileges of the children of God; have his name put upon them, receive the Spirit of adoption; have access to the throne of grace with boldness; are enabled to cry, Abba, Father; are pitied, protected, provided for, and chastened by him as by a father yet never cast off, but are sealed to the day of redemption and inherit the promises, as heirs of everlasting salvation.[1]

There was, however, no basis in the local law for these ideas in the seventeenth century, but if one studies other notions of adoption it seems clear that the Confession's statement draws from Roman law, because only Roman adoption has a content that fully combines the profundities of both the elements of entry into the status of "son" and the incidents of that status, in other words, of becoming a son and being, or behaving as, a son.

Paul is the only New Testament writer to use the metaphor of adoption. He employs it in three places in Romans and once each in Ephesians and Galatians. In Romans 9:4 the place of the Jews as the chosen people is underlined: to them belongs the adoption, the sonship. In Romans 8:15, Ephesians 1:5, and Galatians 4:5 the metaphor points to the selection of believers as sons: their justification is their entry into sonship, and from the point of conversion on they are members of God's family, under His guidance and authority (in legal terms, under his potestas), irrespective of how they actually live. Lastly, the allusion in Romans 8:23 to waiting "for the adoption as sons, the redemption of our bodies," refers to the final transformation at the second resurrection. Then indeed will we have totally passed from our former state into something wholly new.

Naturally not all writers explore Roman law in considering Paul's words. Some are content to see in it only the de facto adoption that existed in British law until the passing of the Adoption Acts in this century.[2] Others refer the concept to Jewish law and even to the deliverance of the children of Israel in the Exodus.[3] It is true that here and there the Roman content of adoption is indicated, but this is not adequately substantiated or developed, and the few more formal suggestions seem not to have been taken up by modern discussion.[4] Of those I have read, only A. A. Hodge approaches the Roman concept, combining justification and sanctification in its present and continuous sense.[5] This is unfortunate. The riches of the concept in Roman law and its weakness in the alternative systems make compelling the suggestion that we must look to Roman law to interpret the notion. Jewish law, the obvious alternative, does not possess the concept, and Greek adoption, existing really as a means of succession, is but a pale shadow of the Roman concept.

Adoption, then, is a device found in many legal systems by which a person leaves his natural family and enters another family. His personal status vis-à-vis his natural and his adopting parents undergoes significant change. In ancient legal systems the fundamental reason for this procedure was to ensure that the family making the adoption would continue—in the absence of the adoption the family line would have died out. Although in the twentieth century ideas have changed, in the legal systems of New Testament times there was usually no suggestion that an adoption was made for the protection, maintenance, or benefit of the adoptee. Adoption was carried out so that the adopting family would continue to be represented before the family god. This was clear in Roman law, where the family cult was all-important, and similar ideas are to be found in Greek law.[6] It is therefore necessary to distinguish adoption from fosterage, where the individual does not enter the family or become part of it in any other than a social sense.

Adoption must also be distinguished from concepts

of *succession*, although it is often connected with it. Succession is a matter of title to property; adoption is a matter of membership in the family. In neither fosterage nor succession does the individual, ipso facto, become part of the family or represent the family for religious purposes. In other words, an individual may succeed to an estate because he is a member of the family of the deceased. That membership is the nexus between himself and the succession, but it is not a reversible equation. Under some circumstances such as where there is no direct heir (cf. Eliezer of Damascus and Abraham, Gen. 15:2), a person who is not a member of a family may succeed to an estate. Such succession does not make him part of the family of the deceased. That would require adoption. Bearing that in mind, let us now turn to the possible sources of Paul's metaphor.

Jewish Law

It is quite clear that adoption as a legal form was unknown to the Jews. No Jewish legal writing contains any provisions that can be rightly construed as adoption[7] and the historical examples some cite from the Old Testament can be explained without bringing in the idea of adoption as part of Jewish law. The instances where God speaks of His relation to the Jews as that of a parent to His children do not help the argument, but we can return to this later. Putting the matter succinctly, the Jews did not need a concept of adoption. The device of adoption was unnecessary and hence unknown in Jewish law. Indeed, adoption is only to be found in modern Israeli law, where it was established by the Adoption of Children Law 1960 (5720/1960). Prior to that it was unknown because the ancient ideas of adoption proceeded on postulates that were unthinkable to the Jewish mind. The basic element of adoption was an assumption of sonship that entitled the adoptee to continue the line of the adopter. Such an idea was quite foreign to the Hebrew. It was a great tragedy that a man might die without offspring, but this was not to be obviated by means of adoption. Instead, two other devices existed to ensure the continuation of the line.[8]

The first of these depended on the proposition that any male child would suffice to represent the family. It was the continuance of the seed of the man, the male line, that was important, the status of the mother being less so.[9] Indeed, the social division of progeny was not made on the basis of legitimacy and illegitimacy (i.e., whether the parents were married to each other or not), but upon the ceremonial fitness for religious purposes of the child.[10] It followed that almost any child of a man could continue his line. Only the child of an idol-worshiping or slave mother was excluded. In all other cases the important factor was the father's acceptance or acknowledgment and identification of his son. An example is the case of Jephthah, whose story is found in Judges 11. Jephthah the Gileadite was the son of a harlot, but his father was Gilead. Although ceremonially unfit, he was nonetheless one of the family, entitled to inherit from Gilead, and for this reason he was driven out by his half-brothers (Judg. 11:2).[11]

Further evidence of the importance of the seed of the male is seen in the genealogies. In most cases the mother is not mentioned and on occasion "subsidiary" marriages carry the line. It was quite proper for a man to have children by a servant (a servant, not a slave), who were then reared as if they were issue of his marriage. One of the clearest instances of this is the giving of Hagar to Abraham by Sarah, where Sarah comments "it may be that I shall obtain children by her" (Gen. 16:2). As in the case of Jephthah, the child born to Hagar, Ishmael, was later driven out (Gen. 21:9–21), though legally he could have claimed a share in the inheritance as a child of Abraham. Be that as it may, Abraham thought that in this way he could bring about the fulfillment of God's promise of an heir and descendants (Gen. 15:1–6; 16:1–4). A similar obtaining of children through servants is found in the case of Jacob and his two wives and their maids in Genesis 30:1–13, but the most extreme application of the idea of the importance of the seed of the male is found in Genesis

19:30–38, where Lot's daughters seek to justify their incest on the grounds that this would preserve their father's seed, although it is clear from the narrative that this was only part of their motivation.

The importance of the continuation of the seed of the male, together with the unimportance of a concept of legitimacy for these purposes, served to diminish the number of occasions when a man would die without leaving a male heir to continue his line. Sometimes, however, a man did succeed in dying without issue, and in that case the institution of levirate marriage, regulated by Deuteronomy 25:5–10, was invoked. This is the closest analogue to adoption in Jewish law, but since it presupposes the death of the "adopter" (the person whose line is to continue), it has no relevance as a source of the Pauline metaphor.

The levirate involved the duty of the brother of the deceased to marry the widow and to raise by her sons for his brother.[12] These children, the product of a man and his deceased brother's widow, then continued the line of the deceased and stood in his place before God. Although an element of this institution was the desire to prevent the inheritance from passing outside the family, the continuation of the name of the deceased brother was important: "And the first son whom she bears shall succeed to the name of his brother who is dead, that his name may not be blotted out of Israel" (Deut. 25:6). It is also interesting to note that this device provided an heir who was genetically as close to being an actual son of the deceased as possible under the circumstances; one half of the genes came from the mother and would thus have been the same, while the other half came from the same gene pool as the deceased. This is very different from the concept of adoption that we know.

In the levirate, substitution of the male was possible after a ceremonial renunciation of the right/duty by the nearest relative. Thus, in the case of Ruth it was of great importance that Boaz was a relative (Ruth 2:20), but Boaz himself properly raised the difficulty of the nearer relative

(Ruth 3:12) and saw to its solution (Ruth 4). However, in the ordinary instance the levirate was the duty of the brother and could only be ignored with peril. In its pure form the ceremony whereby a woman castigated one who failed to take her in levirate marriage is set out in Deuteronomy 25:7–10 and would involve much loss of face for the person concerned. The stigma of the failure to perform his duty then remained with the house of the defaulter forever (Deut. 25:10). However, as can be seen from Ruth 4, quite early the ceremony was modified so as to serve as a release from the duty rather than a punishment for failure to meet the duty.[13]

Final proof of the importance of the institution of the levirate can be obtained from the case of Tamar, the daughter-in-law of Judah, in Genesis 38. She was married first to Er, and then in levirate to Onan, who wilfully failed to give her a son and for this he was slain by God. Judah sent her home to wait until his third son had grown, though the impression given is that he did not wish to risk a third son with her. And indeed, Judah made no move to give her his third son, so finally Tamar took the initiative. Dressing as a harlot she obtained a child by Judah himself. Normally harlotry by a widow was an extremely serious offense, and Judah went to punish her, but the blame she would have incurred was changed to praise when she showed that by playing the harlot she had fulfilled the laws of levirate marriage.

The case of Tamar shows the antiquity of the institution of the levirate and the ideas that lay behind it:[14] the events of Genesis 38 antedate the Deuteronomic provisions by some hundreds of years. But the age of the institution was not a reason for its abolition. The levirate was current in New Testament times and was the source of the conundrum put to Jesus about the multiple husbands and the resurrection (Matt. 22:23–33; Mark 12:18–27; Luke 20:27–38); it passed into disfavor only in Talmudic times and eventually, by the year A.D. 1000, rabbinic opinion repudiated the institution and required the renunciation of the right/duty by the Deuteronomic ceremony in all cases.[15]

The institution of the levirate and the emphasis on the continuance of the seed of the man from whatever maternal source largely eliminated the need for a concept of adoption as a way of continuing a family line in Jewish law. Bearing this in mind we can now consider the other instances in the Old Testament where it looks at first sight as though adoption is involved. Of these, the principal cases, apart from that of Jephthah discussed above, are those of Ephraim and Manasseh, Eliezer of Damascus, Moses, Genubath, Obed, and Esther.

On his deathbed Jacob raised the two sons of Joseph, Ephraim and Manasseh, to equal status with his own progeny (Gen. 48:5–6). But in so doing Jacob was allocating rights of succession among persons who were already within the family. He was not bringing in an outsider. It follows that this is not true adoption. The same would apply to the case of Joseph's great-grandchildren, the children of Machir, the son of Manasseh, who were "born on Joseph's knees" (Gen. 50:23). It is not clear from the text whether there was any question of succession rights or of status involved, but in any event, as in the case of Ephraim and Manasseh, no true adoption is present in this intrafamily occurrence. At most it would seem to be a change of succession rights, as before.

The question of succession is also the kernel of the case of Eliezer of Damascus, the servant of Abraham (Gen. 15:2). There is no evidence that Eliezer's possible succession to Abraham, in the absence of an heir fathered by Abraham, was anything other than a matter of the disposal of Abraham's goods. There is no implication that Eliezer would carry on Abraham's family line. Again, therefore, we are not dealing with an adoption.

One point is common to the next two cases, those of Moses and Genubath, and crops up again with Esther: they occur in alien legal milieus—Egypt in the first two cases, Persia in the last. It may therefore properly be asked whether they provide any evidence as to the Jewish law, apart from any question as to whether adoption is actually involved.

In the case of Moses we are confronted with an instance of fosterage, not adoption. It is true that Moses was reared as one of Pharaoh's house by Pharaoh's daughter. Exodus 2:10 and Jubilees 47:9 are quite categorical: "he became her son." It is also true that Moses remained in the royal circle for forty years (Acts 7:23; Exod. 2:11). However, he seems to have refused to consider himself an Egyptian (cf. Heb. 11:24) and certainly did not feel that his upbringing gave him any special privileges or authority. Faced with the question, "Who made you a prince over us?" he fled (Exod. 2:14). Furthermore, as there is no evidence of formal adoption proceedings, Pharaoh's attitude to him in Exodus 2:15 might be taken (equivocally) to argue their nonexistence.

Genubath is another case of fosterage, but unlike Moses he was related by blood to the Egyptian royal family (1 Kings 11:14–20). His father Hadad, an Edomite and a distant relation of David, had been taken to Egypt when a small boy to escape from the wrath of Joab. He grew to manhood in Egypt and in the course of time married the sister of Tahpenes, the queen. Their child, Genubath, was reared by Tahpenes among the sons of Pharaoh. We are not given sufficient data precisely to define his status, but we can at least say that there is no evidence of his adoption by Pharaoh.

Another example sometimes cited as adoption is that of Obed, the son of Boaz and Ruth. When he was nursed by Naomi, the women of the neighborhood "gave him a name, saying, 'a son has been born to Naomi' " (Ruth 4:17). This might be taken to indicate an adoptive relationship, but Naomi was already in *loco parentis* by reason of the levirate, and in any case, such an adoption would do nothing to ensure the continuance of the male line. What we have here is better explained as merely a recognition of the delight of Naomi in the new arrival, a delight accentuated by her own previous loss of husband and sons.[16]

Obed may also be linked to the cases of Moses and

Genubath, and even to the case of Sarah and Ishmael if it be felt that Sarah was originally intending to adopt the child (Gen. 16:2). In all these cases there may have been an informal adoption—a treating as a son—but this has no importance. These cases are "adoptions" by a female. The seed continued in the male line only. There are in fact only two examples of possible adoptions in the female line. In Ezra 2:61 (= Neh. 7:63) we read of one Barzillai who had taken his wife's name, but he was not to be found in the official genealogies (v. 62). The other example is very intriguing indeed. It is found in 1 Chronicles 2:34–35, where we read of one Sheshan who had no sons, only daughters, and who gave one of his daughters to his Egyptian slave Jarha, in marriage. Their son, Attai, continued the genealogical line (vv. 36ff.). Here the child may have been adopted into the line by the daughter, though adoption by Sheshan seems equally possible. In any event, in this sole instance the family line continued to be recognized in the congregation despite the intrusion of an alien father.

The remaining individual case some have thought to involve adoption is that of Esther. In Esther 2:7 we read that Mordecai, Esther's uncle, had taken his orphaned niece as a daughter, a phraseology that looks very like a formula of adoption. Indeed, the translators of the RSV have no doubt in the matter and translate the clause "Mordecai adopted her as his own daughter." It is likely that Mordecai was a eunuch, which would explain why he was allowed to walk in front of the court of the harem (Esth. 2:11). Adoption would therefore be the only method by which his family line might continue.

But to this two objections can be laid. First, in most ancient legal systems a eunuch might not adopt, for as Justinian (*Institutes* 1.11.4) states, "adoption imitates nature." Someone artificially incapable of fathering children could not acquire a child by adoption (Justinian, *Institutes* 1.11.9). Second, *pace* Sheshan, such an adoption would not have continued Mordecai's family, since Esther was a woman.

Be that as it may, adoption was a concept known in the Babylonian Empire, where its most frequent rationale seems to have been the placing of a child for apprenticeship purposes, since training in a trade was normally given by the father; in the normal instance the child would revert to his previous family at the end of training. But also adoption to continue a family line was not unknown.[17] There is therefore a background to Esther that lends a little substance to the argument that she was adopted by Mordecai.

However, against the possibility of an adoption being involved, and apart from the irrelevance of adopting a girl, the rest of the Book of Esther shows that the girl and her uncle would be unlikely to use a foreign legal device that ran contrary to Jewish thinking. Indeed, one of the complaints of Haman was that the Jews obeyed their own laws though resident in the Babylonian Empire (Esth. 3:8). To my mind these points are sufficient to disallow the possibility of an adoption in this case. However, it does raise the question of the extent to which the Jews knew and tolerated foreign concepts in practice, especially as the remaining examples of adoption may also show Babylonian influences.

The first of these is found in Ezra 10:44. The KJV translation presents no difficulty, but the Hebrew text is acknowledged to be corrupt. The RSV translators, after comparing the Hebrew text with that of 1 Esdras 9:36, produced an ambiguous translation: the men mentioned in the earlier verses had married foreign women "and they put them away with their children." It has been suggested that the correct meaning of this text is that some of the men listed in the earlier verses had married foreign women who already had children by other men, presumably Babylonians, and that the new Jewish husbands had adopted these.[18] This appears plausible, as the people had just returned from Babylon where adoption was known. However, this seems to me to be an unnecessary interpretation. It could well be that the text is much more straightforward and that the men put away their foreign wives and their own children. That seems much more the picture to be inferred from Ezra 9:2 and from the dating sequence of Ezra 8:31; 9:1–2; 10:14; and 10:16–17: at least a year appears to have elapsed. This cannot have been a happy occasion, and it may be that the writer wished to emphasize in Ezra 10:44 that some men put away their own bairns as well as their foreign wives, a measure of their determination to be faithful to God and to the law, which forbad mixed marriages (Exod. 34:11–16; Deut. 7:1–4).

Other Bible passages contain close parallels to the adoption formulae found in Babylonian law. These examples might be further referred to the Nuzi texts, but that seems to be pushing things too far;[19] mere priority in date does not imply influence when the other connections of two legal systems are so slender. Abraham did come from the Nuzi region, but the first example we have is that of Tamar: levirate and not adoption. The connection of the passages with Babylonian law is more distinct, and to my mind is most probable, since there the king was considered to be the adopted son of God. But one need not go on from the instances to be quoted in the next paragraph to postulate a legal device of ordinary use in Jewish law. The other evidence we have already considered is too slender.

What looks rather like adoption formulae are found in the "divine" adoptions. In the New Testament there are God's affirmations of Christ's sonship at His baptism (Matt. 3:17; Mark 1:11; Luke 3:22) and on the Mount of Transfiguration (Matt. 17:5; Mark 9:7; Luke 9:35; cf. Rev. 21:7). Christ's words from the cross to John and his mother (John 19:26–27) have also been cited as resembling an adoption formula.[20] In the Old Testament there are two other very clear instances. In a passage that can refer both to Solomon and to Messiah, God says through Nathan the prophet, "I will be his father, and he shall be my son" (2 Sam. 7:14). An even better case is found in Psalm 2:7, where God says to David (and to Messiah), "You are my son, today I have begotten you." Other less clear examples exist, including Deuteronomy 8:5; Isaiah 1:4; 30:1, 9; Malachi 1:6. All these

Old and New Testament passages contain a declaration by God that someone is His son (cf. 1 John 3:1). Some might add to them the various instances in which God speaks of Himself as a father to His people (cf. Ps. 82:6; Jer. 31:9), but it is preferable to consider the Fatherhood of God as a separate metaphor: the adoption formulae involved declarations of sonship, not of fatherhood.[21]

It does appear that the Old and New Testament declarations of sonship are akin to formulae and concepts found here and there in the ancient world; as I have indicated, Babylon, where the king was considered to be the adopted son of God, is the most obvious source of such language in the Bible.[22] One need not, however, draw these theological metaphors so close together as to postulate a legal device,[23] and the other biblical examples do lead inexorably to the conclusion that adoption was simply not known in Jewish law. The only evidences from secular sources that I am aware of seem to me to indicate only that Jews did on occasion make use of non-Jewish legal forms. Thus, there are not a few instances where inscriptions in the Jewish catacombs in Rome clearly indicate that adoption of and by Jews did occur, but in view of the paucity of the other evidence I believe that it can fairly be taken that these are cases of Jews using the Roman legal forms, not of a Jewish law of adoption.[24] A single case has also been quoted from the Aramaic papyri; the facts are obscure, though the intention to adopt a slave is clear. However, as the transaction takes place in the presence of the Persian garrison commander, it seems likely that Persian and not Jewish law is involved in that instance.[25]

There is, therefore, little evidence for adoption in Jewish law, the case of Sheshan being the only exception. But while the various writers on Jewish law agree on this point, some do draw attention to the existence of a practice of fosterage that might approximate adoption, though lacking the precise legal form. Just as de facto adoption occurred in the United Kingdom long before the Adoption Acts, so it was quite in order, and indeed was considered a work of merit, for a deserted child to be taken into and be brought up within a family as an act of charity.[26] The British experience would lead one to expect that in many cases such a child was treated in practice as a natural child of the family for all purposes, including sharing in the inheritance of the family. But the fact remains that in law the child was not part of the family group and did not have the legal status of a child within it. One proof of this can be seen in the imagery of Ezekiel 16, where the Lord speaks of Himself as having rescued an abandoned child (Ezek. 16:2–7) and later as having married her (Ezek. 16: 8–14). Such a marriage would have been impossible if the child had been adopted or truly become one of the children of the family.

But though there remains a vestigial possibility that in his use of "adoption" Paul was referring to such a fosterage practice or extralegal arrangement, one is left with a large question. Would Paul, a trained lawyer, writing to Greeks and Romans, use an illustration drawn from an informal practice when by the same words he could be referring to a detailed and well-known legal institution? I do not think so.

The question then arises whether an "informal adoption" might have been given a more formal status without the requirement of a normal adoption process. What if the "father" took official steps to acknowledge his "son"? In the Roman or local provincial laws there were two procedures that would seem to make possible such a giving of official status to an informal arrangement. Both would involve registration: a child could be registered as the child of the person registering him either in the local Roman register of births or in the provincial census register that was kept for taxation purposes.[27] In the absence of a proven objection by the natural parent, the appropriate archives, depending on whether the child were a Roman citizen or not, would provide prima facie evidence of the status of the child as a member of a family. I have no evidence that this was ever done—it is rather like asking how many undetected murders happened in Britain last year; the only useful evidence would be that of a challenge to an entry in the register. However, from our knowledge of the legal processes of the time, registration would seem to provide a way of clothing an informal arrangement with some official cloak while remaining less than full formal adoption. It is just possible that the Greek word for adoption in the New Testament, *huiothesia*, which means "placing as son," does in fact conceal such an idea. But again, why should one reject the idea of proper adoption in favor of a partial substitute?

An "Unknown" Referent?

If we accept that Jewish law lacked the concept of adoption, and that it is not probable that Paul was using an informal notion of adoption, it is then necessary to consider what legal system did provide the content for his imagery. The most logical options are either Greek ideas or Roman law. Before considering these, however, we should note that there is the logical possibility that the source of Paul's language is a legal system of which we have no real knowledge. This possibility of an unknown referent resides in the fact that one of his uses of the idea occurs in Galatians 4:5. The Roman jurist Gaius (*Institutes* 1.55) tells us that in his time (c. A.D. 175) the concept of paternal control of a family (*patria potestas*), which is fundamental to Roman family law, was also known in Galatia. It is therefore tempting to speculate that Paul, thanks to his travels and his own legal training, may have had knowledge of a Galatian adoption law, devised to meet the problems raised by the concept of *potestas* and by the perceived need for the continuation of a family line in much the same way the Roman device was created. But this is pure conjecture. Present knowledge does not permit or entitle us to determine this point—it can be but stated, and left.[28]

Roman Law

Rather than considering Greek law as the next possible source of Paul's adoption imagery, I would prefer first to discuss Roman law so that we may later highlight by contrast how far the Greek concepts fall short of the fullness of the Roman. In contrast to the Roman ideas, Greek adoption affords but a pale shadow, having little to do with a real family relationship and amounting to little more than a will.

There are three main reasons for considering Roman law as the source of the idea of adoption in Paul's letters. A first and elementary point is that "adoption" is found in only five places and only in epistles with "Roman" connections. It appears once each in Ephesians (Eph. 1:5) and Galatians (Gal. 4:5), epistles written to churches situated (shown in appendix 4) in centers of population with Roman authority present. Ephesus was the principal city of Asia. If one accepts that the churches of the Epistle to the Galatians were those at Derbe, Lystra, and Iconium (the "South Galatian" theory), they would have had a significant Roman presence by the time of Paul. If Galatians were a letter to Ancyra and related churches in North Galatia, the case is even stronger. The other three uses of "adoption" are found in the epistle to the church in Rome itself (Rom. 8:15, 23; Rom. 9:4). The church there may be assumed to have known its local law, and indeed one might ask whether it is not significant that it is in the Epistle to the Romans that adoption figures most.

The second reason for considering Roman law is that it was the law of Paul's own citizenship. It is possible to argue that Paul would not have known the technicalities of Roman law, since he lived most of his life in a Greek or Jewish milieu, but this is not convincing. Roman law was a prized possession of the citizen. It would have governed the whole of Paul's life, in particular his familial relationships, since Paul's parents were Roman. That point is established because it was required, for citizenship to pass to a son, that both parents be citizens. So when in Acts 22:28 Paul claims to be a Roman by birth, it necessarily follows that his parents were themselves citizens, or that his father was a citizen and that his mother had the right to enter into a Roman marriage (conubium). In such

Re: Paul's Roman citizenship

a Roman family it was Roman law that in the last analysis
would govern, even though the normal life of the family
was Jewish. Roman law would also have controlled the
property rights of the family and have been the legal system under which Paul would have succeeded to his father's estate. That law would therefore be known to a son,
especially to a son with Paul's legal bent.[29]

Lastly, there is a more general point. Adoption in its
Roman form was a concept that was becoming known
even in "non-Roman" areas in the empire; it was the device that had linked Julius Caesar, Augustus, and Tiberius,
largely for the purpose of succession to power in the incipient empire, and that for similar reasons was increasingly used to link other influential Roman families. It can
therefore be argued with some basis that it is likely that
the Roman ideas were widely known and that non-Roman
readers of the Epistles would also interpret such language
in accordance with the Roman notions. *before his own life*

But what did adoption mean in law, in practice, and
hence metaphorically? The profound truth of Roman
adoption was that the adoptee was taken out of his previous state and was placed in a new relationship of son to
his new father, his new paterfamilias. All his old debts
were cancelled, and in effect the adoptee started a new
life as part of his new family. From that time on the paterfamilias had the same control over his new "child" as
he had over his natural offspring. He owned all the property and acquisitions of the adoptee, controlled his personal relationships, and had rights of discipline. On the
other hand, the father was liable for the actions of the
adoptee, and each owed the other reciprocal duties of support and maintenance.

The Roman concept of adoption was rooted in the old
religious basis of the Roman family. Each family had its
own specific cult or *sacra* ("sacred things"). The deities
worshiped by each family varied from case to case, but
they included the *lares* and *penates*, the gods of hearth
and larder, and the spiritualization of that family itself—
its *genius*. In the worship of the *sacra* the head of the

What Roman adoption was! meant

family, the paterfamilias, acted as priest, and this role seems
to have been the basis of his authority over the members
of the family.[30]

It was of importance that the family worship should
continue, since it was an important element in the structure of the formal state worship of the gods of the Roman
state. Where it seemed likely that a cult was about to die
out owing to a lack of persons to carry it on, adoption was
the remedy. By either of two adoption procedures, known
as adoptio and adrogatio, it was possible to bring into the
family a person naturally part of another family, and to
make him by certain ceremonies a member of the new
family in all respects, and in particular to enable him to
carry on the family cult.

Of the two procedures adrogatio is the older, and although it is not very likely that Paul would have had it in
mind as he wrote, since many of its features are sources
of the concept of adoptio and explain its peculiarities, it
is as well to consider it first.

Adrogatio was the adoption of a person who was sui
iuris, that is, not under the legal power or authority of
another person.[31] Since its main original function was to
provide a person who would carry on the family worship,
it is not surprising that the official priests of the state, the
pontiffs, played an important part in the proceedings. They
had to be satisfied in each case that the adrogation should
occur, and to do this they not only inquired into the facts—
e.g., whether in the absence of the adrogation the adopter's
sacra would fall into disuse—but also into the motives of
the parties, the character of the adopter, and the desirability of the proposed course of action in the widest sense.
There were various reasons for this searching inquiry; the
desirability of the preservation of the particular cult was
an important element, but the most important reason for
inquiry was the effect of the adrogation. The person ad-
rogated (the adrogatus) was not the sole person affected—
all those who were under his paternal authority (his potestas) also passed under the power of the new paterfamilias. This meant that perhaps another family, and certainly

a branch of that family, was extinguished to provide for
the continuation of another family cult, a very serious step
to be taken only after solemn consideration.

Once the pontiffs had given their approval to the adrogation, the next stage was the securing of the approval
of the rest of the citizenry. In the early stage of development of *adrogatio* it meant just that: the *comitia calata* met
to consider the matter. This *comitia* was composed of
the citizenry of Rome (though some writers consider that
only the heads of families were members of the council)
and was in fact the Roman legislature, the *comitia curiata*,
meeting under another name for the purposes of regulating the public religion. In this form the *comitia* was pre-
sided over by the high priest, the *pontifex maximus*, who
asked each of the parties if they consented to the adrogation. If they did, the next step was the formal renunciation
of the present family cult or *sacra* of the adoptee (the *de-
testatio sacrorum*), after which the *adrogatus* formally entered into his new family. In passing we may note that
this renunciation is interestingly paralleled by early bap-
tismal practice, where the convert was required first to
renounce the Devil and all his works before his ceremonial
entry by baptism into the family of God.[32]

One of the results of this form of adoption should be
noted separately: all the debts, obligations, and liabilities
of the *adrogatus* were extinguished by the adoption. Paul's
statement in Colossians 2:14, "having canceled the bond
[*cheirographon*] which stood against us," although not
made specifically in connection with adoption, would be
entirely consistent with this aspect of *adrogatio*, since the
Roman *chirographum* was a formal acknowledgment of
indebtedness, signed by the debtor and kept by the creditor.

The other elements of *adrogatio* were shared with
adoptio and can be considered in that connection, but it
should be acknowledged that it is unlikely that Paul had
adrogatio in mind when writing his letters. Although he
makes most use of "adoption" in the Epistle to the Romans, the possibility is remote. In Paul's day *adrogatio*
could only occur in Rome, since in theory it required the

intervention of the *comitia*. In practice the important part of the ceremony was the pontifical enquiry, the people being represented by thirty lictors, but still the Roman environment was essential. It was not until the time of Diocletian (A.D. 284–305) that adrogation was possible by imperial rescript throughout the Empire, but even so, in the Vulgate (the Latin translation of the Bible by Jerome, c. A.D. 400) *adoptio* and not *adrogatio* is the word used for adoption. Jerome is late in legal history and of a period when *adrogatio* was unusual. His knowledge of the law of Paul's day may not be altogether reliable in this detail. However, if *adrogatio* is a possible reference for Paul's language there is one fascinating implication: in adrogation, not only was the adoptee adopted, but all those over whom he had paternal authority also passed into the family of his new father (Gaius, *Institutes* 1.107). This echoes the several instances in the New Testament where we find a man and his family or household converted—for example, Zaccheus (Luke 19:9), Cornelius (Acts 10), Lydia (Acts 16:14–16), the Philippian jailer (Acts 16:29–33), and Crispus (Acts 18:8).

By contrast, *adoptio* was the adoption of a son who was under the legal power and authority of another, who was *alieni iuris*.[33] In its forms and consequences it bears the closest resemblance to theological truth, holding the twin concepts of justification and sanctification together.

There were two stages in the *adoptio* procedure. The first was the destruction of the old *potestas*, the paternal power of the "previous" father. The second stage was the establishing of the paternal power of the "new" father. In order to carry out the first stage the Romans had to resort to what can be rightly described as an abuse of the law. One of the powers of the head of a family, the paterfamilias, was that of selling his offspring into civil bondage (in *mancipio*), making them slaves. Very early in Roman legal history, if the son was then released from slavery (by his owner or otherwise), he automatically passed once again under his father's authority and could be sold into bondage again by him. Accordingly, to avoid this abuse it was laid down in the Twelve Tables (the law established by the second Decemvirate, c. 450 B.C.) that when a son had been sold three times his father ceased to have any authority over him. The *adoptio* procedure was derived from this law. A father would sell his son to a friend who freed him immediately. This meant that the son was returned by law to his father's control. The father then resold the son to the friend, who freed him again, and again he returned to his father's power. Finally the father sold the son to the friend yet again, thus destroying his authority over him.

The proceedings up to this point left the son technically a slave in the power of the friend. The person making the adoption then brought a fictitious claim of ownership against the friend, formally claiming return of the son on the grounds that he was his son. The friend did not oppose the action, and the former father was not a party to the action. In the absence of any defense, counter-claim, or argument, the magistrate gave judgment in favor of the claimant, who therefore became the adoptee's new paterfamilias to whom the adoptee would in due course succeed. Thereafter the adoptee was subject to the authority and direction of his new paterfamilias in all matters.

The metaphor of the legal act of adoption is therefore not to be considered in isolation but as but one of a series of legal metaphors drawn from family life, the position of the child, concepts of inheritance, and so on. These mix with the adoption concept to show that becoming a son by adoption is but the entry into a status that required other things that are also illustrative of theological truth. But in summary we can note there that the position of the "new" child of the family was the same whether he was adopted by *adoptio* or by *adrogatio*. As a son his property and acquisitions, his time and personal life were at the disposal of his father, who had full disciplinary rights. Indeed, in law at any rate, the child was possessor of a status akin to that of a slave, and there was no "coming of age." He was under his father's control until the father freed him or either he or his father died.[34]

Both varieties of Roman adoption, therefore, clearly if metaphorically present salvation and its implications. Christians are the sons and daughters of God, being claimed as such by Him (Gal. 4:4–7), having been bought by the blood of the Lamb (Acts 20:28). They no longer owe obedience to their former master, the head of their old family. Formerly the children of wrath (Eph. 2:3), they have become children of God (John 1:12). All their debts and liabilities are sloughed off in the transaction (Col. 2:14). They pass into a new family and take up new responsibilities in it under the authority of the Head of that family. Their property and personal relationships are all subject to His oversight. All their assets are their Father's. And He has disciplinary rights over His children (Heb. 12:5–11).

All this is exactly what the doctrines of election, justification, and sanctification imply. The believer is taken out of his former state and is put in a new relationship with God. He is part of God's family forever, with reciprocal rights and duties. All his time, property, and energy should from that point on be brought under God's control. The Roman ideas of adoption, with the inherent concept of the father's power, are therefore a peculiarly useful illustration of profound doctrines, affording a depth of understanding and appeal that are simply not present in any other possible interpretation of the language. One can understand the translation from death to life and the truth that coming to God is but the start of a new life, not a terminus. And in all the elements of the metaphor the imagery lays wonderful stress on the personal nature of the relationships involved. We are adopted to become sons of God.

Greek Law

I have already said that I wished to defer consideration of Greek ideas of adoption until after I had dealt with the Roman law, so that the contrast between the fullness of the Roman ideas and the shallowness of the Greek may be clear. It is now time to show what I meant.

Before we begin, however, a preliminary point must be dealt with: the difficulty of discussing the Greek ideas of adoption as they existed at the time Paul was writing. There are three elements here. First, our data on Greek adoption are drawn almost entirely from the orations of Isaeus, who practiced his skills before the Athenian tribunals around 375 B.C., some four to four-and-a-half centuries earlier than Paul.[35] That alone would indicate that one should not place as much reliance on his evidence as does, for example, Von Martitz.[36] Second, it must also be remembered that Isaeus's skills, like those of Demosthenes and Cicero before other tribunals, were not devoted to the exposition of the law in a case but were directed towards the interests of his client. Indeed, judging from the oratorical addresses that have come down to us, it is clear that the actual law was not as important an element in the preparation of a "case" as it is to present-day advocates and barristers. Isaeus was fighting for his side, and none too scrupulously either.[37] One may therefore take leave to doubt his reliability, and that, added to the date of the law of which he is evidence, does devalue his testimony.

Third, we must also note that even by the time of Isaeus adoption was already becoming less common in Greece. As we shall see, an impetus for adoption was a desire to avoid the usual rules of succession, but by the fourth century B.C. it had become possible to do that by an appropriate testamentary writing. One may therefore wonder how vital the concept of adoption was in Greek practice in the time of Paul.[38]

Under Greek law as we know it adoption could occur in one of three ways. It could be carried out inter vivos, through a formal ceremony during the lifetime of the adopter, who would register the adoptee with the latter's consent in the deme (the local government constituency) and the phratria (a social grouping of families) to which the adopting family belonged. Alternatively, it was possible to adopt by will; the adoptee had then to claim his inheritance relying on that will. This latter method, which seems to have become quite common, meant that there was the possibility that the named adoptee might decline the inheritance and thereby frustrate the intention of the deceased.[39] In any event, no filial relationship was brought into being during the lifetime of the adopting parent. In the third kind of adoption the intention of the adopting parent was quite irrelevant. Here the kindred or heirs of an intestate might arrange for someone, usually one of their number, to be made the son of the deceased by a posthumous adoption. The precise rules of this transaction, which would have been useful to clarify a complex situation arising from the intestacy, are obscure.[40]

There were, of course, restrictions on adoption in Greek as in Roman law. Only citizens might adopt or be adopted. At first, only a man without legitimate surviving male issue might adopt, and there were special provisions for the case where he had issue after an adoption—the adoptee was not thereby excluded but had to share with the "normal" heirs. Of course, in many instances the adoption would occur late in a man's life, or as noted, a will might be used for the purpose. There were therefore rules as to the mental capacity of the adopter and safeguards to prevent his being improperly influenced, and these were fruitful sources of dispute.[41]

It seems clear that the original rationale of adoption in Greek law was the same as that in Roman law, viz., the desire to continue a family line and a family cult so that the appropriate ceremonies for the ancestors would be carried out.[42] There were also other purposes to be served, such as the wish of a man to have someone to look after him in his old age or to work the farm, or the need to strengthen a family unit for the purposes of defense and war. But quite soon another element was brought into play: the question of property.

It is evident that a major consideration in the development of the Greek law of adoption was the importance given to matters of property. Under the original ordinary rules of succession, which were quite rigid and could not at that time be departed from by a will, property passed only within the family. This reflected the acute interest the Greeks took in "their" property, exhibiting a "territorial imperative" paralleled only by the Scots. The family unit (the oikos) was considered to consist not only of the persons in it, but also of the land; it was important that the land from which one sprang should remain within the patrimony of one's family and that it should so far as possible remain identifiable. Indeed, the family interest in the property may be seen in that, although the head of the family was in law its owner (kyrios), he was really more to be considered its custodian on behalf of the family than the unfettered owner of Roman law.[43] The interest of the family in the property had also other important social and legal effects, which need not detain us—for example, in the rules regarding the marriage of an heiress (epikleros)[44] Adoption therefore may have begun as a device to ensure the continuity of a family cult, but it prospered as a device to ensure that an estate continued as a separate entity, with its own family, by transmitting it down a line of succession different from that which would have occurred in the absence of the adoption. And even where the actual line of succession was not altered (as sometimes happened, as we shall see), the identity of the separate estate was so preserved.[45]

Often, in fact, the purposes of preserving the cult and the estate would go hand in hand, and practice was to adopt not a complete outsider but someone already within the broader confines of the family. The adoptee might be a blood relative, though not a lineal descendant, a nephew, for example, or a son-in-law, whose adoption, since he was the husband of an heiress daughter (an epikleros), would thus keep her inheritance within the family.[46] Of course, choices within the family tree sometimes meant that the adopted person inherited property that would have come to him in any case under the normal rules of intestate succession, but the adoption served in such instances to maintain the continuity of the family unit. The adoption of relations was, as stated, common.[47] We even know of one case where the claimant, an adopted outsider, strove to show why his adoptive father had adopted him rather than a blood relative. Apparently he felt that such a defense had to be made.[48] To me, all this would lessen the impact of the metaphoric use of the concept—for the whole point is that it is the person outside the family who is adopted by God. Though that was not impossible in Greek law, it appears to have been uncommon in practice to the point of oddity. On the other hand, that very oddity might make the metaphor more striking for some readers.

The relationships between the adoptee and his natural parents and between him and his adopting parent differed in Greek and Roman law, which serves to diminish the utility of Greek law for Paul's purposes, notably because of the by then primary use of adoption as a succession device. The absolute nature of the transaction in Roman law is not found in Greek law: one did not wholly leave one's old relationships or enter into all the relationships in the "new" family that a natural son would be involved in. For example, under Greek law one remained legally related to one's natural mother after adoption, though not to one's natural father, and, though related by the adoption to one's adoptive father, one was not related in law to his wife or his daughters. This explains why a son-in-law could be adopted, or an adopted son could marry a "sister." There were also important effects in succession, for succession through or from a female was fully possible.[49] Further, it seems that one's relationship with one's adopter was not as thorough a passing under his control as in Roman law. This was true at any rate in normal Athenian law, where a child, whether natural or adopted, remained under his father's control only till at puberty he was enrolled as a citizen on the appropriate list of the voting constituency (deme) of which his family was a part.[50] From that date on the power of the father over the child was diminished. The father retained control over property that had been acquired for the family through the child up to that date, but new acquisitions made thereafter by the child were his alone. Similarly, paternal control over the child's civil relationships, whether of status or of contract, was minimal after puberty.[51]

The extent of the contrast between this situation and that found under Roman law will become more apparent when we have discussed other aspects of the relationship between the father and child under Roman law in some of the later chapters, for example, in connection with inheritance. Here it will suffice to point out that the father's control over his child, whether natural or adopted, and "his" property was complete in Roman law and ended, not with the child attaining an age of majority, but with the death of the father or with his conscious and formally expressed decision to release the child from his control. It was therefore quite common for adults of mature years still to be under the control of their fathers in Roman law. The contrast with the Greek position is therefore clear.[52]

But, to return to the immediate point, it must be noted that an adoptee under Greek law, if a child, would be subject to the control of his adoptive father in most respects only until puberty. And if the adoptee were already an adult—which would make some sense, since he would have lived through the perils of childhood and therefore might well outlive his adopter—that adult would pass only under the minimal control a father had over mature issue. A Greek adoption therefore carries fewer implications than a Roman adoption.

There were also other restrictions applied by Greek law to an adopted son, which differentiated him somewhat from the natural heir in ways not found in Roman practice. In the first place, it appears clear (though the details are uncertain) that an adoptee could not himself adopt so as to alter the succession to "his" estate. He could transmit the estate only to his own lawful natural child or to the next heir under the rules of succession. This therefore meant that the adoptee was not the full and unrestricted owner of the estate (oikos), as a natural heir would have been. He was more akin to the holder of a life rent, the eventual onward transmission of the property being fixed by law.[53] This was not a rule of Roman law and may seem a strange provision, but it did have the justifications of ensuring that frequent adoptions did not carry the *oikos* too far from the "original" constitution of the family, and of maintaining the choice of the adoptive father for a further generation, since he would have had that possible line of succession in view when making his original choice of adoptee.

Finally, mention should be made of what can be loosely defined as a "probationary" or "voidable" adoption. There is some evidence from Athens that the property of a family was not usually registered in the name of the adoptee until he himself had fathered a son and registered him in the deme of the family unit of the adoptive father. The rationale of such a provision is understandable: it ensured for the adopter that his heir by adoption should himself have a natural heir and that the succession within the family, over two generations, if not assured, was at least probably settled.[54] This would have been important, especially in view of the prohibition of an adoptee himself adopting. In addition, apart from such a "voidable" adoption, we should also note that on occasion an adoptee, having produced an heir within the family of his adopter, would then leave that family and return to his original family, leaving his natural son within the adopter's family as heir to the adopter.[55] Again, this procedure was not found in Roman law, and it does not seem very useful in interpreting the New Testament.

These then are very interesting legal restrictions on adoption, stemming from a particular view of society and an intriguing belief as to the proprieties. But such restrictions diminish the usefulness of Greek law as a source of the content of the New Testament uses of adoption. For example, the voidability of an adoption seems to build into the New Testament concept a rather unattractive and, from other New Testament texts, erroneous uncertainty. I must, of course, grant that this may be an instance where one should not press the minutiae of a metaphor and its incidental ideas too far. But on balance such considerations require to be taken account of when deliberating on the Greek and Roman concepts.

Greek or Roman Law?

Several elements enter into the judgment whether we should seek to interpret the metaphors of adoption in the Epistles by Greek or Roman law. There is the matter of the evidential base for the content of the metaphor, and the problem of the knowledge of each concept on the part of both the writer and the recipients of the Epistles. Finally, there is the comparative suitability of each source to transmit theological principles whose content we may test by other statements in the New Testament. Let us take these matters in order.

As to Greek and Roman law, there is no doubt that the latter is the better evidenced, particularly on the matter of adoption. Our knowledge of the Greek adoption rules is largely derived from incomplete reports of court oratory, directed to the success of a client and not to an orderly and dispassionate exposition of the law. Further, these accounts, insofar as they are evidence, are evidence of a legal system working some four centuries earlier than New Testament times. Although the processes of legal change were slower in those times, one hesitates to accept that procedures and rationales of the law would not have altered in four centuries.[56] The final major difficulty with the Greek sources is that they are mainly Athenian in origin. While it is likely that there were similarities between the provisions of different Greek city-states, we do know that there were differences, and this must lessen the weight we can place on Athenian evidence. For example, it appears that in Aegina an adoptee may have had to be of the same rank as his adoptive parent, and in Thebes a childless man may have been required to adopt.[57] Such variation may well affect the interpretation of a metaphor of adoption. And these were differences within mainland Greece—one may ask what other differences may well have come into being in other parts of the Graecized Mediterranean region, particularly there where other legal systems could have influenced development, for example, in Asia Minor, Syria, and Galilee.

Such considerations must inevitably lead to the question whether sufficient is known about Greek adoption to allow any conclusions to be drawn as to its use as a metaphor in the New Testament. Of course, even if one considers that there is insufficient evidence for Greek law, that does not necessarily drive one to the Roman provisions. It may just mean that nothing can be said: we do not know enough and can only hope that further discoveries, study, and research by Greek scholars and specialists in ancient legal systems will cast further light in due course. Against that position I would, however, argue that under such circumstances it is not unreasonable to attempt to cast light on the metaphor from other contemporaneous legal systems.

In any event, it is not my opinion that nothing can be said. While there are immense difficulties with the Greek evidence, we do have sufficient information to consider Greek law along with Roman law as a possible source of Paul's metaphors.

The question then arises whether Paul, the user of the adoption metaphors, and those he addressed would have known both systems of law. If it could be established that either Paul or the recipients could not have had a knowledge of one of these legal systems, then there is a prima facie probability that the other system is the one to which the metaphors should be referred for their interpretation.

Unfortunately, this simple solution is not fully available to us. To take Paul first, we already know that he was a Roman citizen and had had legal training.[58] Though that training was Jewish, it seems inconceivable that he would not have known his personal law—even the broad generalities would have included knowledge of an important part of the law of persons. Furthermore, I am prepared to argue that the skill of his use of legal metaphors in the Epistles shows that he had learned Roman law in a more formal way. In Tarsus, where he (perhaps) spent

Paul - knew R. law

his youth and much of his ten-year "silent" period (Acts 11:25; Gal. 1:18—2:1), to say nothing of his travels in the Roman colony cities, Paul would have had opportunity to learn a law that was already the subject of systematic exposition and commentary.

As for Greek law, it would also have been available to Paul. Though Tarsus was a Roman colony, many of the inhabitants would not have been citizens, and local Grecian laws would have been in use. Greek law also ruled in many of the cities through which Paul traveled and, as it were, surrounded the enclaves of Roman law in the colonies. It has also been pointed out to me that Greek law was present close to Judea, in the Greek cities of the Decapolis, just across the Sea of Galilee. It could well have become known to Paul (as to other Jews) from that source, especially given his legal training. If that training fitted him to learn Roman law, it also fitted him to learn Greek law. But I would still argue that he was more likely to have learned his personal law, the law of his nationality and citizenship, and would point out that it was Roman law that was available in taught form and was made the subject of systematic exposition. Greek law remained unsystematic; the only writings on it were the speeches of orators, which were studied for their style, not their content. In short, Paul would have had both Roman and Greek law available to him and at his disposal perhaps—but on balance I consider the Roman the stronger option.

In the case of the recipients of the Epistles, the balance is more clearly on the side of Roman law.[59] Three of the uses of the metaphor of adoption are found in the Epistle to the Romans. While it is possible to argue that the church in Rome may have been largely composed of persons familiar with Greek and not Roman law, that line of argument does not seem very tenable. It necessarily involves the proposition that the church did not contain Roman citizens, for only thus could such familiarity and unfamiliarity be created. There would also have had to be a curious unwillingness to learn anything about the laws governing the community in which one lived. On the other

hand, it might be said that there was a familiarity with
Greek ideas, perhaps from immigrants, and that immigrants formed a large community within the church, retaining the memory, though not perhaps the practice, of
the law of their cities of origin. This is possible, though
Occam's razor still leads me to believe that the law known
to the church in Rome was Roman law, and that Paul,
knowing that law himself, would have used it. Why else
does this technical metaphor find its greatest use in the
Epistle to the Romans?

The other two uses of the metaphor of adoption are
found in the Epistles to the Galatians and to the Ephesians.
Here the possibilities of a Greek reference may be thought
to be greater. The recipients did have Roman law present
in their environments. The churches of Galatia were in
Roman colonies, and Ephesus was a major Roman governmental node, though not a colony. Per contra, its main
legal system was Greek, and the colonies of Galatia were
surrounded by Greek influences. Here we can but balance,
and in my view the triple use of the metaphor of adoption
in Romans offsets the slightly different balance of possibilities in the other Epistles.

Finally, we have to consider which legal system affords a more complete, thorough, or enlightening content
for the metaphors of adoption. In a sense such an argument is lifting oneself by one's own bootstraps, for the
teaching used as criterion is itself in part dependent upon
the metaphor, but I do not think that the argument is
thereby destroyed.

A comparison between the contents of Roman and
Greek adoption is difficult because of the limited knowledge we have of the Greek concept, the possibility of local
variations, and the antiquity of such evidence as we have.
But even given these difficulties, the preceding treatment
of Roman and Greek adoption does seem to show that the
Roman notion affords a better source for the metaphor of
adoption, being richer and more thoroughgoing, both in
itself and in the status of sonship to which it leads. As we
have seen, the break between the adoptee and his former

family is total in Roman but not in Greek law. The relationship with the new family is similarly total in Roman but not in Greek law. When this is added to the divergent views of the relationship between "father" and "son" in the two systems, a reasonable case for Roman law as affording a better content for the metaphor is made. The effect of adoption in Roman law was to place the adoptee, irrespective of his age, in a filial position vis-à-vis his adoptive parent, and that relationship persisted until the father decreed otherwise or died. Under Greek practice, the authority of the father was radically reduced at puberty, when the Greek adolescent came of age, and of course, where the adoption was by will or posthumous there was no real relationship between adoptive father and adopted heir at all.

Finally there is a less settled factor to be considered, that of the "origin" of the adoptee. We have seen that usually in Greek practice a blood relative or someone already linked to the family was adopted. The adoption of a clear outsider was rare. Evidence as to Roman practice is, however, slender. It gives the impression that a prior "familial" connection was not usual, but too much stress cannot be placed on this.

In conclusion, I recognize that the Roman filial relationship may be an unwelcome analogy of one's relationship with God, but that is only if one construes that relationship as in some way demeaning. That is, however, an emotional reaction and not a necessary element of the analogy. A true relationship with God is, I submit, more like that of parent and child within the Roman family than any other.[60] So, given that and the other reasons discussed above, I am content to conclude that, although Greek law is not excluded and does not produce a meaningless metaphor, Roman law was the probable source of Paul's use of adoption as a metaphor.

5

Inheritance

MOST PEOPLE FIND the technicalities of the law of inheritance rivaled only by those of taxation in difficulty and dullness. Certainly in both there is a vast amount of detail, and many difficult distinctions have to be made once one starts to probe below the superficial layer of casual conversation.

"Inheritance" in theology seems to suffer from much the same disease. The imprecisions of normal "lay" usage of the language of inheritance appear to afford a satisfactory grasp of the truths indicated by the term.[1] However, as in the other chapters, if we probe more deeply into the legal rules that are the basis of these metaphors, a richer meaning can be found. The kind of language taking our attention is that of Romans 8:14–17: "For as many as are led by the Spirit of God, they are the sons of God . . . ye have received the Spirit of adoption, whereby we cry, Abba, Father. The Spirit itself beareth witness with our spirit, that we are the children of God: And if children, then heirs; heirs of God, and joint-heirs with Christ" (KJV; cf. Gal. 3:29–4:7).

We must begin by defining terms for the purpose of our discussion, since different people make different uses of the words we need.

The inheritance is the total assets forming the estate of a deceased person. The law of inheritance in a legal

101

system comprises the rules under which these assets are divided—the rules relating to the succession to the deceased's estate. Some would further confine the "law of inheritance" to intestate succession, i.e., the succession to the estate established by rules of law operating in the absence of a valid will or testamentary writing. In that case the estate would go to the heirs by inheritance, and such a disposal of the inheritance is different from any question of arrangement made by the provisions of a will. This is a convenient distinction for us to make, for it keeps quite separate the passing of property by legal rule and the passing of property in accordance with the will of the deceased. It also allows us clearly to identify the heirs. The heirs are those who take the estate by operation of the rules of intestate succession, those who have a "right," independent of the will of the deceased.

In testate succession, that is, where the deceased leaves a valid will, property may pass under the terms of the will to persons who are also heirs under the rules of intestate succession, or it may pass to persons who are not legal "heirs" and who have no claim to participate other than by that will. Passing under will can therefore take us into the idea of the beneficiary under a will and of the fiduciary trust, which forms the substance of the next chapter. In this chapter we are concerned with the imagery of the normal case of inheritance of an estate by the heirs. This requires us to look, first at the inheritance itself, second, at the heir, third, at minority, and last, at the idea of joint heirs.

As with the other metaphors we have looked at, we will refer most of the imagery to Roman law for its content. Inheritance as such we can take more generally, but the technical ideas of heirship need to be located in a single legal system. As we will see, the Roman and the Jewish laws have markedly different concepts of heirship, and the evidence argues for the Roman reference. Briefly, the "heir" in Jewish law does not exist until the death of his ancestor. In Roman law the concept of heir is more profound, the heir having legal existence during the life of his predecessor.

One other preliminary point must be dealt with. Inheritance is a very technical area of the law and it may be questioned whether Paul would have known the detail inherent in it. A possible response is to point out that the uses of inheritance imagery in the Epistles are not unduly technical but exhibit the kind of knowledge that a person such as Paul might be expected to have possessed.

In any event, an argument can be made that Paul had cause to know the technical rules of the Roman law of inheritance.[2] We know that he and his father were Roman citizens, since he claimed to be a Roman by birth (Acts 22:25–27). He therefore probably succeeded to his father under the provisions of Roman law. It does seem that his own inheritance would have been reasonably large. The fact that his family were able to send him to Jerusalem to study with Gamaliel (Acts 22:3) indicates that his family was of means. We know that Paul did work with his hands as a tentmaker to support himself (Acts 18:3; 2 Thess. 3:6–10), but this does not prove his poverty. The learning of a trade was part of the normal upbringing in Jewish education (Mishnah, *Aboth* 5:21), and there are other indications that Paul was not poor. Felix thought it worth his while to keep Paul in jail in the hope of receiving a bribe (Acts 24:26); the text indicates that Felix hoped for a bribe from Paul, not from the church. Of course, he might have thought Paul well off because he had brought much money from the churches of Greece for the poor church at Jerusalem. Felix may have thought the money Paul's own, but some do think that perhaps Paul had inherited his father's estate before going to Jerusalem and was known to be a man of substance in his own right.

Finally, we may add to all this the fact that Paul lived for two whole years in his own hired villa in Rome pending his trial (Acts 28:30). Although the Philippians helped him by the hand of Epaphroditus (Phil. 4:14–18), the implication of the hiring is that, at least by the time of his imprisonment, Paul was of some monetary substance. The

only way this could have happened was by inheritance.
We may be sure that he worked only enough to feed himself and his companions—not to build up a fortune
(1 Thess. 2:9; 2 Thess. 3:7–8). The money to pay for the
hired villa certainly did not come from his ministry, for
he angrily denies having made a financial profit from it.
(1 Cor. 9:1–18, esp. v. 15).

The Inheritance

The inheritance may shortly be defined in law as the
totality of the assets (whether property or intangible assets
such as debts due to him) that are owned by a man and
pass from him to his heirs on his death. Strictly speaking
it is therefore impossible to define the inheritance until
the death of its owner, but the term "inheritance" is often
used figuratively to refer to the ordinary possessions of a
man in a more attractive and gilded way. It was therefore
interesting for me to be told by a reader of an earlier version of these pages that in the Bible the root yarash is used
both for "possession" and for "inheritance," though the
root nachal is also used more particularly for "inheritance." The use of yarash for both the concept of inheritance and that of possession shows how closely these ideas
are interrelated. However, I find that the bulk of the Old
Testament verses I cite below are of the nachal family, and
I have noted those which come from other stables.

In the Bible an "inheritance" usually marks off something special, often because it has been given to its possessor by God. In its broadest use in the Bible, the term
"inheritance" encompasses the whole of God's goodness
to man. Whatever God of His good will gives to an individual is an inheritance. The transmission from God is a
gift and thereafter it passes on from parent to child.

In the Old Testament, an "inheritance" normally consists of specific items. The promise to Abraham of a natural family was a promise of an inheritance (Gen. 15:1–6),
but usually the terminology refers to material things. Thus
the physical possession of goods is a clear inheritance:

"House and wealth are inherited from fathers, but [KJV, and] a prudent wife is from the LORD" (Prov. 19:14).

As any concordance will show, the most frequent use of "inheritance" in the Old Testament is in connection with the Land itself.[3] The string of references begins with the promise of the Land to Abraham in Genesis 15:7 (cf. Gen. 17:8) and runs on through the Scriptures (e.g. Deut. 4:21; 20:16; 1 Kings 8:36; Isa. 60:21; Jer. 3:18). Indeed, the Land was commonly thought of as the inheritance of the Jewish people—an idea that survived the centuries of the Dispersion and eventually resulted in the creation of the State of Israel in 1948.

But not all the Old Testament ideas of inheritance were materialistic. In a beautiful way the Lord was spoken of as being the inheritance of Aaron, the priests, and the Levites (Num. 18:20; Deut. 18:1–2), and the picture is repeated in Ezekiel's vision of the new Israel (Ezek. 44:28). This draws to mind Peter's words, "You are a chosen race, a royal priesthood, a holy nation, God's own people" (1 Peter 2:9).

Actually, the last phrase of that quotation from Peter, "God's own people," inverts the imagery of inheritance. The literal translation of the phrase is "a people for his possession" (cf. RSV mg.) making the inversion very clear. The words take up some of the Old Testament passages in which the Jews are spoken of as the inheritance of God. Such imagery begins with Moses's prayer to God at the second giving of the law that God would take the people as His inheritance (Exod. 34:9) and continues in the prayers of David (Pss. 28:9; 33:12) and Solomon (1 Kings 8:51, 53).

By the time of the New Testament, inheritance had come to mean the whole of God's goodness to man. Thus the promise of the Land made to Abraham in Genesis 17:1–8 becomes a promise to inherit the world in Romans 4:13, perhaps through the prophecy of the spreading inheritance of the children of the afflicted in Isaiah 54:1–3. Some would connect that prophecy with the gospel commission, "Go into all the world and preach the gospel" (Mark 16:15) and "All authority in heaven and on earth has been given to me. Go therefore and make disciples of all nations" (Matt. 28:18–19). In a sense, those who take the commission seriously will be found, and be at home, in all parts of the world, inheriting it. There are also echoes of Matthew 5:5: "Blessed are the meek, for they shall inherit the earth."

The inheritance of places or territories in such a way is relatively easy to appreciate. There is a close congruence between the language and the fact. A far more metaphoric use of the phraseology of inheritance is found in the well-known question put by the rich young ruler (Matt. 19:16; Mark 10:17; Luke 18:18) and by the lawyer whose sophistry gave rise to the parable of the Good Samaritan (Luke 10:25): "Teacher, what shall I do to inherit eternal life?" Jesus Himself used the expression in the Matthean version of His reply to Peter's question about the rewards to be given to those who had left all and followed Him: they who follow Him will receive much to replace what they have left, and they will "inherit eternal life" (Matt. 19:29).

The language is clearly metaphoric. One does not inherit eternal life in any ordinary sense. Yet it is easy to desert the immediate confines of logic and perceive the truth the metaphor communicates. Inheriting the life eternal is not possessing a thing, but it is entering into the fullness of life with God. Like the promise made to Abraham, the inheritance has already been received in the sense that God's promise is sure, yet is also still future. This is substantiated by the way in which the New Testament speaks of eternal life: obtained now, it is fully possessed later (cf. Eph. 1:11, 14, 18; Col. 1:12; 3:24).

Heirs

But who inherits? The heirs. Of course, in one sense Christ is the Heir: the Son whom God "appointed the heir of all things" (Heb. 1:2). However, we may be thankful that the imagery of inheritance is expanded to encompass all Christians.

The language of heirs is used most frequently by Paul

and less frequently by the writer to the Hebrews. In Paul's own writing the bulk of this imagery is found in Galatians (particularly in 3:15–4:7) and in Romans (e.g., Rom. 8:14–17a). It also makes appearances in 1 Corinthians and in Titus, Colossians, and Ephesians. Apart from these instances, James speaks of God choosing "those who are poor in the world to be rich in faith and heirs of the kingdom which he has promised to those who love him" (James 2:5), and Peter exhorts husbands to live with their wives, giving them honor "since you are joint heirs of the grace of life" (1 Peter 3:7). These latter instances are of interest as showing the common use of the metaphor of heirship, though they do not contribute much to the detailed content of the metaphoric device. We must resort to Paul to find the richness of the legal imagery.

For Paul, the Christian is the "heir of God." Romans 8:17 runs together several of the elements of this imagery. If we are the children of God, attested by His Spirit, we then are "heirs; heirs of God and joint-heirs with Christ" (KJV). In other places he says that if one is a son of God one is an heir of God (Gal. 4:7); one of the heirs according to the hope of eternal life (Titus 3:7); one of the fellow heirs of the promise, whether one is Jew or Gentile (Eph. 3:6).

In these short metaphors Paul describes the essential elements of a Christian's hope and assurance: his relationship with God. The words are well worn over the centuries. They are easily said or read, and we do tend to slip over them. Yet we ought not to be so lazy or indifferent. One of the most remarkable phrases in the whole New Testament is that the Christian is the "heir of God." This phrase must give rise to inquiry, for the legal idea it incorporates has no basis in present law. Nor did it have a basis in the Jewish law of Paul's time, and it is this that leads me to refer the images of heirship to Roman law for their interpretation.

We are accustomed to talk loosely of a person being the heir of somebody else, but strictly speaking this is incorrect. In our law and in Jewish law a living person does not have an heir. He may have an heir apparent or an heir presumptive, but not an heir.[4] It is only when a person dies that we can know who is his heir, for until he dies there is always the possibility that his "heir" may predecease him. In Scots and English law this is summed up in the maxim *nemo est heres viventis*—no one is the heir of the living.

The matter comes down to these possibilities. First, the phrase "heir of God" may be a simple colloquialism, devoid of real meaning other than a generalized "glow," where the actual legal relationship between God and His "heir" is uncertain, since it is open to frustration by the death of the "heir" before that of his "Father," and since it is conditional on the death of the "Father," God. (Actual "heirship" is postponed to God's death or is frustrated by our own death). I cannot think that such vagueness was Paul's intention, particularly in view of the apparent technical detail and the conceptual development or progression found in passages such as Romans 8:17, "heirs; heirs of God and joint-heirs with Christ." Such precision appears quite deliberate. Second, anticipating one school of modern theology, the expression may mean that God is dead, for that would be required by a strict Jewish or modern understanding of the legalities involved. Third, it may be possible that the phrase "heir of God" and similar expressions do have a technical significance, carrying a useful meaning under a legal system of the time of Paul. This last is what we find if we look at the meaning of the expressions in Paul's day in the light of the Roman law of inheritance.

The fundamental difference between the Roman rules of succession and those of other legal systems of the time was that under the Roman system the heir was considered to be more than the legal representative of the deceased: he actually continued the latter's legal personality. This notion arose because the original concept of heir in Roman law had reference to the patriarchal system and the family cult (the *sacra*). Each family worshiped its own family gods, the *lares* and *penates*, the gods of hearth and larder, and the spiritualization of that family, its *genius*.[5] The heir was the person entitled to carry on the family cult. This went beyond the idea of a continuity of priesthood, for the "new" priest was considered to be the same person as the former priest, now deceased.

This is a difficult idea for modern thought, but it is not as extraordinary in its context. The word "person" comes from the Latin persona. Its root meaning is clear in the verb per-sonare, "to speak through." In Greek and Roman plays the actors used masks and "spoke through" them: the persona was first the mask, then the character being played, but never the actor himself. However, by the normal processes of language the word did come to mean "person" in the sense of the individual. In the cultic concept the priest was the persona, continuing to serve the family sacra, although the individual "speaking through" the mask might change. He was the "personification" of the family. Again by transference the distinction between the priest and the individual became blurred, and a form of continuity of personality between the individual holders of the priesthood emerged.

The continuity of personality between heir and ancestor in cultic practice was carried over in law into matters affecting the inheritance. Thus, under Roman law the heir did not take the estate minus debts in the way that one does under present-day law, or indeed under Jewish law. Today, if the debts exceed the assets the estate is bankrupt and that is the end of the matter in law. But in Roman law the heir was the same person as the deceased and he was liable for the full amount of the deceased's debts even if they exceeded the assets of the estate. Naturally rules developed under which a person might refuse to accept the inheritance lest he ruin his own financial standing. It was only at that stage that it was possible to talk of the inheritance as something apart from the heir. But even with the development of this equitable device, the technical position of the heir who accepted his inheritance remained that of continuing the legal personality of the deceased.[6]

But the idea of continuity between the heir and the deceased went even further. There was a continuity of legal personality between the heir and his ancestor before the latter's death, for in Roman law the heir existed and had legal standing as heir during the life of his ancestor. In the Roman family a father had control over the person, personal relationships, assets, and property of all those children whom he had not emancipated (set free) from his control. There was no time limit, no legal coming of age and automatic independence. Their legal existence was not separate from his. In a sense, he was they. Their acquisitions in strict law belonged to him. Their acts benefited him and he might be laid under legal liability by their actions. Of course, rules developed to mitigate the harshnesses and absurdities of such a system, but nonetheless, in technical civil law the heir did not have independence from his father.

Those who were released from such patriarchal control on and by the death of their ancestor were called sui heredes and the inheritance passed automatically to them in the absence of a will. In strict civil law children who had been emancipated from control took no part of the inheritance. They were no longer part of the family of heirs. Later the exclusion of emancipated children was done away with, though not by making them again part of the family, but by the praetor giving them other rights of succession. In a case where children had not been emancipated, the father, if he wished to disinherit his heirs, had to do so formally by naming them in his will and in effect excluding them from the family. If there was an attempt to exclude them without using the appropriate formula, the will failed and the estate passed under the rules of intestate succession to these very people (Gaius, Institutes 2.123, 138). In short, a Roman always had an heir if he had children in his family—the point Paul was making when he said "if children, then heirs" (Rom. 8:17). Whether the children were natural children or adopted children was irrelevant; children of either source were heirs.

The existence of heirs in such a situation was therefore not conditional on the death of their ancestor, for they

had existence and status already by virtue of their relationship with him. Birth, not death, constituted heirship—
an appropriate illustration of the gospel faith. We must
further remember the notion of the unity of personality.
Thus, in talking of "heirs of God" Paul is not in any way
assuming that God is dead or will ever die. As long as God
is, His children are His heirs. And does the indwelling
Holy Spirit not mean a continuity of personality between
the Christian and God?

This is not the end of the story. The image of heirship
in Roman law can usefully be pressed yet further. Gaius
(*Institutes* 2.157) says that the *sui heredes,* the children,
"even in their father's lifetime are considered in a manner
owners." Later, one of the most famous writers on Roman
law, Paulus, is quoted by the compilers of the authoritative
statement of the developed law, Justinian's *Digest of Roman Law,* as stating, "On the death of the father the heirs
are not seen to inherit the property as rather to acquire the
free control of their own property" (D. 28.2.11). Further,
Justinian himself says that these heirs "even in the lifetime of the parent are to a certain extent deemed owners
of the inheritance" (*Institutes* 2.19.2). In other words, during the life of the father he and his heirs are coowners of
the property. He has the controlling interest, to use a modern analogy, but ownership is, in a sense, joint.

As "heirs of God" Christians are therefore presented
as coowners with Him of His property, though always subject to His authority (cf. Gen. 1:26; Ps. 8:4–8).

Such an idea of a community of property between the
ancestor and the person who would probably be his heir
(i.e., his heir apparent or presumptive) was not wholly
unknown in Jewish practice. For example, as stated in
note 4, there is the "heir" in the parable of the wicked
vinedressers. Some community of property is also indicated in the parable of the Prodigal Son (Luke 15:11–32).
There is, however, a distinction between the Jewish view
of the matter and the Roman view. The Prodigal is given
his share in the inheritance at his request, goes away, and
returns without apparent change in his legal status as heir,

though he suggests that he has forfeited his status (vv. 19, 21). This would not have been possible under Roman law. For the son to have received his share of the property he would have had to be emancipated from his father's control, thus ceasing to be his heir. We cannot therefore equate the Jewish and Roman understanding of the community of property. It was of course possible for the Roman son to be permitted to go away with some of the father's assets without his being emancipated, but this was strictly speaking an extralegal concession by the father. In the ordinary instance the father might well have given the son some property to deal with (the *peculium*), but this concept is not quite the same as that found in the parable of the Prodigal Son.[7]

Minority

Although the metaphor of heirship does not in Roman law imply the death of God, the technicalities of succession upon a death are also used as figures of speech in the Epistles, notably in Galatians 3:23—4:11, where use is made of the concept of the guardian of a minor heir. This derives from normal human experience, where at the death of the ancestor the heirs might well be underage. In these circumstances a guardian or administrator of the property is usually called for. Jewish law took over from Greek practice the concept of a steward or administrator (the *epitropos* or *apotropos*) for this purpose. Such an administrator could be appointed by a court if necessary, but if the ancestor had expressly directed that his minor heirs should receive their inheritance immediately, no administrator could be appointed. The powers of such Jewish administrators seem to have been limited to dealing with the property of the estate only, and there is some doubt as to its actual date of introduction into Jewish law.[8]

This dubiety of dating is one reason why the famous passage in Galatians 3:23—4:11 cannot really be adequately analyzed by reference to Jewish law. The other reason is a matter of law. As the passage begins, the basic imagery is that the law was the custodian of the immature heirs until Christ came, faith in Him being the evidence of maturity (Gal. 3:24–25). This is explicable under Jewish law, but the rest of the language of the passage goes on to indicate an extent of control on the part of the guardian greater than that available under Jewish law, going beyond property to personality and conduct: "The heir, as long as he is a child, is no better than a slave, though he is the owner of all the estate; but he is under guardians and trustees until the date set by the father" (Gal. 4:1–3). Paul then goes on to dwell on the notion that the underage heir is in effect a slave. The guardianship of the law of Galatians 3:24 becomes perverted into a slavery to the law by the elemental spirits of the universe that use the law as an instrument of oppression (Gal. 4:3; the incidents of such slavery have been discussed earlier in chapter 2, "The Slave and the Freedman"). In short, the picture is one of total dominance. But here it is of interest to note how pointed Paul's concept of the minor heir is. For him the minor heir resembles a slave (Gal. 4:1–3), a resemblance that becomes an identity due to the abuse of the law. To balance this point, it would be well to remember that Paul elsewhere clearly indicates that disregard of the law is not a mark or proof of maturity—rather the reverse (e.g. Rom. 6:1–2, 5–14)—but in the Galatians passage he is attacking legalism, not presenting a balanced exposition.

Paul's notions of the powers of the guardian, the possibilities for abuse, and the status of the minor heir make sense under Roman law, for the tutor or guardian appointed by that law over a minor child had extremely extensive powers. Indeed, it is not inaccurate to equate the status of the minor child under guardianship in Roman law with that of a slave, and there are very close parallels with the power of the father over the child. Of course, as the child grew the practical powers of his guardian diminished, though formally they remained extensive. Clearly therefore, the interpretation of this portion of Galatians gains much by the use of Roman concepts.[9]

But when the heir achieves maturity he is no longer

under guardians and trustees but may take his place as part of the common family, one of the household of God (Eph. 2:16; Gal. 6:10).

> But now that faith has come, we are no longer under a custodian; for in Christ Jesus you are all sons of God, through faith. For as many of you as were baptized into Christ have put on Christ. There is neither Jew nor Greek, there is neither slave nor free, there is neither male nor female; for you are all one in Christ Jesus. And if you are Christ's, then you are Abraham's offspring, heirs according to promise (Gal. 3:25–29).

Joint Heirs

So far this discussion has assumed that there is only one heir involved, but this was not necessarily the case. The civil law of Rome was accustomed to the situation in which there was more than one heir. Those children were heirs who passed out of patriarchal power at the death of the ancestor. In the usual instance this would be a group of brothers. These were the joint heirs of the father and, as in the case of the single heir, were considered to be such during his lifetime. It is therefore perfectly right and proper for Paul to say that the sons of God are "joint-heirs with Christ" (Rom. 8:17), though he is stretching the law slightly, since we are joint heirs by adoption. At first (and perhaps down to the time of Paul, though his use of the analogy may argue the contrary), adoption was not permitted when there were natural sons, "real" heirs, since in that case there was no need to bring an outsider into the family to continue the line. Such an adoption was unnecessary and therefore not permitted.[10] Perhaps this is another area where we should not press metaphor too far.

However, in two areas the metaphor "joint-heirs with Christ" has another message for us. First, it is interesting to note that in both Roman law and Jewish law division of the inheritance amongst the co-heirs on the death of the father was not automatic. In Roman law, just as the inheritance was the common property of the father and the heirs during his life, so that community of property continued after the death. In Jewish law the heirs, once ascertained on the occurrence of the death, took the property in common between them. Division of the inheritance was a separate and subsequent step to be taken on the initiative of an heir. Further, the acquisitions made by the coheirs after the death also fell into the common property of the family in both legal systems. This is certainly true as far as Jewish law is concerned,[11] although there is some slight uncertainty whether this was good Roman law at the time of the Epistles. It is possible that the institution of common property may have fallen out of use in late republican times, although it is mentioned about A.D. 175 as an interesting idea by the Roman legal writer Gaius.[12] But even with that uncertainty, the idea of a community of property of the heirs of God in which the acquisitions of one are for the benefit of all the family could usefully be linked with our present-day notions of Christian stewardship.

The other message from the imagery of being "joint-heirs with Christ" arises from Ephesians 3:6. Gentiles are fellow heirs of the promise along with the Jews. As Paul puts it, they are "fellow heirs, members of the same body"—language that indicates the community among the fellow heirs. Similar expressions are found in Galatians 3:26–29, where Jew, Greek, slave, free, male, and female are thought of as being Abraham's offspring, heirs according to the promise through faith in Christ. The error of allowing feelings of nationality or ethnic prejudice to separate Christians is therefore clear.

Under Roman and Greek law it was perfectly possible for an outsider to be named as heir and thereby inherit. But, as a matter of law, Paul's imagery would run counter to Jewish thinking. The Jew, drawing on the Old Testament imagery, considered that only his people were the heirs of God. It would have been difficult for him to conceive of an outsider becoming one of the heirs, because under the Jewish law of inheritance an outsider could not

inherit, could not be brought into the family relationship
in this way. It was possible for a man in his last will and
testament to give away to outsiders the property that otherwise would have formed part of his estate, the inheritance of his heirs, and he could do this even to the extent
that he gave away all his property so that there was nothing for his heirs to inherit. But such a transfer of his property had to be made in the language of a gift. If he used
the language of inheritance, for example, "let X be my
heir" or "let X inherit my house" and X was not a member
of his family otherwise entitled to inherit, the language
was a nullity: the man would have attempted to do something contrary to the commandments defining the family
and hence his words were void.[13]

Paul is at pains clearly to make the point that *faith* is
the basis of one's familial relationship with Abraham and
with God, which would meet the problems that his imagery would raise in the minds of the orthodox Jew. Consider these representative passages:

> For not all who are descended from Israel belong to
> Israel, and not all are children of Abraham because
> they are his descendants; but "Through Isaac shall
> your descendants be named" [Gen. 21:12]. This means
> that it is not the children of the flesh who are the
> children of God, but the children of the promise are
> reckoned as descendants (Rom. 9:6–8).

> The promise to Abraham and his descendants, that
> they should inherit the world, did not come through
> the law but through the righteousness of faith. If it is
> the adherents of the law who are to be the heirs, faith
> is null and the promise is void. ... That is why it
> depends on faith, in order that the promise may rest
> on grace and be guaranteed to all his descendants—
> not only to the adherents of the law but also to those
> who share the faith of Abraham, for he is the father of
> us all (Rom. 4:13–16).

> Thus Abraham "believed God, and it was reckoned to
> him as righteousness" (Gen. 15:6).

So you see that it is men of faith who are the sons of Abraham. . . . for you are all one in Christ Jesus. And if you are Christ's, then you are Abraham's offspring, heirs according to promise (Gal. 3:6–7, 28b–29).

A man is a child of Abraham and of God by reason of faith, not by reason of genetic succession. If he is one of the family of faith he is one of the heirs of God.

Let me try to draw the ideas of this chapter together. The concepts of inheritance used in the New Testament Epistles transmit many ideas. In summary, the inheritance of the Christian is the totality of God's goodness to him, including the promise of eternal life and of heaven. However, Christians are heirs of God now, without waiting for a death. By the indwelling Holy Spirit there is a form of identity or unity of personality between the Christian and God. As members of the family of faith Christians are, in a sense, coowners with God of God's property and joint heirs with Christ. As such it seems elementary that they should be mature individuals, no longer oppressed by abuse of the law, though not disregarding it.

Taken along with the other legal metaphors, the inheritance metaphors flesh out cold doctrine in a particular way. These ideas require to be thought over with care and to be allowed to do their work in mind and heart. "If children, then heirs; heirs of God, and joint-heirs with Christ" (Rom. 8:17 KJV).

6

The Father's Household

MANY OF THE IDEAS we have considered in the previous chapters find their practical context within the workings of what Paul calls the "household of faith" (Gal. 6:10). Indeed, the true antithesis to being "alienated from the commonwealth of Israel, and strangers to the covenants of promise" is not only fellow citizenship with the saints, but also being a member of the "household of God" (Eph. 2:12, 19). In this chapter I wish therefore to consider the idea of the family household, both in order to draw together some of the fundamentals of the earlier chapters, and to add some material that did not conveniently fit in the earlier discussion. In so doing we will clearly be using an idealized conception of the family, for although such a theoretical "model" family arrangement will explain many of the rules and practices of early social organization, it is unclear whether such an arrangement ever fully existed in practice. To explore the discussions that surround this area would take us well away from the subject of our inquiry, interesting though such a diversion would be. Suffice it to say that there is academic dispute about the theory.[1] However, whether or not the ideal ever existed, the previous chapters show that metaphoric use of ideas of the family and of the household were current and that they still hold meaning. If another example be needed, Augustus was proud to note as one of his major distinctions the fact that the Roman people had given him quite late in life the title of Father of his Country.[2] That metaphor meant much to the old man, perhaps in part because of the tragedies of his own family history.

We will deal mainly with the Roman family. This is not to say that the somewhat different position and authority of the father in Greek or Jewish law would be meaningless as the content of the "father" metaphor, even though in those systems some of the family metaphors would be very obscure or even nonsense, as we have seen in chapter 4 on adoption. However, in both the Jewish and Greek systems there was a concept of "father" that, though more circumscribed in power and authority than in Roman law, was nonetheless of importance and would fill out some of the New Testament language.[3] It might also be a question whether the Roman father would in practice not behave much as the father under the other systems. But in terms of the law and of its implications for the metaphoric use of the ideas of fatherhood and patriarchal authority, the status of the Roman paterfamilias and his extensive powers were markedly different.

The Roman household of New Testament times was a complex association in law. At its head, or perhaps better, at its heart, was the father, the paterfamilias, whose power was all-pervasive. Representing the family before the family gods he was the personification of the family, and this position was the basis and justification of the rest of his powers.[4] As the oldest male ancestor he controlled his descendants as to both their persons and "their" property—in law they had no possessions of their own. He held everything.

Normally entry into such a situation was by birth. The father had power over all his children and over their children so long as he had not formally terminated that association. Only by his specifically freeing those under his control could they become heads of their own family during his life. The main other route into the family was by adoption, either of a person already under the power of another (adoption), or of a person who was free of such control (adrogation). All children of the father obtained by either method were under his authority and remained under his authority until the link was broken by his legal act or by his death. There was no "coming of age" at which the "child" obtained independence as a matter of right. It would be quite possible for a mature and even an old man to be in law still the child of his father and subject to his authority.

But such a status was not necessarily negative or constricting. In the ideal situation, the father would give his child capital (the *peculium*) with which to trade and prosper. He would set him up in business or support him in a useful career within society. Mutual obligations or care would operate and be discharged gladly. Unlike the present day, independence was not an absolute goal; rather, the reciprocal interaction of the two personalities would be natural and enriching. This "lack" of independence of adults may be rather difficult to accept, given our modern social context, which would hold such an arrangement as oppressive and demeaning, but if the image is interpreted in terms of our relationship with God it makes sense.

For many today such a message should come as a relief. As children of God, Christians are never to be sent out on their own to do what they can. On the contrary, their Father will care for them and supervise their way. He will not cast them off or fail to acknowledge them. They will never be adopted or "freed" from the authority of God. Such security allows the development of a personality to the fullest extent of its potential. Made for God, we are at our best in Him.

One element was clearly common to the familial systems of New Testament times. They were agreed that the family was not a democratic unit; the authority of the father was final. There was no sense in which he was bound by a majority vote of the family. It might be that the family was to a greater degree independent of his control in Greek or Jewish law, but where he had the power to decide his decision was in law final. This is natural, for democracy was invented to control the abuse of power. Where there

is confidence that authority vested in an individual will
not be abused there is no need to fragment or disseminate
power among the group. Families that are running well
reflect this confidence, and naturally, this is preeminently
the case with the family of God. One can trust God to do
right.

Of course, this is not necessarily to argue that the
family is not consulted or has no opinion to put forward
on a matter. A patriarchal family need not and should not
be dictatorially organized. The father should seek to weigh
the family's feeling. Yet in the last resort the decisions are
those of the father. To take the analogy, in the Christian
life there is a duty laid upon Christians to play an active
part through prayer. This does not infringe on the sovereignty of God, for He has commanded it. There are problems in putting the matter as simply as that, but it will
suffice for present purposes.

To pursue that theme a little, it is clear also from the
family metaphor that participation in prayer should not
be formalized. In a family it is the personal relationship
expressed through communication, discussion, and interest that matters. It would be strange to live in the same
house as one's family and to communicate only by sending birthday cards. It is a mark of a broken family connection when contacts between members are staid and
ritualistic. The same is true of one's relationship with God
(cf. Isa. 1:10–17). It is also true in the horizontal relationships of life. The Christian family, the church, is a necessary part of Christian life. Solitary Christians who stay
aloof and separate are to that extent betraying their joint
heirship.

Participation in the family councils is of course but
one of the privileges of sonship. Roman sonship involved
also the allied thought of the community of property among
coheirs and between the father and his family. This may
afford one possible way of understanding the *peculium*
already mentioned. An idea of common interest in the
property of the family would lead to an expectation that
the other members of the family should be allowed to act

freely with a proportion of the family assets, even though in strict law the final rights of ownership were reserved to the father. Which of these elements is most helpfully brought out of a given text will depend upon the circumstances in which the metaphor is being invoked. Some need to be encouraged to grow in maturity. Others need to be kept within bounds. It is the function of a true ministry to provide the necessary instruction for all types of people and circumstances.

The authority of the head of a household extended not only over his children, but also over his wife. The authority over the wife was rather special and evoked a great amount of legal debate. At first sight such authority would seem to provide a ready source of legal metaphors, but marriage and marital relationships do not form a large body of imagery in the New Testament. The image is potent, though the proportionate use of marital images is small.

The major use of marriage in the New Testament is in the description of the church as the bride of Christ, particularly in Revelation (e.g. Rev. 18:23; 21:2, 9; 22:17). Considerably more work needs to be done on the status of women under Roman and Jewish law before it is absolutely clear which is the most useful legal system to use in interpreting such language.[5] The common reference is to Jewish customs, because of the clear parallels between the language of Revelation and the prophetic words of Hosea, who saw Israel as the faithless wife, and of Ezekiel in relation to Jerusalem's backsliding (Ezek. 16:1–63). There are further parallels with the traditional interpretation of the Song of Solomon. Such references do invoke the pictures of the traditional Eastern ceremonial and are informative. Whether one can or should go beyond their surface to the legal rights and duties involved is a different matter.

One place in the Epistles where a clearly legal metaphor of marriage is used is Romans 7:1–4, which has been comprehensively and convincingly discussed from the point of view of Jewish law by Professor J. D. M. Derrett.[6]

His exposition of the passage as speaking of the law as ruling the individual only during life, and of the death of the individual through baptism into Christ (Rom. 6:4), freeing from the law in order that one should consort with Christ, is attractive and coherent in its analysis. I would point out only that if they did not know the Jewish law in any detail, the recipients of Romans were likely to refer to their own domestic law for the interpretation of the analogy, which gives the same result.

Under Roman law the husband of a Roman citizen, who had married her in one of three traditional ways, had powers over his wife more extensive than those available under Jewish law. These powers, comprised in the concept of manus, essentially placed her in the same legal position vis-a-vis her husband as one of her children (cf. above). In practice the right of the husband over his wife was somewhat more restricted than the right of the father over the child, but this was not so in law. It follows that there was a degree of control over the wife, which would provide a background against which Romans 7:1–4 could be interpreted. In view of Paul's warnings elsewhere about the perils of enslavement to the law (e.g. Gal. 5:1–15 and 4:1–7), a possible interpretation of the passage is that the law as husband abuses its authority. Through baptism into the death of Christ the "wife" ceases to be under the authority of that husband and is then freed in order to come under the true authority of Jesus "in order that we may bear fruit for God" (Rom. 7:4).[7]

The final group under the authority of the head of the Roman household were the slaves. Perhaps because of the social composition of the early church, or perhaps because the slave status was so stark, many New Testament images are drawn from the law of slavery.

In Roman law the authority and power exercised by the head of a household over his slaves was that of ownership. It is known as dominica potestas, the word dominus meaning "owner." Such language indicates the degree of control the master had. Technically the slave was a chattel, though a valuable one, and was traded by special for-

malities as were other valuable assets in early Roman law.
As a chattel the very life of the slave was at the command
of the owner, and such laws as did exist to protect the
slave as a matter of humanity were capable of avoidance.
In other words, the slave life might be miserable and de-
manding. It would seem to be this severe aspect of the law
that Paul makes use of in characterizing the life under the
law (e.g. Gal. 5:1) or the life before conversion. The slave
was totally at the disposal of his master and was, or ought
to have been, a malleable instrument of his master's will
(Rom. 6:15–23).

On the other hand, for certain individuals the slave
life might not be as bad as it could have been. The will of
the master might be for good, and subservience to him
enriching. The good master would look after his slaves,
even entrusting them, like his sons, with some capital with
which to trade (the peculium). In the last analysis any
profits made by the slave would belong to the master. Yet
it was not unusual for the master to allow the slave to
"keep" his profits and save them up, so that he might
eventually "buy" his freedom. The transaction was illogical in that the master received only what was already his,
but such practices are useful in thinking of such exhor-
tations as "work out your own salvation with fear and
trembling; for God is at work in you, both to will and to
work for his good pleasure" (Phil. 2:12–13). The analogy
of the slave "buying" his freedom allows the twin truths
of the sovereignty of God and the responsibility of man to
be kept in fruitful balance.

Other elements might be taken from the law of slavery, as we have done already in chapter 2. Of these, two
can be selected here. First, there was the element of mutual care, seen not only in the relationship of master and
servant; but also in the continuing link between the freedman and his former owner, his patron. Second, there was
the potential for the future in the relationship. A slave
might be freed into full citizenship of Rome. It is therefore
possible to see a progression of analogies from slave to
freedman and citizen. Indeed, in law the progression might

go further, for it was possible for a freed slave to be adopted and/or made heir. But these possibilities cannot be taken too far. Adoption of a slave was rare, and making a slave an heir was usually done only to throw on him the disgrace of a bankrupt estate. However, we can note that for the Christian slave there was no conceptual barrier to thinking of himself as the son or heir of God.

The household therefore consisted of the father, his wife, children (either natural or adopted), their children and wives if any, and the slaves. Ideally it was bound together by the natural familial bonds of feeling and love, each member fulfilling his or her duties within the family. The legal framework was, however, more absolute, with the authority and power of the paterfamilias being the central basis of the community formed by the family group. In form, as we have seen, all the assets and losses of the group were the assets and losses of the father. But we have so far only hinted at one important element of any family association, that of discipline.

Discipline within the family of God is the point of several of the legal metaphors of the New Testament. One clear example is the warning to masters to treat their slaves justly and fairly, since they themselves have a Master in heaven (Col. 4:1). Other examples are drawn more clearly from the family situation. A good father will be concerned that his children should grow up to be of good character. He will therefore discipline them when (not if) necessary. That is the point of Hebrews 12:5–11. Discipline is a mark of sonship and a necessary element of training. It is also a mark of the father's care for his children, which Paul takes up in not a few passages. Timothy and Titus are his "sons" who are given advice and exhortation (1 Tim. 1:2; 2 Tim. 1:2; Titus 1:4). Occasionally he justifies his encouragement and his criticism of a church by claiming a father's privileges (e.g., 1 Thess. 2:7, 11; 2 Cor. 6:13). He hints at a father's interest in Philemon 10, but the clearest picture is in Galatians 4:19. "My little children, with whom I am again in travail until Christ be formed in you," which, though the image of a mother and not a father, cannot be left out of consideration.

But discipline is discretionary—which is not the same as arbitrary. Different forms of discipline are appropriate at different times, and it may be that discipline is in fact unnecessary where the child knows it has done wrong and learns thereby. I can see such a principle at work with my own children. What is important is that the child be led back into fellowship with the father. Sometimes "punishment" may be the route—sometimes it may not. (Of course, for those troubled by logic, all sin has to be punished, but that is done in and through the death of Christ.) Discipline thus may or may not look like punishment, is never arbitrary in true fact, and is for good (Heb. 12:9–11).

This can be illustrated from the rights of discipline given to the father under Roman law, summed up in saying that he had the right of life and death, the *ius vitae necisque*, over those in his power. This right was not exercised arbitrarily but seems to have required the authorization of a family council before the death penalty was enforced. Thus Tacitus relates how, in A.D. 57, Pomponia Graecina was tried before such a family council for practicing a foreign superstition which may have been Christianity.[8] There was therefore some formal check upon the free and arbitrary use of powers of discipline. Public opinion would also have had a role to play. Such a requirement of a formal procedure would have had some restraining force upon the vagaries of an unpredictable paterfamilias (cf. Heb. 12:9). Some principles upon which discipline was exercised did develop down the years.

The other element that I take from one of the discussions on the matter is that the power was that of life and death. Many take the element of life to refer to the ability of the father effectively to confer life by his decision to recognize a newborn child as his, thus saving it from exposure. Professor Reuven Yaron points out that it can also mean the right to pardon an offender otherwise subject to punishment.[9] This would fit well with the graciousness

inherent in the disciplining of a family, mercy coming in
to mitigate the terrors of the law.

An interesting sidelight on the matter of discipline is
an action for damages for personal injury discussed in
Justinian's Digest (9.2.5.3). Though not the basis of a New
Testament metaphor, the case provides a useful illustration. Justinian quotes a passage from a book by Ulpian
that asks, "What is the liability of a teacher or instructor
who kills or wounds a slave in the course of teaching him
his craft? Has he incurred liability on the grounds of in-
flicting unlawful damage?" Ulpian's own opinion is that
an action for wrongful damage would lie, but he quotes
also the opinion of Julian concerning damage done to a
freeborn pupil whose eye was put out when his instructor,
displeased with his execution of a task, struck him on the
back of the head. There has been much ink spilled on the
question of this liability, but it is interesting to find that
both Ulpian and Julian indicate that the instructor, whether
of a slave or a freeborn person, has a right to inflict reasonable castigation upon his pupil. The punishment was
technically known as *levis castigatio*.

Given Paul's use of Roman law as the primary referent
of his metaphors, it is tempting to construct a pseudo-
Pauline metaphor on the basis of this legal principle: God
is our Instructor, whose purpose it is to teach Christians
and to prepare them for daily life in His kingdom. He has
to use discipline, but His discipline is *levis castigatio*—it
is reasonable chastisement to keep us in order, or to train
us properly to execute the tasks set before us. Once the
lessons are learned, the Christian will himself be a master
of his craft, and that will involve "an eternal weight of
glory beyond all comparison" (cf. 2 Cor. 4:17; Rom. 8:18).[10]

To summarize, the discipline presented to us in the
Bible is not a matter of punishment without regard to humanity and mercy, but rather a response to the precise
requirements of the individual, calling him or her back
into a proper, personal, "father and child" relationship
with God. The closer that relationship is, and the more
easily it is reconstituted, the less the individual is likely

to fear or be careless, and (dare we say) the less discipline
will seem punishment. On the other hand, the more formal
the relationship, or the more it is forgotten about and ignored, the greater the likelihood of complaint that the
eventual discipline is "arbitrary" and "unfair." But in it
all, it is the care of a father for his child that is being
evidenced. In the last analysis he will not permit his children to go their own way into final disaster.

But what about hell? I view hell as God's final act of
grace to those who will have nothing to do with Him, that
is, to those who are not His children. Like C. S. Lewis, I
can envisage that existence in hell is better somehow than
nonexistence, and that hell is a form of tourniquet, a limit
on the fissiparousness of evil.[11] It is not a pleasant thought
and has been rejected by many, but it is one of those things
the Bible tells us is a fact, whether or not we like or at
present understand it.

All the ideas of discipline and of the interactions of
the family that we have considered so far are really of the
vertical or patriarchal relationship of God and the Christian. But membership in the household of God operates in
the horizontal plane as well. As noted earlier in this chapter, the family ought to associate with each other. Solitary
Christians who are unwilling to fit or be fitted into any
fellowship are to that extent cut off and cutting themselves
off from the family. It is one thing to be a loner where
there is no company of fellow heirs. It is another deliberately to stand aloof, too conscious of the faults of others,
where there is a family gathering.

Children of God are heirs of God, joint heirs with
Christ (Rom. 8:17). Under our elder brother we owe a duty
of care and concern among ourselves within the family,
and where such an attitude is even partially developed,
there will develop a caring church that is more a family
than an ecclesiastical association or organization. Such
fellow feeling does away with considerations of race (Gal.
3:28; cf. Col. 3:11). Paul, the Jew, speaks of Titus, the Greek
(Gal. 2:3), as his brother (2 Cor. 2:13) and uses the same
term of Philemon, another Greek, and of Onesimus, a run-

away slave (Philem. 16, 20). Whether this last use can be tied in with Paul's having "fathered" Onesimus as well (Philem. 10), I know not, but the fact remains that for Paul brotherhood had a depth of caring quality it may have now lost through its too facile use in evangelical jargon.

So then we are left with the family as the community, a creation of care and concern that included discipline, centered upon the father and the relationship with him, but not excluding the interrelationships of the children. These are all spoken of in the legal language of the family, but in truth are rooted in the love of a father for his children.

What happens to those outside the family? One answer is that they should be brought within the family, through adoption, as we saw in chapter 4. However, there is one other entirely separate legal metaphor that Paul sometimes uses, the notion of trust, to which we now turn.

7

Trust: The Faith of Christ

A̲s WE NOTED towards the end of chapter 5, under Jewish law it was not possible for an outsider to inherit under a will. He might take property that had been gifted to him in the context of the will, but the transfer of the property to him had to be couched in the language of gift. If the language of inheritance was used, the words were legally void. So long as the difficulty of language was avoided, the outsider could share in the property that otherwise would have formed part of the inheritance.

It is perhaps curious to find that this legal technicality does not directly form the basis of one of the legal metaphors used in the Epistles, though the omission may simply add to the reasons why Jewish law is not to be taken as a usual source of legal images. Salvation through faith is spoken of as being the gift of God in Ephesians 2:8, and in Romans 5:15–21 and 6:23 eternal life is spoken of as being the gift of God. It is possible in exposition to couple these instances with other passages, where faith is seen as establishing the link between Abraham and his true sons, thus bringing them into the inheritance (e.g., Rom. 4:13–15; Gal. 3:6–9). Nonetheless, the passages in Romans 5–6 and Ephesians 2:8 do not occur in the context of an inheritance metaphor where we might expect the use of the language of "gift" to avoid the difficulty raised by the Jewish law.

However, although in Jewish law gift was the only mechanism by which the strict rules of inheritance might be avoided, there was at the time a device in another legal system by which outsiders could be brought in to share in the inheritance; the fiduciary trust of Roman law. The existence of this device was drawn to the attention of the world of New Testament scholarship in 1966 by Professor G. M. Taylor in an article that does not seem to have had the impact it deserves.[1] Professor Taylor's suggestion is very interesting and contributes not only to our understanding of the technicalities of the New Testament metaphors but also can be taken as the basis of a slightly more generalized inquiry into faith. In brief, his contention is that on occasion in Galatians the phrase "the faith of Christ" refers to Christ's faithfulness to the terms of a fiduciary trust rather than the Christian's faith in Christ. A subsidiary argument is that the concept of the fiduciary trust also allows Paul to present Abraham and Christ as successive testamentary heirs, receiving the inheritance in trust for others.[2]

This suggestion is important because the metaphor of the fiduciary trust (the *fidei commissum* as it is known) supplements the metaphor of adoption. It speaks to the person who may not feel that he is the child of God, although the metaphor of adoption tells his mind that he is. The fiduciary trust portrays his new relationship with God in a different way, stressing the fact that what is important is not so much the strength or quality of his faith in Jesus as Jesus' faithfulness. Of itself this can be reassuring and it helps the Christian to avoid thinking that, unless he can work himself up into a particular emotional state of "feeling his belief" in Jesus, there is something wrong with his relationship with God. Christians are therefore to be encouraged in their confidence in God's provision for those who are not naturally His children.

The metaphor of the fiduciary trust, the *fidei commissum*, refers to an institution peculiar to Roman law and not found in Jewish or Greek law, although no doubt it would have been familiar to those Jews or Greeks who paid attention to interesting developments outside their own national law. It is, for example, probable that a Jew would have become acquainted with a device that would allow him to avoid the strictness of his own law. We will come back to this point later.

The *fidei commissum* bears some resemblance to the modern law of trust that can be found in Anglo-American laws of succession. Metaphorically, it presents the Christian as obtaining the grace of God and access to the inheritance through the "faith of Jesus Christ" (Gal. 3:22 KJV)—"the faith of Christ" translating the ambiguous Greek phrase *pistis Christou* and meaning in this context "Christ's faithfulness to His Father's will."

Such a rendering runs contrary to many modern translations that take the phrase as meaning "the Christian's faith in Christ," and much scholarly ink has been expended in discussing which translation is correct. The ambiguity arises from the fact that in Greek the genitive case can express a number of relationships; grammatically, the words *pistis Christou* can therefore mean either "faith *in* Christ" or "faith *of* Christ," i.e., "Christ's faith." "Christ's faith" could further refer to either His faith in His Father or His faithfulness to His Father.

There is a very clear distinction between something occurring through the faith *of* Christ and something occurring through faith *in* Christ. Certainly not all the occurrences of "faith of/in Christ" are to be considered as bearing the possible legal meaning of a *fidei commissum.* There are, however, a number of passages in which Paul is clearly arguing juridically and which contain this or similar phraseology. There are a sufficient number of these passages to suggest that the phrase is used with a technical meaning in some of them.

It may therefore be that the possible presence of such a technical legal metaphor can contribute to the continuing argument in scholarly circles as to the "faith of Christ." This argument goes a long way back into New Testament scholarship,[3] although its most recent manifestation began with an article by Dr. Gabriel Hebert, published in

1955.[4] It is not necessary for the purposes of this book to go into this debate in any detail, even were I competent to do so. It is however interesting to find that recently theologians have tried to establish some kind of balance in this question and have sought to show that it comprises a variety of elements: the faith of the believer, the faithfulness of Christ, and the faithfulness of God Himself.[5] I would suggest that this approach is supported by the possibility that on occasion *pistis* can be interpreted by the legal device of the fiduciary trust.

As noted earlier, the suggestion that the phrase *pistis Christou*, the faith of/in Christ, refers to the Roman device of *fidei commissum* was made by Professor Taylor. He discussed in particular the use of the expression as it is found in Galatians, but what he says is capable of more extended reference. Professor Taylor points out that *pistis* occurs ninety-three times in the epistles usually credited to Paul, that fifty-eight of these instances are in Romans and Galatians, where Paul is dealing with the relationship of the Christian to the law, and that thirty-five of these uses are in two specialized passages where the argument is pursued in legal language (Rom. 3:22–5:2 and Gal. 2:16–3:26). He goes on to give examples from various first- and second-century Roman writings that are available also in contemporary Greek. These show that the Greek work *pistis* was used to translate the technical Roman term *fidei commissum*. A preliminary case for the occasional correspondence of the two terms has therefore been made. Professor Taylor then discusses in some detail the argument of Galatians 2–3, which involves the analogy of the *diatheke*, a technical term often used to mean the testamentary will, and the technical application of the concept of *fidei commissum* in relation to the testament of a deceased person. He then points out that in Paul's time *fidei commissum* was a device familiar to non-Romans with no particular technical competence, and that the interpretation of *pistis* as being a *fidei commissum*, referring to the faithfulness of Christ rather than faith in Christ, fits the argument of Galatians. Finally he suggests that, since Paul could have

known of the *fidei commissum* and such a metaphor fitted
his argument, the use of the analogy may have been conscious and deliberate.

Professor Taylor's argument is attractive, but as I wish
to avoid any accusation of plagiarism I must put it slightly
differently. First we will look at the difficulties Paul is
dealing with and then at the institution of *fidei commissum* as we know it to have been round about the time of
Paul. We can then see the extent to which the Roman idea
meets the needs of Paul's mode of expression.

By using the image of the testamentary will in such
passages as Galatians 2–3, Paul has to deal with a related
legal idea that might occur to some of his readers; the legal
inability of someone outside the family to take part in the
inheritance. Paul does this in two ways. On the one hand
he is at pains to say that Abraham and his seed participated in the inheritance by promise and not by law (Gal.
3:6–9, 27). Under the law, Jesus as God's Son is God's heir,
and Abraham and his seed could not be included in the
inheritance by the normal law of inheritance. In a sense
all, both Jew and Gentile, are outsiders.

On the other hand, if Abraham and his seed (including Christ) are the beneficiaries under God's will and in-
heritors of the inheritance through His testament, others—
the Gentiles to whom Paul is writing—would be excluded. They, being aliens and strangers (Eph. 2:12;
4:17–18), could not come in to the benefit granted under
the law. How could Gentiles therefore partake with the
lawful heirs? As we saw at the end of chapter 5, one way
is for Paul to say that believers are the sons of Abraham
(e.g., Gal. 3:7; Rom. 9:6–8). Another way would be for the
inheritance to be transferred to the outsiders by gift, as I
have suggested might be one interpretation of Romans
5:15–21 and 6:23.

But a question still remains whether there was another legal device that Paul could properly have used as
a metaphor to get across this point and meet both difficulties, allowing him to show both Jew and Gentile as
partakers in the inheritance. In modern law the matter

could easily have been solved by the appropriate words in a will, but such devices were not available in the first century, with the single exception of the Roman *fidei commissum*, the fiduciary trust.

One advantage of the fiduciary trust was that it enabled a testator to leave his property to pass first to one person and then to another after the first heir's death. It therefore was a suitable way for Paul to explain how one could grasp the point that Abraham received the inheritance by promise, and yet Christ as his successor was able to open up the inheritance to other outsiders.[6] The question of successive heirs is therefore an element of the language, but its main force lies in the opening up of the estate.

In Roman law the precise function of the fiduciary trust was to allow persons who were otherwise barred by the ordinary law from participating in an inheritance to avoid that prohibition and to receive benefit from the estate of a dead friend. It was accomplished by the testator requesting, but not ordering, the heir to do such and such or to give something to so and so. In short, performance of the request was committed (*commissum*) to the faithfulness (*fides*) of the heir—hence, *fidei commissum*.

Under the ordinary Roman law of succession only a person possessed of the *ius commercium* (commercial rights) could take property by a Roman will. This *ius* was automatically one of the rights held by a citizen and was frequently extended by treaty to certain noncitizens. Possession of the *ius commercium* was in a sense a privilege, but a lesser privilege than the grant of full citizenship. Further, even where the *ius commercium* was extended to noncitizens, the right to take under a Roman will was occasionally excluded. All these difficulties meant that it was not usually possible to leave a legacy to an alien.[7] Other groups of persons were similarly excluded from taking under a will by specific legislation that seems occasionally to have depended on imperial whim; for example, at one point actresses were excluded from taking legacies.

In these circumstances the device of the *fidei commissum* was invented towards the end of the first century B.C. As indicated, it was a committal to the faithfulness of the heir, a request to him to do something, which he was not bound by law to honor. However, given the normal well-developed Roman sense of honor, it came to be expected that an honest man would comply with the stated wishes of his ancestor, so long as the request was not actually illegal.

But not all proved honorable. In his *Institutes* of A.D. 533 (2.23.1) Justinian suggests that one reason why *fidei commissa* were given binding force was because of some notorious cases of perfidy. Be that as it may, Augustus, according to Justinian, made the fiduciary trust binding on an heir. Apparently one Lentulus appointed Augustus as his heir and imposed various *fidei commissa* on him by codicil. At that time neither *fidei commissa* nor codicils were legally effective, but Augustus ordered the *fidei commissa* to be carried out and, having consulted the jurists, the senior lawyers of the time, commanded both codicils and fiduciary trusts to be given limited legal status.[8]

At first this meant that the fiduciary trust should be enforced only where it appeared that justice required that it should be complied with. However, as one might expect, the discretionary element present in such a ruling vanished in practice, and the device of the *fidei commissum* rapidly became recognized as the normal legal instrument and a special official the *praetor fidei commissarius*, had to be appointed to oversee the execution of these trusts, much as American courts today supervise executries and check the executor's accounts before discharging him from office.[9]

Of course, the argument that Paul was referring to such fiduciary trusts in some of his writing faces one major question: how far had knowledge of the device spread into the provinces? The legality of *fidei commissa* had only been established for some fifty years when Paul was writing, and some might consider that this was a fairly short period for knowledge of such a technical device to have spread throughout the empire in the way that would seem necessary for Paul to have used it freely as an image.

Various counterarguments can be put. First, some of the uses of the image are in the Epistle to the Romans (e.g., Rom. 3:22–5:2). It seems obvious that the church would refer this to its local law. Second, there is evidence that the device was used in the province of Egypt by relatively poor people, showing that it was known not just to the upper classes.[10] Third, Greek writings refer to the *fidei commissum* without explanation. Greek authors apparently could assume that their readers would be aware of the meaning of the term.[11] Fourth, it is the sort of device that would have intrigued the legal staff of provincial governors who would have carried it with them on their tours of duty. Indeed, it is quite possible that some of the legal officials of the governor's staff might have spent time either as the praetor appointed to oversee the execution of fiduciary trusts or as assistant to such a praetor before proceeding to the provinces.[12] They would certainly have knowledge of such a device, and that leads us to the weightiest and last argument.

The *fidei commissum* was the one way in which an alien or a person not possessed of the *ius commercium* could benefit under the provisions of a Roman will. It was the means of avoiding one of the major penalties of lack of citizenship, and it seems to have been popular. The emperor Vespasian (A.D. 69–79) abolished *fidei commissa* as a means by which aliens might benefit. He decreed that only fiduciary trust by Greeks to Greeks or by Romans to Romans were legal. Trusts across the division of citizenship were made ineffective.[13] Gaius (*Institutes* 2.285) tells us that later Hadrian enacted that such trusts should be claimed for the state exchequer. These legal changes show that the device was known and used between Greeks (i.e., between noncitizens), and also that the device of the fiduciary trust was a popular way of avoiding the strict requirements of the formal law; had this not been the case, there would have been no need to make the change. It follows that the device of *fidei commissum*, allowing transfers of property to persons not possessed of the *ius com-mercium*, had spread significantly throughout the Empire,[14] and Paul, writing before these changes, could well have made use of the device as a metaphor in the way that is being suggested.

We are then back to the familiar argument. Paul, a citizen, would probably have himself inherited under Roman rules and he would therefore have known of the possibilities.[15] Even if he did not so inherit, the device was doubtlessly known in Tarsus, a provincial capital. Further, this device is one that would have delighted Paul's legally trained mind. It is therefore difficult to think that he did not consciously use it as a metaphor of the Christian's entry into the inheritance. Let us therefore see precisely what it conveys.

We can take elements of Galatians 2:15–3:26 as a model to illustrate the use of the fiduciary trust as a metaphor. At intervals throughout the passage we find the ambiguity of faith in/of Christ. This may readily be detected by comparing the passage in the KJV with a translation such as the RSV;[16] the divergences of translation indicate clearly where the ambiguity occurs.

As indicated, one of the problems Paul has to explain is the inclusion of the Gentiles in the promise given to Abraham. Thus, in Galatians 3:13–14 it is said that Christ has redeemed all Christians through His death, "being made a curse for us. ... That the blessing of Abraham might come on the Gentiles through Jesus Christ" (KJV). The intervention of Jesus is necessary and is instrumental in bringing in the Gentiles to inherit the promise. But how is that intervention to be understood?

The other key verse is Galatians 2:16, where it is made clear that it is belief in Jesus that brings about the justification of the Christian. Even the Jew is not justified by the law "but through faith in [KJV, by the faith of] Jesus Christ, even we have believed in Christ Jesus, in order to be justified by faith in [KJV, by the faith of] Christ, and not by works of the law, because by works of the law shall no one be justified."

No one would quarrel with the principle that faith in

Jesus is necessary to work the justification of the sinner. The reference to our faith in Him, which is the interpretation of the ambiguity in the Greek text adopted by the RSV, is not inaccurate. But the selection of that single possibility from the ambiguity of the text obscures another primary element in the transaction—Jesus' faith. On a fundamental level justification is accomplished by His faithfulness to what His Father has committed to Him, by His faithfulness to that death that works salvation for those who believe (Gal. 3:13–14).

The faithfulness to death is not, however, the only element of this passage. There is also the point to be taken from the language that the heir has been asked to do something with his inheritance—he has been asked to share it with persons who are not entitled to share under the formal rules of inheritance. What is involved may therefore by understood, though not fully explained, as the performance of the *fidei commissum*, bringing in outsiders, aliens, persons who by nature would not be qualified to enjoy the inheritance, to share in it.

The picture fits. The entry of the Christian into the inheritance is not a matter of right but is a matter of the faithfulness and of the grace of the Heir (cf. Titus 3:3–8).

But what about the death of the ancestor? There the metaphor does not quite apply in one sense, for the death involved in this *fidei commissum* is not the death of the *fidei commissor*, God, but the death of the heir. Yet the death of Christ may also be understood as the death of God, being the death of the second person of the Trinity. It therefore is not improper to see the death on the cross as bringing into operation in every sense the fiduciary trust upon which those outside the family may rely.

This picture of the fiduciary trust may then be seen as a metaphor given for the encouragement of Christians. It is not a narrative of the mechanics of salvation, but helps Christians better to understand, grasp, and accept what has been done by gracious love. Christians are to have faith in Jesus' faithfulness to His Father. They need not

work themselves up into an emotional state of "faith" nor
be anxious about the quality of their feelings as some kind
of index of the reliability of their faith. It is Christ's faithfulness that is important, and He may be trusted fully:
"God is faithful, by whom you were called into the fellowship of his Son, Jesus Christ our Lord" (1 Cor. 1:9; cf. vv.
4–8); "He who calls you is faithful, and he will do it"
(1 Thess. 5:24); "For by grace you have been saved through
faith; and this is not your own doing, it is the gift of God"
(Eph. 2:8); "Let us hold fast the confession of our hope
without wavering, for he who promised is faithful" (Heb.
10:23).

8

Mercantile Images

Very good

the NT writers personalize this way of legal ideas

THE WRITERS OF THE NEW TESTAMENT EPISTLES drew their legal imagery almost entirely from the law of persons. Not for them a cold presentation of the facts of salvation as a formal legal transaction—on the contrary, the deep personal relationship between man and God, which is of the essence of salvation, brought to their minds images of the ordinary interpersonal legal relationships and correlative notions of status: adoption and sonship (with the inherent concept of the Fatherhood of God), slavery and redemption, alienage and citizenship. Even such use as is made of the "drier" law of inheritance and succession deals with these matters in personal terms. It is interesting therefore to find that generally a similar "personal" use is made of the more technical mercantile or business metaphors of partnership, earnest, and the seal.

Partnership

The concept of partnership is not really found in a developed sense in the New Testament, although the idea of the joint heirs is very akin to it. Indeed, most people consider that the idea of partnership found in Roman law began with consortium, the community of property among brothers, which continued to exist in limited form for a considerable period after New Testament times. This con-

143

sortium seems to have been the origin of the *societas omnium bonorum*, the general partnership, which was the only form of commercial association in New Testament times.[1] Partnership was and is a voluntary association of persons for profit. It involves a common purpose and a contribution of time, money, and/or effort by the partners, with profits and losses divided by agreement or by law.

As such, partnership was certainly known in Jewish law, although there is a lack of information as to its precise content.[2] In the Bible it is referred to in Proverbs 29:24, where one is warned about being the partner of a thief, and in Luke 5:10, where we find that James and John the sons of Zebedee were partners with Simon Peter in their trade as fishermen. But these references tell us only that the concept was known; they say nothing about its details, such as the extent of the partnership or the division of profits. A similar passing reference is made to Titus, whom Paul calls his "partner and fellow worker" in the service of the Corinthians (2 Cor. 8:23), but again there is lack of any specification.

However, matters are taken a little further in the short Epistle to Philemon, where Paul makes some play with the concepts and incidents of partnership in verses 17–19. He asks Philemon in verses 15–16 to take back the runaway slave Onesimus. Paul then says that if Philemon considers Paul his partner he ought to receive Onesimus as he would his partner. Further, Paul instructs him as his partner to charge to his (Paul's) debit in the partnership accounts any wrongs or debts Onesimus owes to Philemon. In verse 19 Paul then guarantees in writing that he will pay this debt between partners, clearly showing that it was possible for the conditions of partnership to be altered from the usual equality, so that one partner would pay a particular debt even to the other partner.

The image is clear: Paul and Philemon as Christians were in partnership, working for a common purpose. The contributions to the partnership made by Paul and Philemon clearly differed: the one traveled and preached, the other provided a center for a local church (Philem. 2), but both were devoting themselves to the same "business." But though Christians may be partners, it is interesting to note that the Bible nowhere talks of the Christian as the "partner" of Christ. He "partakes" of Christ's sufferings (2 Cor. 1:7), and Peter refers to a partaking in the glory that is to be revealed (1 Peter 5:1) and a partaking of the divine nature (2 Peter 1:4). The language is that of partnership, but in these verses there is not that community of participation, that equality of contribution and purpose, which a full partnership would require. Christians are Christ's servants, not His equal partners.

Nonetheless, Paul speaks of a notion similar to partnership in discussing the Lord's Supper. In 1 Corinthians 10:14–22 Paul deals with the worship of idols, and in verse 18 he points out that those who participated in the sacrifices of the Old Testament were partners in the altar; similarly, there is a participation in the body of Christ in taking communion (v. 16). He therefore warns his friends: the food offered to idols is not of itself important, but the offering is made to demons, and he does not want them to be the partners of demons (vv. 19–21). And, as pointed out above, partnership implies a common contribution and a common purpose. The point is plain.

Earnest

In three places Paul speaks of the Christian having "the earnest of the Spirit" (KJV). In two of these, 2 Corinthians 1:22 (conjoined with the imagery of the seal) and 5:5, the earnest is the guarantee of the agreement or bargain with God, while in Ephesians 1:14 (again along with the seal) the Christian's possession of the Holy Spirit is "the guarantee of our inheritance until we acquire possession of it."

"Earnest" is a concept found in many legal systems. For example, under the Statute of Frauds in English and American law it had a function in validating certain verbal or parole contracts.[3] It is a concept whose roots reach back into antiquity.

It is not possible to fix the source of Paul's use of the idea with certainty. The concept of earnest was known in Jewish law as *erabon*, and many think that it was invented by the Jews, passing into Greek law as *arrabon* and into Roman law as *arra* or *arrha*. In any event, the similarity of the language does indicate a common root. Though there are interesting differences between the Roman and Greek concepts, earnest could arise in both systems of law where a bargain involved an obligation to be performed later—as in sale with a postponed payment of the price or delivery of the goods[4]

In Roman law the *arra* was a nonessential part of the contract of buying and selling.[5] One of the parties to a sale (normally but not necessarily the purchaser) gave the other a sum of money or some valuable token, quite often a ring. Some would argue that originally it was this transaction that completed the bargain. However, it is clear that by the time of Paul the *arra* did not perfect the bargain but was simply evidence that the bargain had been struck. In other words, if the *arra* were absent the bargain was not void but could be proved in another way.

Applying this Roman content of the idea of earnest to Paul's language, we see that the earnest of the Spirit is proof of the "bargain" between God and the Christian. We need not strain the analogy in this instance in an attempt to decide whether the seller or purchaser is the giver of the earnest. It is surely enough that the bargain is made and is proved by the gift to the Christian of a valuable earnest—the indwelling Holy Spirit.

Arra in Greek law was a wider concept than that of Roman law.[6] In the Greek legal systems (so far as we know them) its function was not only to act as evidence of the conclusion of a bargain but also to act as a possible penalty, thus ensuring in the ordinary instance the performance of an agreement. The earnest was in a sense a hostage. At the conclusion of the bargain the purchaser gave to the seller something of value as a token that he would perform his obligation. If he failed, the *arra* was forfeit, entirely apart from any question of an action to

compel him to comply with his bargain. It appears that
the practice arose of giving a sum of money as *arra*, in
which case it later might be treated as a partial payment
of the purchase price. Where the *arra* was not money but
a valuable object, it had to be returned by the seller when
the purchaser met his obligation.

Applying this content to Paul's language we can see
the Holy Spirit given to the Christian as a guarantee of his
redemption. The Christian is purchased by blood (Acts
20:28). If God were to fail, the Christian would be entitled
to keep the earnest—God the Holy Spirit. Such an idea
functions as a *reductio ad absurdum* of the possibility that
God could or would renege on his bargain. If God were to
fail the Christian would be left as possessor of God the
Spirit. It is difficult to see what other legal figure could
better present the utter reliability that undergirds the faith
of the Christian.

It is not really necessary to take this concept further,
though I am intrigued with the possible light these ideas
may shed on the life after death. Is the indwelling Holy
Spirit to be thought of as some sort of partial payment or
partial fulfillment of the heavenly destiny of the Christian? Do we have to give him back when the bargain is
performed and we are in heaven? Or is the bargain rather
to be considered as a continuing matter so that the earnest
is never withdrawn? My own impression is that the Spirit
is not withdrawn from the saints in heaven and must be
considered a "partial payment." Perhaps when we are in
heaven with God and no longer troubled by the remains
of a fallen nature, that fullness of experience will make
the present earnest of the Spirit in our hearts seem but the
preliminary experience of heaven. There are two passages
in favorite books of mine that put this thought well. In the
foreword to *Voices and Echoes from the Braes of Bennachie*,
the dying James Stark, a biographer of some notable men
of the northeast of Scotland, says: "Heaven will not be so
very different from earth . . . not where Christ has been."
The other comes from C. S. Lewis's introduction to *The
Great Divorce*: "Earth I think, will not be found by anyone

to be in the end a very distinct place. I think earth, if
chosen instead of Heaven, will turn out to have been, all
along, only a region in Hell: and earth, if put second to
Heaven, to have been from the beginning a part of Heaven
itself."[7]

Seal   (3)

One biblical metaphor that is obviously drawn from
legal procedure is that of the seal.[8] Seals have many uses
in the law, and all of them find some sort of employment
in the imagery of the Old and New Testaments. Since the
seal was widespread throughout the ancient world as one
would expect in a time when reading and writing were
not general accomplishments, there is no need to try to
determine its source. Thus, although George Horowitz indicates that "sealing" really meant attestation of a deed by
a witness and not the actual use of a seal,[9] this slight
evidence does not rule out a Jewish source. The basic notions of each legal system in respect to seals were akin
because they were conditioned by the same need for a
sealing procedure.

A seal may perform one or more of several functions.
It may be used to close up a document or a repository; it
may indicate a finished transaction or the completion of
something; and it may act as an authentication, as an identification, or as a statement or claim of ownership. In that
connection it is interesting to note that the language of
sealing occurs along with the concept of the earnest twice
in the Pauline Epistles (2 Cor. 1:22; Eph. 1:13–14). However, common to all the functions of the seal is the idea
that the presence of a seal gives some sort of security or
assurance to the person dealing with material that has
been sealed. By it he may know that all is in order and the
material has not been tampered with.

One of the basic functions of a seal was to close something up, either to keep it shut or to have proof if it were
opened, much as one seals a registered letter. Thus Darius
sealed the entrance to the lion's den (Dan. 6:17), the tomb

was sealed (Matt. 27:66), and in the vision of John the Devil was cast into the bottom of the pit and it was sealed (Rev. 20:3). From these it is but a short step to the seal that closes up a book or a piece of writing. Revelation 4 and the following chapters tell of the opening of the book with the seven seals. Later John is instructed to seal up a particular vision and not to write about it (Rev. 10:4), but at the end of his vision he is told not to seal up the prophecies of the revelation, presumably so that they may be read (Rev. 22:10). A similar use of the seal is made in Daniel 12:4 and Isaiah 8:16, where the prophets are told to seal up the book of the prophecy and the law respectively.

The idea of sealing up a book also includes the idea that its contents are finished or complete. One of the earliest references to sealing in the Old Testament shows this clearly and is found in a legal context in Jeremiah 32. Jeremiah was told to buy the field at Anathoth as near-kinsman to his cousin and then to hide both copies of the title deed to show prophetically that though the Jews were to be taken from the Land, yet in due time, when the Jews had returned from captivity, such titles would still be valid. Verses 10–12 tell how Jeremiah took a copy of the title deed that was sealed and one that was open and gave them to his secretary Baruch with instructions to deposit them suitably (v. 14). These verses state a simple procedural device: deeds of sale were made in two copies, one closed by means of a seal to prevent alteration, the other open so that its contents were public knowledge. In so doing Jeremiah was using the two "document" procedure well known to us from other legal systems of antiquity. For example, it is likely that Paul's certificate of citizenship existed in a closed and in an open form, the open form being possibly carried by Paul wherever he went as proof of his citizenship.[10]

In the case of Jeremiah's title deeds the presence of his seal also indicated that the transaction was completed—a finished work—which has importance in the New Testament uses of the imagery of sealing. Jeremiah's seal also acted as an authentication that the document had been validly executed by him. Jeremiah subscribed the evidence of the purchase and sealed it (Jer. 32:11, cf. v. 44). The seal was proof that he had personally acted in the transaction.

This element of authentication by the seal is found more clearly in the Old Testament references to the seal of particular monarchs. A clear example occurs in the Book of Esther, where the possession of the king's ring allowed first Haman and then Mordecai full powers to legislate without further reference to the monarch (Esth. 3:10; 8:2). Any document sealed with the king's signet was legally valid throughout the Persian Empire.

Authentication can come in various ways. The seal may be affixed by a party to a transaction indicating, as in Jeremiah's case, that he has acted.[11] It may further be evidence of a party's solemn willingness to be bound by a contract. Thus, in Nehemiah 9:38–10:26 we read of the sealing of the covenant with God under which the returning Jews bound themselves to keep the law after the return.

On other occasions the seal may be applied simply as a mark of ownership, as when a company puts its name on vehicles. Of course, there is a certain advertising value involved in this apart from the question of ownership, but that advertising value may not be irrelevant in questions of Christianity. In Revelation 7:2–8 and 9:4 we are told of a multitude having the seal of God on their foreheads (cf. Ezek. 9:4) and there is the parallel "mark of the beast" (Rev. 13:16–17; 14:9; 19:20). Both ownership and advertising elements are present.

The seal may also be affixed by a witness authenticating and proving the validity of a documented transaction.[12] Analogously, Jesus speaks of Himself as authenticated and validated by God (John 6:27). We can also interpret in this sense Paul's statement that the circumcising of Abraham was a seal of the faith that he had already before circumcision—a proof of its existence (Rom. 4:11). Paul also speaks of the Corinthian Christians as being the seal of his apostleship, a proof of its validity (1 Cor.

202 when th "law" became (Must!!) & Jus

X : Lacking th Temple (a center) ∴ Ends th Law
became central; ∴ what & Synagogue

the rules Ezra — th "Men of th Great assembly"
203 & finally th origin of th Sanhedrin 300 BC
∴ what th Talmud is (what with th Torah)

204   midrah — midhalah etc

205   Maimonides
       is popular
208 th Sadducee / Pharisee split 75 BC – 70 AD

206 circa 100–150 BC

208 re "th lawyers" of th Gospels

211 how Rome related administratively to it
        subject govts

213+14 The history of rulers in Palestine — th Herods
        etc — but also Felix; Festus (Acts 24, 25,
        on Acts 17:5 f   28
                19:34 f
           16   16:21
215 "Colony of heaven" 14 & Roman Colonies
           Phil 2

229 th origin of th "Great Mother" cult
                     adopted by Rome
X   Mt 2da 204 B.C. —

241-24 th 5 "stages of life" in Judaism —; th education
        system in Jerus. in Paul's time X

108 re: "legal _personality_" re: heir.

~~X~~ ava 109 "persona" = 'to speak thru'
w. to mark, the & character, etc

faith in X&l & th' faith & XL — see
note p. 287 re Gal 2.d —
! ch 7 & the th bod

143 "Consortuin" = general partnership

178 whereas "criminal law" needs "proof
beyond reasonable doubt" — "civil law"
does not so require — but why empirical
evidence to make a decision —

1C D & & 50 wh chooses' th wits & D&l
freedoms

183 re: interpreting "metaphors" in NT
(very good)

185 CS Lewis 14": "Flatland" wh 2 dimensions —
no Reptile, cf th Secular bred vein

†201 f. The "Jewish "law" (Tirah) differs fr.
Western law (traylla) in that it reached
into every area of a Jew's life
"   "   called "th trad & th elders" (MA)

This
good
material 201 Th "Oral law", Jan'n interp, in who
Moses taught Joshua & who 202 Exile
Became and effective after th tr Ex Do. 203

9:2). In both these instances Paul is saying that the facts of the case show that God has put His seal of approval upon His servants. Such an idea may also lie behind the words that the man who receives the testimony of Him who comes from above "sets his seal to this, that God is true" (John 3:33; cf. John 6:27, above): when a person has received Christ's testimony he, in his turn, witnesses or gives his seal to the statement that God is true.

Before we finish with the idea of the seal, there are three other passages in the Bible that use the seal figuratively. The first is a simile; in Job 38:14 God talks of shaping the earth, which is "changed like clay under a seal"; while not expressed directly, we may see in this both God's finished work (Gen. 2:2) and the indelible mark of His ownership. The second example is similar, and deep. In Hebrews 1:3 Christ is spoken of as the "express image" of God (KJV) or as bearing "the very stamp" of God's nature.

The third example may indicate one way by which Christians in the Roman Empire, towards the end of Paul's life when the persecutions were getting under way, identified each other and signaled their faith to their fellows. It was common practice in the ancient world, as it is today, for a seal to have a device or a short phrase, such as a family motto, cut into it, so that the impression left on the wax by the seal would be identifiable. In 2 Timothy 2:19 Paul speaks of God's foundation standing firm and sure, "bearing this seal: 'The Lord knows those who are his,' and, 'let every one who names the name of the Lord [Christ] depart from iniquity.' " Paul is saying that the seal of the foundation of God has a motto on it, and he gives two examples. For Paul, anyone using these particular sentences used a password akin to that of the sign of the fish—he too was a brother.

Finally, bearing all the foregoing in mind we can look at Ephesians 4:30, in which Paul's use of the seal as an image seems to embrace almost every one of the possible uses of the seal. He asks the Ephesians not to grieve the Holy Spirit of God "in whom you were sealed for the day of redemption" or "whereby ye are sealed unto the day of

redemption" (KJV). If one accepts that either of these ren-
derings is permissible, then one can read into the language
the whole gamut of the imagery of the seal. The Holy
Spirit's presence in the Christian indicates a finished
transaction to which nothing can be added. He authenti-
cates God's acts. He is the badge and proof of God's ownership. He changes the character by the impress of Christ.
And, safe in him, the Christian can await the final redemption with absolute confidence.

9

Redemption

now are true to Jewish, not Roman law — Only Jews knew of redemption given by revelation

Up to this point our book has had two major theses: First, that the legal metaphors of the Epistles shed greater light when the law from which they were drawn is understood; and second, that in the bulk of the instances Roman law is both the probable source of the metaphor and provides the richest content for the legal language involved. Accordingly, in the preceding chapters we have interpreted the metaphors discussed largely by Roman law. That second thesis—the reference to Roman law, has been almost exhausted, and may be taken as finishing with the discussion of the mercantile images in the last chapter.

There remains the multifaceted concept of redemption, which is itself a legal idea. Redemption is of fundamental importance to the biblical message and is integral to the other legal metaphors. Slave and freed status, alienage and citizenship, adoption, sonship and heirship, trust, and the commercial metaphors are summed up in the simple "belonging or not belonging to the family of God." They all speak of the existence or nonexistence of a personal relationship between the individual and God. Redemption is concerned with the creation of that relationship.

The Bible teaches that man was created for fellowship with God. By sin that original closeness became impossible because man, created in the image of God, went out-

side the limits of God's nature and became other than
good. The relationship with God was therefore broken.

Redemption is the reconstitution of man's relationship with God. A holy God could not ignore, repeal, or
"magic away" sin—it had to be dealt with. The wrath of
God for sin had to be met and in the technical sense "satisfied." It is as though the occurrence of sin had brought
into being an electrical charge of wrath that had to be
safely earthed, and the only way that that could happen
was for it to be properly discharged. Ordinarily that would
involve the punishment of the sinner, yet God provided
a Savior and His anger was, for those who believe, discharged on and through His Son, Jesus. To take another
analogy, as matter and antimatter combine to form nothing, so in the sinless Christ the holy wrath of God com-
bined with the "antiholy" (sin) and annihilated it. Thus,
for Christians, the barrier of sin was destroyed and the
broken relationship with God was restored.

The concepts of the earlier chapters then transmit
ideas of being in the family or outside it, of loving God or
being a stranger to Him. These ideas are essentially ideas
of status. Redemption has to do with change of status, the
actual movement from out to in, from hostility to love. Yet
redemption is also a matter of relationship, for it is not aid
given by some altruistic stranger: the basis of the idea of
redemption is that it is a family matter. Salvation is not a
business transaction; it is the act of our heavenly Father
and our elder Brother, an act of those who love us better
than any blood relation. The language is that of ransom,
atonement, expiation, and salvation, all grounded in law,
yet still speaking of a living love. It is help and rescue by
a member of one's family.

Of all the legal notions that are taken up and used in
the Bible to illustrate and communicate God's ways of
dealing with mankind, that of redemption is preeminent.
The death of Jesus procuring the redemption of believers
is the main focus of the story. Salient points of the biblical
narrative show this clearly. The promise of the Redeemer
was given at the time of the Fall (Gen. 3:15). The blood of

the Passover lamb preserved the people when the firstborn of Egypt were slain as a judgment on Pharaoh (Exod. 12). Both the Passover and the Exodus are interpreted in redemptive terms in the Old and New Testaments. The various Levitical sacrifices are also representations of the redemptive process, apart from their function in postponing God's judgment on sin. The Epistle to the Hebrews, particularly chapter 9, most clearly states the connection between these ceremonies and the work of Christ. After the Land was occupied, the coming of the Redeemer sent by God was made increasingly clearer to the prophets. They foresaw the Captivity and the return, events that are in themselves analogies of redemption when looked at from the point of view of the person being redeemed. They also foresaw the coming of the Redeemer, who would have to suffer to procure the redemption, the clearest revelation being found in Isaiah 53.

In the New Testament, the events of Jesus' life, particularly the week prior to the Crucifixion, parallel the Old Testament concepts. Thereafter the Epistles celebrate the death of Christ as working the redemption of believers and interpret the whole of Old Testament history and prophecy in its light. From that time to this, the main burden of theological enquiry has been a consideration of the idea or ideas of redemption.

No other religious system contains a doctrine of redemption as found either in Judaism or in Christianity[1] On occasion other religions speak of a god or the gods coming to deliver their worshipers, but these ideas lack the fullness or care and the element of the free grace of God that is to be found in the biblical narratives. In the Bible the initiative lies with God. He intervenes to save His oppressed people in the Book of Exodus and in the prophetic literature. In other religions deliverance is forthcoming upon proper worship;[2] the Christian worships because he is redeemed.

There are also massive differences between the idea of "the dying god" and the death of Christ. Many religions contain tales of a dying god. There is the myth of Balder

the Beautiful, slain by the cunning of Loki, in Norse myth-
ology. He does not rise again, but occasionally these dying
gods are resurrected by one means or another. Osiris is
resurrected thanks to the devotion of Isis, and there are
many other examples to be found, collected in J. G. Frazer's *The Golden Bough*, particularly in the volume devoted to "The Dying God."[3] In none of these religions,
however, is there the suggestion that the death of the god
works the redemption of his worshipers in anything other
than a rather crude journalistic sense. In the main, such
religions may be considered explanations or representations of the death of the sun in winter and its rebirth in
the spring, or of the death and rebirth of vegetation in
those seasons. There is only a faint prospective echo of
the Christian teaching. In other religions the death of the
god is procured by the worshipers in order that they may
be saved from Chaos. It is a major step beyond such ideas
to consider that the death of God, occurring on the initiative of God, redeems in the way found in the Christian
tradition. For the Christian the purpose of redemption,
occurring on the initiative of God, is the returning of man
to the function and the place which but for the Fall he
would have occupied in God's economy. It is the constitution, or reconstitution, of a permanent living relationship between God and the believer rather than a rescue
from Chaos after which the believer is permitted to carry
on as suits him. And it happens by a redemptive act, an
act falling within and explained by concepts of law relating to the protection and salvation of the weak and the
oppressed.[4]

So far, however, I have been rather simplistic in my
use of the term *redemption*. It is a complex notion with
many facets, all of which are taken up to a greater or lesser
extent in both the Old and New Testaments. Although
redemption is primarily a legal notion, it has also social
and philosophical aspects, which can equally contribute
to a theological understanding of its implications. As is
only to be expected with such an important topic, redemption is a matter on which many have written, and I

cannot pretend to have mastered or even read all the different treatments. As this book is intended to shed some light on the possible legal backgrounds to New Testament metaphors, it will suffice to restrict the compass of our investigation to the law. The question of course arises, which law?

As in other legal metaphors, the choice of law for the interpretation of redemption metaphors is basically three-fold: Roman law, Greek law, or Jewish law. However, in this instance there can be no doubt that it is Jewish law that provides the broadest and richest content for the concept. I have myself been persuaded of this as a result of reading Professors David Daube and J. D. M. Derrett.[5] Both writers have fascinating discussions of the legal concept of redemption as known in the Old Testament, in rabbinic study, and in New Testament times. Indeed, I am strongly tempted simply to refer to these discussions and to abandon any attempt to discuss the legal content of redemption myself. However, as to do so would be to omit one of the major legal ideas of the New Testament, I will simply deal with my own understanding of the topic and would refer those who would wish a more scholarly treatment to Professors Daube and Derrett.

One last preliminary point: as in previous chapters, we are dealing with living relationships. Under Jewish law redemption was basically a family matter. It was neither a cold "third party" business transaction nor an act of charity between friends. It was an outworking of a fundamental familial relationship, more profound than pity or charity, stemming from the deeper reaches of love. The personal nature of the transactions should not be forgotten in the ensuing discussion.

Apart from the redemption of a captive, Jewish law made provision for redemption in four basic situations.[6] There was redemption of a person from civil bondage caused by debt, the redemption of land sold to meet a debt, levirate marriage, and lastly, the role of the avenger of blood. In each of these four categories it was provided that someone other than the person immediately affected by the circumstances might intervene to act as his "defender" or "redeemer." This intervener was the go'el of the person, his claimant or vindicator (vindex). It is apparent from the four situations covered in the Pentateuch that normally the go'el was expected to be kinsman of the person who (or whose property) was to be redeemed, and that there was a fairly strict hierarchy of duty, the nearer kinsmen having the first responsibility to act. That responsibility was, however, social and not legal. Failure to act did not attract legal penalty, nor could a man be compelled by legal process to act. There was no legal duty imposed upon the go'el, though if he failed to discharge his responsibility there would be various social consequences. For example, the failure to discharge an obligation of levirate marriage originally resulted in the kinsman being subjected to a rather debasing and insulting ceremony (Deut. 25:9). Failure to do one's duty as go'el attracted opprobrium but that was all. One could not be sued for breach of that duty.

Redemption from Civil Bondage

Redemption from civil bondage is dealt with in Leviticus 25:47–55. The rules for calculating the price of redemption are set out in verses 50–55,[7] but we need not go into these technicalities. The general principle of the legislation is set out in verses 47–49 in these words:

> If a stranger or sojourner with you becomes rich, and your brother beside him becomes poor and sells himself to the stranger or sojourner with you, or to a member of the stranger's family, then after he is sold he may be redeemed; one of his brothers may redeem him, or his uncle, or his cousin may redeem him, or a near kinsman belonging to his family may redeem him; or if he grows rich he may redeem himself.

In other words, when a person had been reduced to bondage, the law provided that he might be bought out of it either by himself, when he became rich, or by the go'el,

the near kinsman. This provision was important because
the reduction of a debtor or his family to bondage was a
normal pattern of the times. Such bondage was not quite
the same as slavery because the individual could recover
his freedom if the debt was paid off, while in the case of
a Hebrew owning Hebrews the rules of Jubilee applied
(Exod. 21:2; Deut. 15:12–18).[8]

An example of such a situation is found in 2 Kings
4:1–7, the well-known story of the widow and the cruse
of oil. The woman's deceased husband had been heavily
in debt and the creditor had arrived to take her sons as
slaves to work off that debt. Elisha, the prophet, told the
woman to get basins and buckets, and she continued to
pour oil from her little jar until all the containers she could
obtain were full. She was then able to sell this oil to pay
off the debt. The story has been the basis of many evan-
gelistic sermons, but what is important for us is the underlying legal structure. Elisha did not deny the justice of the
law by which the creditor could have taken the sons; he
ensured that the widow was able to meet her obligations—
in itself a form of redemption.

Redemption of Land

On occasion land was sold to meet debts, and the
buying back of such land was a fundamental part of the
land law of the Jews.[9] Redemption became the duty of the
near kinsman if the original seller could not redeem his
property. In Leviticus 25:23–25 God says, "The land shall
not be sold in perpetuity, for the land is mine; for you are
strangers and sojourners with me. And in all the country
you possess, you shall grant a redemption of the land. If
your brother becomes poor, and sells part of his property,
then his next of kin shall come and redeem what his brother
has sold."

Redemption of the land operated originally to retain
the tribal property in the hands of the tribe. It was not
possible at first to sell property in perpetuity, though, as
might be expected, the lawyers did invent ways of avoid-

ing the prohibition, which we need not go into. It is enough
here to observe that the redemption of land was built into
the basic concepts of Jewish land law. Redemption was
normative.

An example of a parable based on this provision of
the land law is found in Jeremiah 32:6–15, where Jeremiah
as next of kin bought the field at Anathoth on the invita-
tion of his cousin. Through this God showed that after the
coming Captivity He would bring His people back to the
Land and the title to the field would be honored. This is
an important prophecy in normal biblical study. Our interest lies in it being firmly rooted in the law of redemption. If Jeremiah's cousin had sold the land to a stranger,
Jeremiah would have had a duty to redeem it.

Another classical example of redemption of property
is found in the fourth chapter of the Book of Ruth, where
the nearest of kin of the deceased Elimelech was given the
opportunity to redeem the property of his kinsman. This
he was willing to do until he realized he would have to
take the widow of Elimelech's son as well (Ruth 4:1–6).

Levirate Marriage

Mention of Ruth takes us to the third example of redemption regulated by, or perhaps more accurately, recognized in the Old Testament.[10] We have already discussed
this institution fairly extensively in relation to adoption
in chapter 4, but briefly, the levirate was the duty of a man
to take in marriage the widow of his brother who had died
without issue, and to raise a son by her who would carry
on the name and line of the deceased.

In levirate marriage, therefore, provision was made
for the continuation of the familial line in the congregation
of Israel (Deut. 25:6). The family was thus "redeemed"
from extinction and would continue with a close genetic
resemblance to the family line that would have come into
being if the deceased man had had a son. The taking of
the widow of the deceased is of course rather foreign to
modern ideas, but it was an ancient practice, the idea of

the levirate existing long before the Deuteronomic provisions. The case of Tamar in Genesis 38 establishes its antiquity, and the example of Ruth shows how the institution operated in practice. Although the institution finally fell into disfavor by the time of Maimonides (c. A.D. 1000), it was current in the time of Jesus. One of the conundrums the Sadducees put to Him turned on the technicalities of the levirate. Rather cynically, since they did not themselves believe in a resurrection, the Sadducees asked Christ about a woman who had had seven husbands by reason of the rules of the levirate—whose wife would she be in the resurrection? Christ's answer that in the resurrection there would be no marrying or giving in marriage destroyed the premise of the question, but the fact that the question could be put shows the vitality of the levirate in biblical times (Matt. 22:23–33; Mark 12:18–27; Luke 20:27–38).

The Avenger of Blood

The role of the avenger of blood is found in provisions dealing with murder, manslaughter, and the institution of the cities of refuge, principally in Numbers 35:9–34 and Deuteronomy 19:1–13.[11] There is a certain amount of doubt as to how these provisions worked in practice,[12] but the main lines seem to be that there were six cities of refuge, one for each major area of the land. In the case of accidental homicide the slayer could flee to take refuge in one of these cities. He had to remain there until the death of the high priest, after which he could return to his own village (Num. 35:28). If he went beyond the boundary of the city of refuge and the avenger of blood found him there, the avenger might slay him guiltlessly (Num. 35:26–27). In the case of murder the death penalty was mandatory (Exod. 21:12–14; Num. 35:16–21). In cases of doubt as to whether a killing was murder, the congregation (which probably means the local council) had to determine whether the slaying was accidental or not (Num. 35:22–25). Where it was determined that the killing was murder, the murderer was to be surrendered from the city of refuge to the avenger of blood who could kill him (Deut. 19:11–13). The provisions as enunciated were absolute. The murderer could not be ransomed from death, nor could the accidental killer be ransomed from the requirement of residence in the city of refuge (Num. 35:31–32).

But it was not anyone who could act as avenger. The avenger of blood was the go'el hadam, go'el meaning "near kinsman" as before, and hadam, "blood." The avenger of blood in any given case was a near kinsman of the deceased who had by virtue of the relationship the right and duty to slay the killer. From the biblical texts it appears that the avenger was a well-known person in Hebrew life, for the passages in Deuteronomy 19 and Numbers 35 do not define who he is. Apparently this was unnecessary, proving that the passages were not inventing new law but were setting out or revising an existing practice.

The concept of the avenger of blood was taken as an image into prophetic utterance, as we shall see, but the role of the avenger continued in ordinary society at least until David's day. When Joab was trying to influence David to bring back Absalom he made use of a trick to show David his inconsistency in not forgiving Absalom. That point need not detain us, but the content of his ruse depended upon the institution of the avenger of blood. Joab got a woman of Tekoa to go to David to say that she was about to lose her remaining son, who had killed his brother; the avenger of blood was seeking his life (2 Sam. 14:1–24). Of course in this instance the avenger was the next heir, and the result of his exacting of the lawful vengeance would have been to get the inheritance for himself. This fabricated complaint did indeed stir David's sense of injustice with important other effects, but for our purposes it is clear that the role of the avenger was not obsolete at least down to David's day. Even if it did become obsolete in practice after that its presence in the texts means that it would have been known to Jews. The next later fact of practice we have is that the Romans reserved to themselves the right to carry out the death penalty (John 18:31).

Where is the element of redemption in the concept of the avenger of blood and amid such slaughter? The killing of the manslayer had several functions. The shedding of blood was seen as polluting the land, and that pollution could only be removed by expiation through the blood of the slayer (Num. 35:33–34). It appears that the spilling of blood attracted the judgment of God and there was the special ceremony of the sacrifice of a heifer by the elders of the nearest city in the case of a man found slain by a person or persons unknown (Deut. 21:1–9). In other circumstances the act of the avenger turned away the wrath of God (Deut. 19:13).

The religious duty of making expiation for the blood that had been shed was therefore part of the role of the avenger of blood. Another important element in his function was the social requirement of the exaction of punishment for murder, and this element should not be forgotten. But in addition to these two purposes the avenger of blood also acted in a way to redeem. We speak easily of "taking life," an expression that reflects the idea that a person killing another has in some way taken control over him and deprived others—his family—of him. The killing of the killer by the near kinsman, the avenger of blood, "brings back" or "releases" the blood. The execution redeems the slain. Such ideas may seem somewhat odd to modern minds reared in a society in which the individuality of each person is stressed, but when it is remembered that the Near-Eastern family structure was closely knit, redemption through avenging a death is not so strange.

The Redeemer

Redemption, whether of the poor, of the possessions of the poor, of the familial line by levirate marriage, or of blood by the avenger of blood, was to be carried out by a near kinsman. But the concept of the "redeemer" involved more than intervening in the four desperate situations we have looked at. The redeemer had other duties. In par-

ticular, he had to take his relation's part in law suits. This
is part of the point of Job's cry; his argument is not getting
on very well, but he knows that his redeemer lives and
will come to his aid, "whom I shall see on my side" (Job
19:25–27). The redeemer had to help all his poor relatives.
He had to defend them against oppression and plead their
cases.

Pleading the cause of a relative is exactly what Christ,
our Redeemer, does (cf. Heb. 7:25). There is, however, another application of this metaphor. Pleading another's
cause through prayer is the only way in which the individual Christian can act as the redeemer of another. Of
course, on a lesser plane we can "redeem" in the physical
sense. We must succor the poor and help the needy, for
they as fellow human beings are our kin. But in spiritual
terms we cannot deliver from oppression or, as we shall
see, pay their debts. Our work in the spiritual realm can
only be that of intercession, and to omit that duty vitiates
and may even negate all that we do by way of social relief.

Of course, fallen human nature is not good at doing
its duty to the poor of this world, and so the cry has gone
up for an ideal go'el, who can defend the poor with both
compassion and authority: a king. Psalm 72:12–14 tells
how this ideal king is worthy of praise and glory: "For he
delivers the needy when he calls, the poor and him who
has no helper. He has pity of the weak and the needy, and
saves the life of the needy. From oppression and violence
he redeems their life; and precious is their blood in his
sight." Nowadays, this passage speaks to us of Christ,
though David was speaking primarily of his son Solomon
and of his hopes for Solomon's reign. But the Jews also
saw beyond the idea of the ideal king to God, the God who
would defend the poor when their human relatives failed
to do so. Thus Proverbs 23:10-11 states, "Do not remove
an ancient landmark or enter the fields of the fatherless;
for their Redeemer is strong; he will plead their cause
against you." David, in peril, asks God to plead his cause
in Psalm 35:1: "Contend, O LORD, with those who contend
with me." Jeremiah argues that as God has pleaded his

case and redeemed his life in the past, He should now go on to crush His enemies (Lam. 3:55–66). And in Psalm 119:153–154, the psalmist prays, "Look on my affliction and deliver me, for I do not forget thy law. Plead my cause and redeem me; give me life according to thy promise." Such redemptive acts were the privilege and duty of near kinsmen, and it is awesome to realize that God's intervention is being spoken of as that of a relative.

Jewish tradition, anticipating Christianity, is quite clear on this. God is our "superrelative." Created by Him in His own image (Gen. 1:26), we are even more His relatives than we are the relatives of our human relations. A claim of relationship underlies the earliest and the most confident affirmation of redemption, found in the words of Job: "For I know that my Redeemer lives, and at last he will stand upon the earth; and after my skin has been thus destroyed, then from my flesh I shall see God, whom I shall see on my side, and my eyes shall behold, and not another" (Job 19:25–27). There are other examples. God asserted his claim to Israel by redeeming Israel from Pharaoh's domination on the grounds that He was Israel's Father. Exodus 4:22–23 says, "And you [Moses] shall say to Pharaoh, 'Thus says the Lord, Israel is my first-born son, and I say to you "Let my son go that he may serve me." ' " In the middle of a passage lamenting the unfaithfulness of the people, their treatment of the prophets, and God's failure to bring them to heel, Isaiah points out that God should act: "For thou art our Father, though Abraham does not know us and Israel does not acknowledge us; thou, O LORD, art our Father, our Redeemer from of old is thy name" (Isa. 63:16). The grounding of this passage in ideas of kinship is underlined by the fact that the word "acknowledge"—"Israel does not acknowledge us"—is a technical term for recognizing one's duty to a kinsman.

Earlier in the same chapter Isaiah has seen God (Christ) coming in crimson garments from Edom "announcing vindication, mighty to save" (Isa. 63:1). "Vindication" here is also a technical term meaning the taking of one's kinsman's part. Why has God done this? Because there was

no other redeemer, no near kinsman either able or willing
to redeem his relative.

> For the day of vengeance was in my heart, and the
> year of my redeemed has come. I looked, but there was
> no one to help; I was appalled, but there was no one
> to uphold [i.e., no redeemer]; so my own arm brought
> me victory, and my wrath upheld me (Isa. 63:4–5).

This passage is an outworking of the vision of Isaiah
59:12–20:

> Our transgressions are multiplied before thee, and our
> sins testify against us; ... Yea, truth faileth; and he
> that departeth from evil maketh himself a prey. And
> the LORD saw it, and it displeased him that there was
> no judgment. And he saw that there was no man, and
> wondered that there was no intercessor [i.e., no re-
> deemer]; therefore his arm brought salvation unto him;
> and his righteousness sustained him. For he put on
> righteousness as a breastplate, and a helmet of salva-
> tion upon his head; and he put on the garments of
> vengeance for clothing, and was clad with zeal as a
> cloak. According to their deeds, accordingly he will
> repay, fury to his adversaries, recompense to his ene-
> mies; ... So shall they fear the name of the LORD
> ... And the Redeemer shall come to Zion and unto
> those who turn from transgression in Jacob, saith the
> LORD (KJV).

Of course, not all the instances of redemption language make it obvious that God is acting as our relative.
In some cases it is not at all clear in what capacity or for
what reason God acts. In some cases the concept of redemption is the simple idea of getting back one's own
property. There is a redemption in this sense in Leviticus
25:24–34, under which a man could redeem immovable
property by repaying a proportion of the sale price based
on the number of years to the Jubilee. This corresponds
with the usual idea of redemption in the English language,

but it is unfortunate that our notion usually includes an idea of "buying back" (the literal meaning of the Latin *redemptio*, from which we derive our word "redemption"). But the Jewish idea did not always involve repayment. In Isaiah 52:3 God says of Jerusalem, "You were sold for nothing and you shall be redeemed without money." According to Leviticus 25, in the case of sale of a person or property, both transactions were cancelled automatically at the Jubilee without any question of money passing. Indeed, even more simply, merely to assert one's title to one's property was a form of redemption, a bringing back under one's control of something belonging to one. This gives rise to a confusion of images in Isaiah 43:1: "But now thus says the LORD, he who created you, O Jacob, he who formed you, O Israel: 'Fear not, for I have redeemed you; I have called you by name, you are mine.'" Here a variety of images are drawn upon. In law, creation gives title, forming gives title, redemption gives title, and the calling by name is a clear assertion of title. In this verse God is not necessarily acting as a relative. He may simply be acting as owner, but the instances in the Bible where God acts by reason of familial relationship far outweigh those in which He enforces a right of property.

The passages from Isaiah 59 and 63 indicate that on occasion the redeemer might take the initiative and need not wait until his aid was asked for. When this happens it usually means that God is not only going to plead the case but that He is also going to do something more to get justice for His poor oppressed people. We have seen the example of the Exodus. Another instance is to be found in Jeremiah 50:33–34, where we read: "Thus says the LORD of hosts: The people of Israel are oppressed, and the people of Judah with them; all who took them captive have held them fast, they refuse to let them go. Their Redeemer is strong; The LORD of hosts is his name. He will surely plead their cause, that he may give rest to the earth, but unrest to the inhabitants of Babylon."

The need for redemption seems to have arisen most frequently from debt, causing either the sale of possessions or the self-sale of a debtor until he had worked off the debt. This is capable of immediate use as a metaphor teaching the truth of the gospel and is the cardinal use that Paul makes of the idea. We are all in debt because of sin. Entirely apart from the sin of Adam, breach of the covenant of Mount Sinai has put us all in debt—a debt that we cannot work off. But there is a Redeemer. As Paul puts the matter in Galatians 3:10–13,

> For all who rely on works of the law are under a curse; for it is written, "Cursed be everyone who does not abide by all things written in the book of the law, and do them." Now it is evident that no man is justified before God by the law; for "He who through faith is righteous shall live"; but the law does not rest on faith, for "He who does them shall live by them." Christ redeemed us from the curse of the law, having become a curse for us.

This is the fuller statement of what Paul expresses also in Romans 3:24, 1 Corinthians 1:30, and Galatians 4:4–5. In terms of Christian theology, as it has been worked out over the years, Christ has redeemed us from the debt that we ourselves had no hope of satisfying.

It is but a short step from the idea of redemption from debt to the idea of redemption from any form of control by a hostile power. This is exactly how the Jews interpreted the Exodus, for God Himself presents the Exodus as redemption.[13] In Exodus 6:1–8 God says to Moses that He has heard the groans of His people and that He will bring them out from Egypt. In verse 6 He continues: "Say therefore to the people of Israel, 'I am the LORD, and I will bring you out from under the burdens of the Egyptians, and I will deliver you from their bondage, and I will redeem you with an outstretched arm and with great acts of judgment.' "

This may be compared with the song of Moses after the crossing of the Red Sea, where Edom, Moab, and the Canaanites are said to dread, to be dismayed and terrified, and to be "as still as a stone, till thy people, O LORD, pass by, till the people pass by whom thou hast purchased" (Exod. 15:16). To such language could be added many psalms and the other examples already given where the Lord is spoken of as having redeemed His people from their enemies.

The idea of redemption from captivity or from hostile forces is taken up by Paul in the New Testament and, used in conjunction with the idea of freeing from slavery in a more strict sense, ideally illustrates what Christ has done for us.[14] *Thoredeend we owf ounlves to our Redeemer.*

In the case of redemption of property or redemption from a hostile power, one important point is occasionally overlooked. In neither instance was the person redeemed free from obligation. Until the redemption price had been repaid to the redeemer, the person redeemed was subject to certain restrictions; he could not just go off and do as he pleased thereafter. In the case of the redemption of an individual from hostile control, the salvation given him through his redemption meant that he was, to a degree, under his redeemer's control.[15] This is one of the few instances in which the Roman law of redemption can supplement and illustrate the Jewish law.

Where a Roman citizen had been captured in war he was automatically reduced to slavery. As far as the Roman legal system was concerned he was civilly dead. However, if he returned to Roman territory thereafter (provided that his capture was genuine, i.e., that he had not deserted to the enemy), most of his former rights revived. This was known as the *ius postliminium, limen* being the Latin for "threshold"; the term thus refers to crossing back over the threshold of the Roman state. But if his return to Roman soil was the result of his having been redeemed, his civil rights did not revive until his redemption price had been repaid to his redeemer. He was, we are told, "pledged" to his redeemer until this happened.[16]

In this Roman instance and in the more general Jewish instance of redemption, we see that the redeemed individual is not wholly free until he has paid off his

cf return q a 'backslides' ?—

redemption price. Of course, in the theological analogy repayment of the Christian's redemption price is impossible. He is therefore always under obligation to his Redeemer. There is an echo of this in Romans 6:22: "You have been set free from sin and have become slaves of God." "He has delivered us from the dominion of darkness and transferred us to the kingdom of his beloved Son" (Col. 1:13). Therefore, "Live as free men, yet without using your freedom as a pretext for evil; but live as servants of God" (1 Peter 2:16; cf. 1 Cor. 7:22–23). Redemption from slavery to sin means that the Christian has a new Master.[17] An analogous train of thought occurs in Ezekiel 16, where Jerusalem is pictured as a cast-out child that was cared for, reared, and later married by God. Her subsequent unfaithfulness was aggravated by her previous history. Redeemed from distress, she should not have disregarded the obligations her redemption laid upon her. The parallel with our earlier discussion is not quite exact, but, in Jewish terms, it is close.

From our standpoint in time it seems natural that the prophets took up the ideas of redemption from debt and redemption from a hostile power and came to see God, not only as the Redeemer who redeemed Israel from other nations, but also as the Redeemer from the power most hostile to man that they knew—death itself. For example, Hosea reports God saying, "I am the LORD your God from the land of Egypt; you know no God but me, and besides me there is no savior" (Hos. 13:4). Then, after again reciting how the Jews had gone astray, God asks, "Shall I ransom them from the power of Sheol? Shall I redeem them from Death?" (Hos. 13:14). The answer is made clear in Hosea 14:4–8 and begins, "I will heal their faithlessness; I will love them freely, for my anger has turned from them." An alternative picture is found in Isaiah 35 where, following the depiction of the vengeance of the Lord on the enemies of Israel, the glory of the coming kingdom is spoken of in terms going beyond this world: "A highway shall be there, and it shall be called the Holy Way; . . . the redeemed shall walk there" (Isa. 35:8,9). And there is Job, penetrating beyond the grave; "I know that my Redeemer lives, and at last he will stand upon the earth; and after my skin has been thus destroyed, then from my flesh I shall see God, whom I shall see on my side, and my eyes shall behold, and not another" (Job 19:25–27). God redeems from death itself, making it but a gateway to Himself.

Assurance

That God redeems from the power of death is a bold assertion for the Bible to make. Can we rely on it? Can the Christian trust his Redeemer? This raises another element of redemption that is explored in measure in the New Testament. It is implicit in most of the preceding discussion but deserves to be further drawn out. The question is one of confidence, of reliability, of surety. The obligation or duty to redeem a kinsman from debt or control was based on the idea that the group was responsible for the debt and welfare of all its members.[18] This gives rise to the idea of surety or guarantee in three distinct ways. First, there must be confidence that the redeemer can redeem; second, that the redeemer will redeem; and third, that the redemption is judicially final.

The Bible warns against too easily guaranteeing the debts of another. To take some examples from Proverbs, Proverbs 6:1–5 urges the son to free himself from a guarantee thoughtlessly given. Proverbs 11:15 says: "He who gives surety for a stranger will smart for it, but he who hates suretyship is secure." Proverbs 17:18 is blunter: "A man without sense gives a pledge, and becomes surety in the presence of his neighbor." And there is the amusing yet realistic instruction of Proverbs 22:26–27: "Be not one of those who give pledges, who become surety for debts. If you have nothing with which to pay, why should your bed be taken from under you?"

Surety was and is not something to be entered into without great consideration, for only a person with sufficient assets can be a trustworthy redeemer—only he can pay the debt (cf. 1 Tim. 2:5–6; Heb. 8:6; 9:15). When the debt has been paid, the redeemer further guarantees that there will be no new falling into debt. Again his ability to guarantee is dependent on his assets. Once more these precise ideas are to be found in the Old Testament. Thus Job asks God to be his guarantor: "Lay down a pledge for me with thyself; who is there that will give surety for me?" (Job 17:3). Isaiah says: "O Lord, I am oppressed; be thou my security" (Isa. 38:14b). And the psalmist prays: "Be surety for thy servant for good; let not the godless oppress me" (Ps. 119:122). In these pleas there is a clear understanding that God is the Redeemer *par excellence*. He alone has the power, the wealth, and the resources to guarantee the life and property of those He redeems. There is no possibility that His substance will be wasted and that the Christian will pass once more under the power of another.

The second element of the Christian's confidence is that the Redeemer will act. As noted earlier, the obligation of the redeemer was a social obligation, not a legal duty. In the event of a failure to act there was no way in which the unredeemed could compel the redeemer to intervene. In human terms, the Jew could not trust his relations and friends to act on his behalf. They might not be able for financial reasons, or they might be unwilling. The rules of levirate marriage specifically provided for the instance of a refusal to undertake the duty (Deut. 25:7–9). Boaz was not the nearest relative to Ruth. The nearest relative turned her down (Ruth 4:6). But God, our "superrelative," can be relied on. He will not fail the Christian. With Him, social duties are never broken. As Isaiah said, "Israel does not acknowledge us; thou, O LORD, art our Father, our Redeemer from of old is thy name" (Isa. 63:16).

The third element of the Christian's confidence lies in the finality of the judgment that declares him free of debt. This is therefore different from the idea of the redeemer being able to guarantee that the debtor will not again fall into debt, but it is allied to it. By decree of the judge, who also happens to be the creditor—a not uncommon practice in the Orient—the debtor is declared to be free of debt. This decree, based either upon the idea of Jesus' death having paid the debt or upon the concept of

"faith" being reckoned as righteousness, is final. There
can be no appeal against it. It may be relied upon whenever the Accuser seeks once more to drag up matters that
have been dealt with (Rev. 12:10; cf. Zech. 3:1–3).[19]

To summarize: The redemption through the death of
Christ we read of in the Bible has three elements that are
highlighted by the legal metaphors that are used to explain it. First, there is the guarantee that the Christian will
not be returned to the hostile control or bondage of his
previous state. It is this guarantee that gives the Christian
confidence to live his life in the world.

Second, the corollary is that he has been released from
being controlled by hostile forces. He has been "ransomed
from the futile ways inherited from [his] fathers, not with
perishable things such as silver or gold, but with the precious blood of Christ" (1 Peter 1:18–19). Other passages
in the New Testament express this freeing from hostile
control by the idea of being freed from slavery in a more
strict sense (cf. Rom. 6:18, 22; 7:23; 1 Cor. 15:57; Gal. 4:5;
5:1; Col. 2:14; Eph. 4:8).

Third, redemption from slavery or bondage due to
debt involves the payment of the redemption price or of
the debt. Here, of course, we run into a mixture of images,
with the contrasting and yet complementary ideas of debt
and expiation. I consider that it is unnecessary and undesirable to attempt here to separate the elements of debt
and expiation in redemption, although it is possible both
to do so and to argue about their balance and meaning. It
is unnecessary because these ideas are well known and
undesirable because to do so is to devalue the truth that
is communicated by keeping them together. The whole is
more than the sum of the parts. If we will listen, if we will
hear, the metaphors we are given tell us that the debt of
sin has been paid in the civil sense and that expiation has
been made in the criminal sense (Rom. 3:21–26—are we
still in the realm of metaphor?). In God's economy His
Son can discharge our responsibility for our sin. We lose
so much by being so proud and nobly tragic, caviling at
the idea of another taking our responsibility by being crim-

inally punished—executed—in our place. To quibble thus
is suicidally arrogant and devilishly self-regarding. The
picture that we have been given is that Christ is the Redeemer. We may not entirely comprehend how this is effected. We are, however, given sufficient information to
allow us to accept it and to find that it works.

These pictures of our redemption may be sufficient
for us, but the "levirate" and "avenger" ideas need not be
forgotten. The levirate may be referred to in Romans 7:1–6
with the inference that Christians should bear fruit for
their new husband (vv. 4–5). This is a difficult passage
and many other interpretations are possible. However, the
avenger image is clearer. In a sense, man has been killed
by sin: "For sin, finding opportunity in the command-
ment, deceived me and by it killed me" (Rom. 7:11). We
may ask, Who plotted this murder? From whom is our
blood required? The very first promise of the Redeemer
answers that question: "The LORD God said to the serpent,
'Because you have done this . . . I will put enmity between
you and the woman, and between your seed and her seed;
he shall bruise your head, and you shall bruise his heel' "
(Gen. 3:14–15). The promise of the Kinsman-Redeemer
in the Garden of Eden is also a promise of the Kinsman-
Avenger-Redeemer (Rev. 20:7–10).

Such, then, are some of the implications and nuances
hiding in the metaphor of the legal idea of redemption. It
is a complex bundle of notions, many of which can communicate profound truths. This is perhaps easiest seen in
a short compass in Isaiah 52–53, where redemption and
the Redeemer are foreseen by Isaiah in mingled imagery.
(Many will recall the setting by Handel in *The Messiah*.)

Given this background, many verses in the New Testament coruscate and gleam as they tell us of God's love
for His fallen creation:

In Christ God was reconciling the world to himself.
. . . For our sake he made him to be sin who knew no

sin, so that in him we might become the righteousness
of God (2 Cor. 5:19, 21).

You know that you were ransomed from the futile ways
inherited from your fathers, not with perishable things
. . . but with the precious blood of Christ, like that of
a lamb without blemish or spot (1 Peter 1:18–19).

And, picking up other legal ideas now, I hope, familiar:

I mean that the heir, as long as he is a child, is no
better than a slave, though he is the owner of all the
estate; but he is under guardians and trustees until the
date set by the father. . . . But when the time had fully
come, God sent forth his Son, born of woman, born
under the law, to redeem those who were under the
law, so that we might receive adoption as sons. . . . So
through God you are no longer a slave but a son, and
if a son then an heir (Gal. 4:1–7).

10

Conclusion

In CONCLUSION I would summarize and comment on three points. First, the preceding pages show that there is room for further research into, and consideration of, the insights to be obtained from the legal systems of New Testament times as sources of some of the metaphors found in the Epistles. Even at a very superficial level the content of the law affects the interpretation of the metaphors. To pass over that content in silence is to act in error.

Second, the case for the investigation of the detail and technicalities of the law that forms the source of each metaphor is strong. Certainly some of the language, loosely used, would transmit some meaning, but we require to know and understand the degree of correspondence and of difference between the concepts in the different legal systems before we can choose to remain at the merely superficial level. When we do carry out such an investigation we find that, while there is in some areas an apparent correspondence of provision that would communicate generalities, there are important differences between the systems, which cannot be ignored, and sometimes only one legal system provides a sensible meaning for the metaphor. For example, the relationship of adoptee and adopting parent, of the freedman and his patron, and the status and liberty of the Roman, the citizen of the empire, transmit meaning only within the context of Roman law. In chapters 2 through 8 we have shown that the precisions of the Roman law communicate a breadth and depth of meaning when the several metaphors there dealt with are considered in its light. In short, we can get more out of the words and out of the passages by taking a technical approach to the language involved. I have not been able to make the same case for Greek law.

However, third, and with regret, I reckon that I cannot claim to have proved conclusively that Paul was using Roman law in all his legal metaphors. The fact that chapter 9 explores the concepts of redemption in the context of Jewish law involves conceding that there is more than one possible source of the legal metaphors under discussion in this book. It may be, therefore, that others will be able to show that Greek law has a stronger claim than I have established for it.

The matter at this stage, therefore, remains one of opinion and judgment. The standard of proof required by different readers will, of course, vary. The standard I would apply here is that of the civil law, which is not that of proof "beyond reasonable doubt" found in the criminal law. It is rather a matter of considering whether there is sufficient evidence to permit a decision, and then, if it is felt that there is, of weighing the evidence available and coming to a decision. Some may say that the evidence I have adduced in these pages is insufficient. Naturally I think otherwise, but I hope that, in any case, I have fairly provided the materials from another discipline that will allow theological scholars to perform their own tests.

My own view (which takes account also of the material in the Appendices) may be summarized in this way. There are metaphors in the New Testament Epistles, particularly in the Pauline epistles, that are drawn from the concepts of law. In the main these metaphors are used in letters to churches known to Paul, churches where Roman law was either the ruling law or immediately available. Legal metaphors are fewer in letters to churches that were unknown to the writer and in the personal letters, with the exception of Philemon, where there is much play on

and with legal ideas—it reads like the badinage of two old
friends secure in the knowledge that the technical language being used is communicating. In the case of the
Epistle to the Romans, Roman law is an obvious referent.

There is the problem that not all inhabitants of the
empire were citizens, but the law of that empire was a link
between the churches. Further, Paul himself was a Roman
citizen and had legal training. Though that training was
in the first instance in Jewish law, Paul would have had
cause to know the law of his citizenship. In his epistles
the legal material is used with assurance and often in ways
in which the technical content of the Roman law adds
both to the data communicated and to the impact of the
analogy. It follows that Roman law should be investigated
in the case of all legal metaphors in the Epistles for the
light it may afford.

If, then, in the bulk of the instances the technical content of the analogies fit and further illuminate the message, and if the law providing that technical meaning was
available both to the writer and the recipients of the Epistles, there is a likelihood that the writer used these metaphors with full knowledge and intention.

We moderns should, therefore, pay attention to these
metaphors, as they contribute to our knowledge and appreciation of the gospel.

Appendices

Appendix 1

Of Metaphors and Analogies

THE NATURE AND FUNCTION of metaphors and analogies in
the New Testament make it desirable and indeed necessary that
we should seek to explore and understand the facts that are the
basis of such figures of speech before we seek to interpret them.[1]
What a metaphor does, and how it does it, make it essential first
to understand the language of the metaphor in its nonmetaphoric sense. Only with that background can we rightly appreciate the force of the metaphor.

Stated broadly, the function of metaphors and analogies
both in theology and in biblical writings is to enlarge understanding by depicting something unknown in terms of something known. There is however a discontinuity between that
which is known and that which is unknown. The metaphor does
not function to extend information logically—rather, it is an aid
to intuition. The metaphor shows a point without quite arguing
it out.

Metaphors may be grouped into two categories. There are
those that illuminate the mind by speaking to the intellect and
thus may be said to be directed towards cognition. The other
group is directed towards the heart, emotions, and affections
and has a rhetorical or poetic function. Through either group an
alteration of action or belief may be produced by a perception
of truth through head or heart, reason or affections. Thus the
"Lamb of God," seen in its true cultural context as a sacrificial
animal and not as a cuddly toy, is appreciated almost entirely
intellectually. On the other hand, "The Lord is my Shepherd"
speaks of care and concern through the emotions. While neither
of these examples is pure in that each has elements of appeal in
the other category, the basic thrust of each is to head and heart
respectively.

Between the major groups of cognitive and rhetorical/poetic
metaphors there are of course many overlaps. Indeed, the bulk
of the metaphors considered in this book bridge the categories.
This is because they are directed toward the instruction of their
readers and hearers, enabling them to appreciate and grasp by
faith the truths of the gospel. For some the intellectual element
is uppermost. Legal notions obviously appeal first to the mind,

but for those accustomed to thinking in and of such concepts, legal notions can easily appeal to the emotions. One sees through the technical language to the personal relationships that are delineated and regulated by, and are the basis of, these concepts.

Metaphors and analogies that are intended to instruct illuminate by picturing something that is unknown or imperfectly appreciated as being "like" something that is known to the person being instructed. Aspects of the unknown are presented in terms with which we are already familiar. The familiar is used to depict the unfamiliar. This may be done by offering a partial explanation of something in terms of something else, or by a description in similar terms. Of course, such depiction may be very imprecise, but by the building up of the effects of a number of metaphors and analogies one may come to appreciate and grasp a truth without necessarily being able to explain or understand that truth in nonmetaphoric terms. In other words, the process of instruction or description of truth by analogy or metaphor leads toward the understanding and grasping of a phenomenon or a truth, not toward its scientific explanation. In using metaphors and analogies the biblical writers are trying to aid in the apprehension of truth, not fact. Those addressed are asked to understand or grasp, not to know in an analytical way. They are asked to perceive the meaning of the metaphor as being indicative of the truth, not as the pure reality of the truth.

Let me present this by means of another metaphor. Just as a painting is more than blotches of color and lines, so the meaning of the metaphor goes beyond its technical components. What we appreciate is more than we see. The meaning of the metaphor transcends the facts that make up the content of the metaphor. It must therefore always be recognized that the factual basis and the meaning of the metaphor are two different things. Sometimes the same language may transmit both elements, but often they are quite separable.

As indicated above, it is possible for a single metaphor to be directed towards both heart and mind. Where this is the case, different people will accept the instruction of the metaphor differently. What appeals more to one man's mind than his heart may appeal to another's heart rather than his mind: the diverse make-up and abilities of men are met in this way. But for both it is important to know the factual basis or root of the metaphor.

The distinction between the significance of a metaphor and a scientific and analytical explanation of the truth to which it

points can lead to two equal and opposite errors. First, there is
the error of failing to perceive the distinction, which results in
a distortion of our knowledge and appreciation of the truth.
Second, the opposite error is to allow this distinction too much
prominence and to recoil from analogies and metaphors as being
merely shadows, with a consequent impoverishment of one's
grasp of truth. Let me take these in their order.

1. The first error in approach to metaphor is a failure to
perceive the distinction between a metaphor and the reality or
truth to which it points. This can result in three major categories
of distortion in our appreciation of the truth.

First, it is possible that a metaphor that contributes to our
perception of truth is taken as a scientific explanation of that
truth, or in some way as a narrative of the process or mechanics
by which that truth operates. This could happen, for example,
as a superficial reaction to the metaphor of adoption.

Second, distortion may occur by an attempt to synthesize
different but related metaphorical ideas to try to make them one
self-consistent whole. This can happen, for example, if it is attempted to bring too many of the different metaphors of redemption together. This is a clear instance where the whole is
more than the sum of the parts and in which an attempt to
synthesize the parts results in something far less than even the
totality of those parts.[2]

It seems to me that the correct approach to such problems
is to accept that we are talking in metaphoric terms of deep
theological truths. Our words and concepts represent aspects of
a totally consistent theological truth that exists in a dimension
of thought different from that available to finite minds.

To take an analogy beloved of the late C. S. Lewis, we can
consider Abbott's *Flatland*.[3] In Flatland the world is two-
dimensional, having length and breadth but no height. The inhabitants of Flatland are capable of appreciating only those parts
of a three-dimensional world that intersect with their own two-
dimensional world. Thus, if their world lies at a certain level in
a three-dimensional world, to them a table would consist of four
separate units (the legs in plane), set at certain distances from
each other. Were it revealed to the inhabitants of Flatland that
these separate units are interconnected as being part of some
greater "truth," no doubt some would attempt to bring the separate elements together. They would probably find this process
impossible, and many would conclude that it was therefore in-

correct to say that these "four truths" were connected. Others might find it possible to bring these "truths" together by some form of higher mathematics, but an attempt to force these truths together would produce a distorted reality. In our analogy their efforts would result in a warped truth—though of course, a warped truth may be better than no truth at all.

The other possibility is for the Flatlanders simply to accept the "reality" that has been presented to them as "representative of" the true reality, even though they cannot quite comprehend this true reality themselves. They would then believe that the four elements of which they are conscious are interconnected and interdependent in a different (or true) frame of reality, although they would normally consider such elements as separate within their own frame of reference. The four parts "represent" aspects of the truth of the three-dimensional table.

To my mind, this is the proper approach when considering theological truth. Theological truth is bound to be presented to us analogically. Finite minds are incapable of fully comprehending infinite truths. I would not, however, suggest that we Flatlanders should simply accept things as they are and never seek to discern what we may about true reality. We have been given our minds to use them. But there comes a point at which the juxtaposing and wilful synthesizing of certain metaphors is counterproductive in terms of its contribution to our grasp of truth. This danger is most acute when synthesis is conjoined with a mechanistic approach and people seek to deal with the metaphors we have been given, not as aids to the perception of truth, but as an explanation of truth. *science*

We must also remember that it is likely that what we consider to be the meaning of a metaphor is less than the reality to which it points. We are talking in terms of blueprints or models and have to be careful how we interconnect the different blueprints in our attempt to perceive or grasp reality.

The third category of this type of distortion comes by pressing a single analogy or metaphor too far. Here, the main elements of the truth are communicated through the main elements of the metaphor or analogy. Distortion arises when subsidiary or incidental aspects of the metaphor are either unduly stressed or, in some instances, taken into account at all. There is a real danger of pressing the metaphor too far and of distorting the truth the metaphor transmits, through trying to squeeze the last drop of meaning from it. This is a trap of which I have been conscious in writing of the legal ideas in the Epistles. Whether or not I have always succeeded in avoiding the danger is a matter for you to judge. The danger is that one gets so taken up with the peripheral notions of the metaphor that one may even forget the core that points to the truth, or more probably, that one comes up with an interpretation of the metaphor that runs contrary to some other truth.

Another way in which this difficulty arises is when people read into a particular word the content of that word as they themselves are aware of it in their experience. They fail to recognize that the word had a slightly or subtly different meaning when it was first used.[4] Thus, I feel that many people nowadays read the metaphors drawn from the law of slavery far too superficially. Because slavery does not exist in the Western world it has gained a romantic tinge. Slavery in the time of Paul was normally something rather different. Similarly, the concepts of citizenship, sonship, and inheritance spring to mind as examples where the modern notions are sufficiently different from those of New Testament times to impede the proper transmission of truth by them.

But at what point should we decide that we have gone far enough in seeking to synthesize particular metaphors? At what point are we to know that the incidents surrounding a particular metaphor are no longer contributing to our understanding? When does one abandon the analogy as being a deficient representation of the truth it is communicating?

The answer would seem to be that the analogy or metaphor is to be abandoned at the point where pressing further with it will clearly distort the truth being communicated by the main elements of that analogy or by another analogy. We have not been given only one metaphor for each theological truth. The process of balancing analogies to produce a balanced grasp of truth is one that has been perhaps too often forgotten. Of course, this means that one has to be confident as to one's selection of the factual basis of the metaphor as being true. But that is a point which we had better leave until we look at the alternative pitfalls surrounding metaphor.

2. The opportunity for the alternative error in dealing with metaphor lies in the knowledge that one is dealing with and thinking in terms of metaphor and analogy, that one's thoughts are of shadows and not of substance. The difficulty here is that the intellectual mind in particular (or the pretentious mind) can

become impatient with the shadows of the traditional pictures and may abandon them in a frantic search for "reality." There are many examples in recent theological writing. In intellectual theology there has been a stampede away from the familiar images of the Fatherhood of God in an attempt to provide us with new language. Unfortunately, the new language and images by which the writers seek to replace the old familiar pictures are themselves still metaphoric, and most people find the innovations far more impoverished and lacking in substance than the older ideas they seek to replace.

The undue quest for reality at the back of metaphor may, like its opposite danger, be traced to a desire for a scientific explanation of truth rather than a perception or grasp of truth. Instead of grasping and using truths there is an attempt to make them objects of analysis to be carefully laid out in exhibition cases. It is also often a consequence of a theological position that does not accept traditional views of biblical revelation, which hold that God, in His revelation to man, has provided man with those metaphors and analogies that best illuminate and communicate truth, since the pure truth itself is unknowable.[5]

This takes us back to the question of balancing analogies and metaphors, for I consider that God's revelation must be the base from which one works, both in the selection of the metaphors that are to be taken to speak of truth and in the process of balancing metaphors. The language of the Scriptures does permit the creation of a more or less systematic body of theological knowledge, drawing theological propositions from what we are told in the Bible. We have been provided with representations of theological truth that allow us to grasp what God has done and is doing. The initiative lies with God. He has revealed Himself. Man has not found Him out. It follows that the final criterion in matters of selection and balance are given in revelation. Of course, some would then ask, "Does this mean revelation in Christ, the Word made flesh, or revelation in the words of the Scriptures?" To me this is a false antithesis, for the Bible is the word of God speaking of Christ, the Word made flesh. I am afraid that the only advantage that I can see in making a distinction between the Scriptures and Christ is that on occasion it allows one to avoid some inconvenient biblical teaching on the grounds that it "does not truly represent the mind of Christ," but I do not wish here to enter into that particular controversy. Suffice it to say that my view is that God Himself has provided representations of theological truths that allow us to grasp what has happened. We are to employ these pictures, not as explanations, but as illuminations through which the great truths are transposed down to the level of our apprehension.[6]

One fascinating question, which I do not intend to explore in any detail here, is the extent to which a metaphor may represent truth. Are there theological metaphors that are so close to the reality of which they speak as to be indistinguishable from it? And if so, which metaphors are they? A similar question is, which way round do our analogies work? For example, there is a tendency to say that the Fatherhood of God is an analogy drawn from our experience. But may it not be that the Fatherhood of God is the reality of which our human fatherhood is the shadow? Might it not be that the sonship of believers constituted through adoption is rather closer to the truth (particularly if interpreted in terms of Roman law) than we might perhaps care or wish to believe? This is a difficult area, but it is a problem that ought to be remembered when we are looking at the legal metaphors.[7]

To conclude: the legal metaphors and analogies discussed in this book illuminate theological truths. It is therefore desirable, if not necessary, to seek to understand the legal principles involved before one seeks to go beyond these principles to appreciate or grasp the truths involved. There are, of course, dangers in dealing with metaphors and analogies. We may take things too far. We may fail to maintain a proper balance between different aspects of truth. But if we know that these dangers exist, we are then in a position to cope with them. On no account should we allow these dangers to put us off. "Man's chief end is to glorify God, and enjoy Him for ever"—the language is archaic but the meaning is clear.[8] We exist to appreciate God. We exist so that each of us may show in special measure a particular facet of Christ the Son to the Father. In order to do so properly it is necessary that we should know God, and this is done by paying attention to what He has said.

I suggest that some of God's revelation has been expressed in the legal language of one particular legal system, Roman law. Even if this is not the case, this legal system does allow us to draw a richer truth from some of the language used in the Bible. In history some Christians must have used Roman law to interpret these metaphors. It is interesting to see what they may have seen.

The Systems of Law

THE WRITERS OF THE NEW TESTAMENT EPISTLES could draw on three main sources for the legal language, analogies, and metaphors they used: Roman law, Jewish law, and the disparate systems which we, for the sake of convenience, call Greek law. Of these the Roman was the best developed and most widespread legal system, and we have the best evidence as to its content. Greek or Hellenistic law is the most difficult to discuss, as we shall see, and of the three appears to be the least likely source.

As the probabilities of a reference to each system can best be considered in relation to particular ideas, this appendix seeks only to give a general and rather simplified outline of the three legal systems. However, it will be useful to give some greater detail of the processes by which the laws of the Roman system were created, as these have a direct bearing on the spread of knowledge of Roman law throughout the empire, though even this detail is comparatively simplified. The minutiae of the Roman system were very complex and variable. In appendix 4 we will look at the organization of the empire and consider the extent to which these three legal systems were available as a stock of examples meaningful to both writer and reader.

Roman Law

The Roman system of law is one of the highest achievements of the human mind. From its earliest forms to the end of the massive codification work of Justinian in A.D. 528–555, Roman law developed from a primitive customary law to a remarkably wide-ranging instrument, governing the affairs of the major empire of the world. Even after the passing of that empire, Roman law continued to influence legal development, particularly on the Continent, but also in Scotland, and forms an intellectual foundation for many modern legal systems.

At the time the New Testament was being written, Roman law was entering upon the classical phase of its development— the golden age of the first two and one-half centuries after Christ. The main lines of Roman law had, however, already been firmly established. Although there were to be later innovations, particularly in constitutional law, with the establishment of a consciously imperial form of government, Roman civil law was not subject to similar drastic change until well after the period that interests us in these pages.

Roman law began as a primitive customary law governing a people resident in a small area of Italy after the founding of Rome, traditionally dated 753 B.C. Little is known, though much is conjectured, about the content of this early law. The period of the kings (753–510 B.C.) has not left many legal traces, and the first fixed date we need refer to is the adoption of the Twelve Tables in 450 B.C. The Tables appear to have been proposals by a commission known as the decemviri (the "ten men"), which functioned during a period of conflict between the patricians and the plebeians (the lower classes), at the end of which the higher offices of government were opened to the plebs. One of the grounds of unrest among the plebeians was that the law of the community was not freely available to all the people. Knowledge of its detail and operation was at that time entrusted only to the priests of the community, the pontifices, who were drawn exclusively from the patrician order. In an attempt to meet this complaint, the decemviri published a code in Ten Tables, to which a further two were later added. The Tables appear to have been a partial codification of the law of Rome as it then existed; the areas covered are procedure, reparation (tort), succession, guardianship, and the powers of a head of family (patria potestas). On the restoration of the usual forms of government the Twelve Tables were retained and continued to have an influence in Roman life. This influence was diffuse, yet fundamental; the Twelve Tables continued to be revered, despite the onward progress and development of the law, in much the same way as we view the Magna Carta today. Thus Cicero said, "We learned the Twelve Tables in our boyhood as a required formula; though no one learns it nowadays."[1] The Twelve Tables therefore form "the foundation of the whole fabric of Roman law," but like all good foundations are well buried.[2] Thereafter, during the Republic, different methods of lawmaking evolved, some direct and some indirect.

Within the area of direct legislation three forms came to be of importance: the lex (plural leges), enacted upon the proposal of magistrates by an assembly of all the citizens; the plebiscitum,

enacted by the plebeian assembly; and the *senatusconsultum*, a
resolution of the Senate, which clearly had the force of general
law by the end of the Republic. These forms of legislation were
continued by the emperor Augustus (31 B.C.–A.D. 14) who strove
to give the appearance of maintaining the forms of a republican
government. One of the ways in which he did this was to have
himself appointed to several of the republican magistracies, and
he was thus able to amend and develop the law by the use of
the magisterial powers of these different positions (these powers
will be outlined shortly). In addition, both Augustus and his
successors developed a practice of lawmaking through *decreta*
and *rescripta*, which at first were merely imperial responses to
particular situations, but obviously, once the emperor's will
was known in a particular situation there was a tendency to
treat it as a general proposition of law. Further, it became standard practice for proclamations made by the emperor to be treated
as substantive legislation. The major uses of these latter powers,
however, lie later than our period.

The indirect methods of lawmaking in the Roman Republic
were the necessary outcome of the developing political structure
of the Roman state. In the time of the kings (753 – 510 B.C.), the
powers of state in fullest measure were vested in the king. These
powers were collectively known as his *imperium*. When the Republic was established the powers of the head of state were
transferred to two magistrates, whom we know as "consuls,"
although there is doubt whether that name was used at first. The
two consuls were elected annually and held office for one year
only. The joint holding of the supreme power of the state, coupled with the annual rotation of personnel, served to restrict the
use that could be made of the *imperium*, and other limited restrictions were added by legislation over the years. But despite
such practical and legal restrictions, the *imperium*, the power of
the consul, remained in large measure undefined and retained
importance as the supreme power of the state available to deal
with any matter.

The consuls were, however, mere men, and the range of
their responsibilities was so large that other magistracies had to
be created in order to accomplish the business of state. At first
the day-to-day running of the city of Rome, and later the administration of the expanding Roman Empire, had to be dealt with
efficiently. Accordingly, various functions of the consuls were

entrusted to particular magistracies, of which the more important were the praetorship, the aedileship, and the quaestorship.[4]

As we will see, the praetorship was invented to take over the duties of the consuls in relation to the operation of the civil law. The aedileship was responsible for the running of the city in such matters as sanitation, highways, water supply, public buildings, public places, and so on. The aediles were also responsible for controlling certain of the public games and public functions and had a limited responsibility for police matters. The quaestorship was responsible for the financial organization of the city and of the empire. Naturally, as responsibilities in relation to the empire increased, specialization occurred, both with regard to territory and in the precise responsibility of different quaestors. However, it may be noted that as the quaestor was more clearly an aide to the consul or, in a province, to the governor, both of whom had in theory full imperium, the quaestors in the provinces did come to be entrusted with all kinds of military, administrative, and judicial duties and might even be given complete responsibility for the governing of a territory. This junior magistracy therefore came in later years to be very important in training for the highest offices of state.

Every Roman magistrate had the ius edicendi, that is, the right to issue edicts dealing with matters within the sphere of his competence, and many branches of law were developed by the edicts of the appropriate magistracies, forming a class of law known as the ius honorarium (magisterial law).[5] One example is the development of significant aspects of the Roman law of sale through the edicts of the curule aediles, the aedilitian edict. One of the functions of the aediles was the supervision of the city market and the transactions that occurred there. Their edict was therefore the appropriate place to deal with matters of the law of sale.[6]

The office that carried the greatest opportunity to develop magisterial law was that of the praetor, created in 367 B.C. under the Leges Liciniae Sextiae, which marked another stage in the struggle of the classes. These laws were of profound social and constitutional importance, since they provided that from that time forward one of the consuls and one-half of the membership of the priestly colleges always had to be of plebeian origin. Another provision was the creation of the praetorship, largely in order to free the consuls from their responsibilities in the administration of the civil law.

As established in 367 B.C., the praetorship was an elective office held for one year, and the praetor was entrusted with the power to allow actions to proceed to trial. A second praetorship was added in 242 B.C., and these two praetorships continued to have jurisdiction within the city of Rome. Following each of the First and Second Punic wars, two additional praetorships were created for the specific purpose of providing governors for territories taken from the Carthaginians. In 227 B.C. praetorships were created for Sicily and Sardinia and in 197 B.C. for the two new Spanish provinces. However, this device was not further used to provide governors for the later provinces until the reforms of Sulla around 80 B.C. As part of his reconstruction of the administration of the empire, Sulla arranged for the principal officers of state to consist of the two consuls and eight praetors, each being elected annually. The eight praetors remained in Rome during their year of office, two having a specific jurisdiction in civil law and two with specific jurisdiction in criminal law. Only at the expiry of their period of office did they take up governorship of provinces abroad.

Of the praetors, it was those with civil jurisdiction who had the greatest effect upon the development of the law. Technically, the praetor did not have legislative power, but as a magistrate he had the authority to issue edicts indicating his interpretation of his function. By the use of this edict and by his key position in the day-to-day functioning of the civil court system, the original praetor was able to innovate in the interests of justice. However, as long as his role was confined to permitting actions based on enacted laws (leges) to proceed, the possibilities of interpretation were somewhat restricted, although real. In actions based on leges strict adherence to certain words was absolutely necessary.

The power to develop the law through interpretation became more apparent following the creation of the second praetorship in 242 B.C.[7] The introduction of the second praetorship was necessary because the extension of Roman dominion resulted in more and more noncitizens coming to reside within the Roman territory, and provision had to be made for the legal problems of these noncitizens (peregrines). The original praetor was thus left with responsibility for actions between citizens, and he was therefore called praetor urbanus; the second praetor was given special responsibility for law between citizens and aliens and between foreigners, as was indicated by his title, praetor peregrinus. The praetor urbanus was therefore concerned with the strict civil law that was applicable only to Roman citizens and hence called ius civile. The praetor peregrinus, on the other hand, was concerned with obtaining just solutions to problems arising between foreigners and between foreigners and citizens. This meant that he had to take account of the different legal systems represented by the parties coming before him and also of the rules that were thought to be common to mankind, the so-called ius gentium.

The form of procedure of the praetor peregrinus was much more flexible than that of the praetor urbanus, as he was not confined to dealing with actions based upon enacted law. He was, therefore, more able in the interests of justice to incorporate new ideas into the law he administered. This could be done in the actual conduct of actions or in the granting of new remedies.

In the case of actions, the procedure that made development more easy and possible was that of the formula. In formulary procedure an abstract statement of the case between the parties was agreed upon and presented to the praetor in a stylized form (the formula) for his approval. If the formula was approved by the praetor, it was then put to the judge (the iudex), whose position was really more that of arbiter than judge since he had jurisdiction over matters of fact only. Argument was put to him by skilled orators, but their functions lay within the context of the abstract formulation of the formula. Thus, a formula might run, "Let Marcus be judge. If it appears that Stichus has promised to pay a thousand sesterces to Balbus, condemn him to pay that amount. If it does not so appear, absolve him." In other words, the judge was given a statement of the law and was required to decide in one way if he found certain facts proved, and in another if not. Of course, before giving his approval to the formula, the praetor would have to be convinced that there was something to the claim, but this was broadly construed. Indeed, the best modern analogy to this part of the praetor's role would be a cross between the clerk of the court, certifying that the papers in a case are in order, and the deliberations of a legal aid committee in the United Kingdom, trying to decide whether or not to assist a person who wishes to raise an action. For this committee the test is not whether the action is bound to succeed, but simply whether there is a probable ground for action.

Since the praetor's approval of the *formula* was essential, his views on what should or should not be made the subject of litigation were of great weight. By altering the accepted *formulae* the praetor was able to ensure that the legal process would produce a more just solution to a dispute. Thus, the *formula* was extended by the use of the *exceptio* and by the fictitious use of existing concepts. In the *exceptio* there was added to the normal *formula* an instruction to the judge to find in favor of the defense if certain allegations were found proved. For example, if a bargain correct in form was proved to have been induced by fraud, the judge was instructed to reject an action seeking to enforce the bargain. In the fictitious situation the judge was instructed to treat one set of facts "as if" it were another. Thus, the idea of acquisition by long possession was invented by the praetor instructing the judge to treat a nonowner, who had in good faith possessed a disputed object, even land, for a stated period, "as if" he were the owner. The technical nonowner would therefore, in practice, be given all the rights and protections available to an owner under the normal law because no one could successfully bring an action against him. Another example of this device was the use of the fiction that a noncitizen (a peregrine) was a citizen for the purposes of a particular action. In this way, peregrines were allowed some access to Roman legal procedures, though not to the full *ius civile*, the civil law of citizens.

The development of the law by such instructions to the judge and by interpretation of the law was first mapped out by the original praetors working within the framework of the *ius civile*. The development was, however, considerably accelerated by infusion of ideas from the *ius gentium*, administered by the *praetor peregrinus*, whose more flexible formulary procedure gave him greater freedom of innovation. The *praetor peregrinus* introduced many principles dictated by general common sense. Simplified conveyancing, trusts, property rights, and certain rights of succession were so recognized, and when in 145 B.C. a Lex Aebutia made the formulary procedure of the *praetor peregrinus* available before the praetor urbanus (some say the *lex* merely ratified existing practice), change and development in both courts was accelerated.

But not all praetorian development of the law occurred

through actions before the courts. Procedural developments and remedies were also important agencies of change. For example, a praetor had power to insist that a person promise that if a particular event occurred he would pay a sum of money to another individual. Thus, if A feared that B's house was likely to collapse and damage his own house, he could ask for B to be made to promise to pay so much money if the house did collapse. If the house then did fall, A could enforce the promise and recover damages far more easily than through the old form of action, which would have required proof of negligence. This procedure, known as the *cautio damni infecti*, quite superseded the older form of law. Also, the praetor, by inventing various interdicts (injunctions) and by authorizing people to take possession of property, whether real or personal, heritable or moveable, was able to protect the interests of individuals whose standing in the ordinary civil law was dubious. These remedies and procedures also favored the protected individual if an action was brought against him in an attack on the position he had been given by the praetor's *imperium*. Major advances in land law were brought about in this way, as was further development in the law of succession and in other areas.

In summary, therefore, the position of the praetor in the functioning of the civil law of Rome (that is, civil as opposed to criminal) allowed him both to develop that civil law, the *ius civile*, and to construct a parallel system of law based on different ideas, presuppositions, and concepts, which supplemented the civil law and in some areas in practice replaced it. This new law, which was called magisterial law or the *ius honorarium*, was available to all and in general avoided the possible injustices of the older civil law, though that law was still available to citizens if they so chose.

All these developments in the law, whether through actions or remedies, were announced by use of the edict. As noted, all magistrates had the right to issue edicts on matters under their jurisdiction. In the case of the praetor, practice called for each praetor to issue an edict on taking office, indicating in broad terms the conditions under which he would be prepared to approve a *formula* in a legal action and the factual situations he would allow to go to trial during his year of office or on which he would grant a remedy. The edict, valid for the one year of office of the praetor (*edictum perpetuum*), was not a closed cat-

egory, but failure to bring one's action or complaint within the
instances cited would normally mean that nothing could be
done. The development of the edict and its categories gave rise
to magisterial law as it became usual for each praetor to take
over the bulk of his predecessor's edict (*edictum tralaticium*).
Alterations to the edict were made on the advice of jurists and
commentators, but such alterations became fewer as the difficulties of edictal law were ironed out and this "continuing"
body of law, largely grounded in equity, became extremely important in Roman jurisprudence. It was after all the effective
law, the summary of enforceable rights and duties. Eventually,
on the orders of Hadrian (after the period of greatest interest to
us), the praetor's edict was revised and codified as a permanent
body of law by one of the leading jurists, Julian (Salvius Jul-
ianus), and was enacted as such by the Senate in A.D. 130.[8]

But it would not do for an academic lawyer to leave the
impression that only officials were active or important in the
creation of legal principles and institutions. Mention of Julian
leads us to the role of the jurists in the development of Roman
law. Although the golden age of the jurists lies in the first two
and one-half centuries after Christ, the jurist was a well-known
institution by New Testament times. The advice of the jurist had
been sought in cases since early times, and Augustus gave a
special status to the response (*responsum*) of certain jurists to
legal queries from judges in cases. Whether their *responsa* as to
the law were at first binding on the judge in a case is not completely clear, but by the time of Hadrian this had been provided
by formal enactment. The jurists were also engaged in conduct-
ing lawsuits and carrying out legal transactions, but they were
not professional lawyers as we would understand that term.
Unlike the orators, the jurists were not paid but carried out legal
work in the course of their careers in public affairs. They advised
on legal questions and taught the law, probably through allowing pupils to be present at advising sessions and discussions.
They wrote books on legal matters, often by way of commentary
on the praetorian edicts or on particular areas of the law. In
their theoretical elaboration of the principles of the law, and
through acting as advisers to magistrates, including the praetors,
and to parties, the jurists were able to play a very important part
in legal development, their actual advice in cases and their
clashes of opinion clarifying legal principle. Naturally the jurists

did not always agree, and there evolved at least two important schools of juristic thought, the Sabinians and the Proculians, which date from the time of Augustus.[9]

The work of the jurists is important for this book in two ways. First, the jurists were clearly important in that they developed the law by their activities. Second, they are of particular importance in that their writings provide evidence as to the actual content of the law on precise topics, though that evidence is not always complete. A main source is Justinian's *Digest of the Civil Law* (A.D. 533), which consists of extracts from the works of the jurists, arranged by subject matter. Occasionally these extracts quote the exact terms of legislation, and all form a useful body of evidence as to the law of the time they were written. However, some caution has to be observed in using such sources, since the compilers of the *Digest* attempted to state the law as it existed at the time of their own labors. This required the revision and alteration of some of the jurists' writings they used, and as in biblical studies, there is quite an industry devoted to the establishment of the original text. None of this, however, is of major importance for the present inquiry. There is sufficient evidence of the tenor of the law.

Apart from the *Digest*, other manuscripts containing the works of jurists have come down to us—some more fragmentary than others. Of these the most interesting for our purposes are the *Institutes*, written by Gaius around A.D. 161, a copy of which came to light in Verona in 1812. This work, a short elementary teaching manual in four books, is unusual in being almost complete. Little is known of Gaius—not even his full name—but his works, particularly the *Institutes,* are invaluable because of his historical approach, which provides evidence as to the law of the previous century, the period of the New Testament.[10]

Jewish Law

At first sight it would seem obvious that a main source of legal metaphors in the New Testament Epistles is Jewish law. I certainly would not deny that Jewish thinking underlies the message of the Epistles. By this I do not mean that in some way "truth" has been filtered, and therefore distorted, in its passage through the minds of the writers—that is a separate argument, which massively divides scholarship and into which we need not venture. But even though the theology of the Epistles may be rooted in Judaism, since the writers present Jesus as the fulfillment of the law (Rom. 10:4), it is quite a different thing to say that the imagery involved in disseminating that theology was drawn from Jewish law. Metaphors may express and illuminate an idea without sharing its origin. Indeed, in most cases the use of symbols that are not factually connected with the point drives the message home.

Jewish law, as we know it, was a complex matter. As Herzog says: "Jewish Law is of an infinitely larger scope than what would be warranted by the term 'law' in modern usage. 'The Law' as the title of the Pentateuch (Hebrew, *Torah*), already gives the general reader, familiar with the contents of that part of the Hebrew Bible, an adequate idea of the wide ambit of Jewish Law."[11] For the Jew, the law was an all-embracing set of rules and instructions governing the whole of life. Part of the law was directed towards the regulation of man's relationship with man in the modern Anglo-American sense of "law": contract, reparation (tort), succession, and so on. Another part of the law was concerned with moral relations between persons. Yet other parts of the law were concerned with religious observances, ceremonial purity, and man's relationship with God as expressed through temple rituals. The Levitical prescriptions as interpreted and developed through the ages were of great importance because they indicated the ways in which a Jew could keep right with God. All these elements formed "the Law." In speaking of Jewish law, therefore, we must recognize the extent of its meaning, going far beyond "law" in the current Western usage, reaching all departments of life.

The stream of Jewish law had two distinct channels, the written law and the oral law. As we will see shortly, the accepted doctrine was that both the written and oral law had the same starting point—the giving of the Law, the Torah, by God to Moses at Sinai. This law was partially reduced to writing by Moses himself, forming a written Torah substantially like the Pentateuch as we have it. The remainder he told to Joshua.

We have no evidence for the content of the orally transmitted law until after the time of the Exile. We do have, however, the evidence of the Old Testament books as to the treatment of the written law in this period. At times it was given practical importance, and times it was not—it had, for example, to be "rediscovered" in Josiah's day, despite the reforms of Hezekiah

(2 Kings 22:8–10; 2 Chron. 34:14–18). When the written law was known to individuals it was often revered as an oracle (cf. Ps. 119). In general, however, it was without practical importance throughout much of Jewish history down to the Exile. This is seen particularly clearly just before the Exile, when the complaints of the prophets show that there was considerable doubt as to the content, extent, and operation of the Torah.

One result of the Exile was that greater attention was paid to the provisions of the written law. The coming of the disasters prophesied by Moses, inter alia in Deuteronomy 28:15–68, led to a lively interest in the detailed commands of the Torah. Before the Exile prophets such as Isaiah and Jeremiah had drawn attention to the imminence of punishment. During the Exile prophets such as Ezekiel were active underlining the lessons to be learned. The written law was therefore exalted both as an explanation of the Jews' present situation and as showing the way to the return.

Prophetic activity was not the only manifestation of this interest. There were also new developments in formal study. Oral commentary on the law and a new body of teaching, the oral law or the tradition, began to emerge. Oral commentary upon the written law started because in Babylon there was no possibility of performing the appropriate temple worship, which had been the central manifestation of the Jewish religion. All that was left to the people was the Law and round it there developed the institution that we know as the synagogue. This was a meeting for worship at which a central place was given to the reading of the Law, supplemented by exposition. Accepted expositions of parts of the Law began to form the body of oral commentary, accepted itself as a form of doctrine.

However, attention to the written law and its elaboration by commentary were not the only content of the studies begun in the synagogue. It is from this point that we have knowledge of the oral law. This, the "tradition of the elders," was a body of teaching said to contain principles that God had given to Moses at the time of the giving of the written Torah; these had been transmitted by Moses to Joshua and hence orally down the centuries by the elders of the people, together with the commentaries of the elders on these principles.[12] This oral tradition was supplemental to the Torah, the written law, elaborating its provisions and where necessary dealing with situations for which the Torah did not make express provision.

Following the return and the "reestablishment" of the Law by Ezra (Neh. 7:73–8:18), skill in the Torah and in the tradition came to be much prized, both for its intrinsic merit and its social and religious utility. This development lay not so much with the hereditary priesthood but with laymen, since Ezra's actions had the effect of giving the Law to the whole people and not just to the priests. These laymen were called the scribes (the *soferim*), and are known to all readers of the Gospels. Acknowledged masters of the law were called rabbis, and we call the product of their efforts rabbinic law, which was a major element in rabbinic Judaism.[13]

Interest in the law therefore developed, both as a "legal" interest, which takes our attention here, and also on a more general religious basis. Thus there are such works as the Book of Jubilees (c. 100 B.C.), which reworks the biblical story from Genesis to Sinai so as to exalt the Law. We now also have the evidence from Qumran of the rules of the community of the Essenes, showing their interest in the Law, which interest took religious observance far beyond anything found elsewhere.[14] But be that as it may, our interest here is in the formal development of the rules of ordinary law governing the ordinary life of the Jews.

From the return onward, development of the law took place by practical application and by theoretical discussion. These may be separated for the purposes of our consideration, but in fact they overlapped to a considerable degree. In practical terms, development could occur through case law and legislation.[15] Each village and town had a court or courts dealing with all matters of the law, which would act on the advice of local rabbis; in later years at least two to four of its members had to be learned in the law. Such courts were small sanhedrins and also had local government functions. These courts were not wholly independent. Official and semiofficial councils and assemblies were set up to supervise the operation of the law. The most important of these councils and assemblies immediately after the return was that known as the "Men of the Great Assembly," which seems to have functioned from the time of Ezra down to about 300 B.C. In the second century B.C., the Great Sanhedrin composed of seventy-one members was established. This Sanhedrin had many functions and powers. It had an advisory function in government, acting as a council of state, and also had legislative, administrative, and judicial powers. The Great Sanhedrin also sat as a supreme court with both appellate and original jurisdiction (cf. the trials of Jesus, Stephen, and Paul). According to the Mishnah (*Aboth* 1.3–13), pairs of outstanding scholars "stood at the head" of this Sanhedrin in each generation, the last of the pairs being Hillel and Shammai, who were active during the reign of Herod I (c. 35 B.C.). The Great Sanhedrin and the other lesser courts continued to be important beyond that time, however, and the Sanhedrin continued to exist during the periods of Roman hegemony over Palestine.[16] Apart from judicial activity, the councils and assemblies, including the Sanhedrin, made it their duty to fix the text of the Pentateuch,[17] to regulate worship, to apply the law, and to legislate.

A major purpose of Jewish legislation was to place a "fence" round the Torah lest any man should offend against the law by accident. This was also a main point of the theoretical elaboration of the law, which was largely the work of the scribes. They further developed the law, whether written Torah or oral tradition, by interpretation and logical deduction, by commentary and explanation. Such "academic" development of the law was termed Halakah and took two forms. Where the development was by commentary on or interpretation of a given text, it was known as midrash. Where the teaching was given in a systematic arrangement by topic, with or without citation of basic texts from the Scripture, it was known as mishnah. In New Testament times this elaboration of the law was still in an oral form, but it is interesting to see how the techniques of elaboration developed. In the second century A.D. a series of rabbis culminating with Rabbi Judah collated and harmonized the Halakah into what is known as the Mishnah. The Mishnah is not a complete textbook;[18] it presupposes considerable other knowledge, and it was supplemented in its turn by further commentary. Its importance for our purposes is that it does provide historical evidence as to the content of earlier law. The commentary on the Mishnah, known as the Gemara, was reduced to writing in the sixth century A.D. The whole body of Torah, tradition, commentary, and illustration is known as Talmud. In particular the Babylonian Talmud (c. A.D. 500) contains the authoritative collection of talmudic material dealing with the principles and rules mostly of the oral Torah, but without excluding the written Torah.[19] Yet again, commentary and exposition began. Schools of interpreters resident in the Babylonian empire acted as final courts of appeal and also exercised an advisory jurisdiction. Once the Babylonian schools began to decline around the year 1000 A.D., the role of instruction, collation, commentary, and development passed to the Jewish communities of Western Europe. Many commentaries were written, containing and continuing the development of ages, and these are commonly accepted to culminate in the great *Mishneh Torah* of Maimonides (A.D. 1135–1204).[20]

Of course, there has been considerable development in Jewish law since Maimonides. This development has not been entirely systematic, different groups of Jews in different countries taking different lines, and the harmonization of laws from these different sources has been a problem for the State of Israel. But for our purposes it is unnecessary to look at developments after the first Mishnah, let alone the Babylonian Talmud. Further, though both do contain interesting data as to the law in New Testament times, the information must be treated with caution. Even with the Mishnah of the second century A.D., which is at most one hundred years removed from New Testament times, there are problems. As has been said, one of the advantages of the Mishnah is that it does contain a compilation of oral tradition going back to the centuries before Christ. However, it must be acknowledged that the Mishnah and the later Babylonian Talmud reflect for historical reasons only the opinion of one group within the Jewish people, the Pharisees.

A major doctrinal split amongst Jewish thinkers occurred some 100 to 150 years B.C., giving rise to the two schools of thought known to us as the Pharisees and the Sadducees. Other groups—for example, the Essenes—were also formed, but although it is arguable that these had importance in theological thinking (some people argue that John the Baptist was an Essene), they were of less importance in the normal development of law.

In contrast to the Pharisees, the Sadducees rejected the oral tradition and considered that they were bound to observe only the written Torah. There were, of course, other differences between the two parties. For example, the Sadducees rejected any

idea of an afterlife and the division between the two parties on
this point was sharp (cf. Acts 23:6–9). The Sadducees also tended
to be much more severe in punishments exacted for breach of
law.[21] But of the areas of contention between the Pharisees and
the Sadducees, the most important for our purposes is the con-
flicting attitude towards the tradition, for the rejection of the
tradition by the Sadducees would lead them to develop, and
perhaps to apply, concepts of law different from those of the
Pharisees. As the Sadducees were active and indeed largely
dominant in the period from Herod I (c. 35 B.C.) to the destruction of Jerusalem in A.D. 70, there would appear to have been
every possibility that the law in force in the period would reflect
their preconceptions. However, the destruction of the city was
the end of the Sadducean sect. Only the Pharisees remained,
and they made it a holy duty to continue the vitality of the law,
expanding it by tradition and commentary, as we have seen.
The Mishnah and other compilations are therefore works of the
Pharisaic tradition. Little trace of Sadducean opinion is to be
found in them, and such mention as is made of it is usually
unfavorable. We therefore simply do not know the extent, if any,
to which the daily law in Palestine at the time of the Epistles
contained rules based on Sadducean thinking. Still less do we
have any idea as to the content of these rules.[22] A further difficulty in the evidences of Jewish law is that the Mishnah and
other Pharisaic works are not factually accurate in all respects.
The Mishnah occasionally records what would ideally have been
true, rather than reporting what actually happened in the administration of the law.[23]
    In short, we know that evidence as to one school of legal
thought has been suppressed and that the evidence available as
to the other schools is sometimes inaccurate. It follows that we
have no certain knowledge of the precise content of the law
applied in practice in New Testament times. The law found in
the Mishnah may or may not be an accurate guide in interpreting
the legal metaphors of the Epistles. One is therefore in some
difficulty. A metaphor that does not connect up with the Jewish
law we know might actually connect with some legal rule of
which no trace has come down to us. Alternatively, some
expression that may find echoes in the Mishnah may not represent actual practice and may have been meaningless on that
ground to an ordinary reader. Clearly this exposes a vast field

of possible legal and theological research and indicates that statements as to Jewish law, where the points being made are technical and precise, must in many instances be treated with caution. Broad principles are clear, but the minutiae may well be contentious.[24]

There are, therefore, difficulties in assessing the content of Jewish law on particular topics at the time the New Testament Epistles were being written. In view, however, of the success of Professor J. D. M. Derrett's book *Law in the New Testament*, which explores the law found in the Gospels, I would not wish to overstate this difficulty. But in reading the Epistles there is another problem: with the arguable exception of the Epistle to the Hebrews, none of the Epistles were written to Jews in Palestine. This does therefore raise the question of the degree to which the Jewish law of Palestine was identical with the law of the communities of the Dispersion.[25] On the one hand it seems reasonable to suggest that the nature of Judaism was such as to preserve a considerable degree of harmony in the law, brighter Jewish boys being sent to Jerusalem to study (e.g., Paul) and then returning to their own communities. But it might not be so. The Jewish communities of the Dispersion, the Diaspora, are known to have developed their own individualities. In that case legal metaphors might receive differing interpretations in Judea and elsewhere. But even if there was homogeneity of Jewish law, questions must still remain as to the extent to which Jewish law was active within Jewish communities outside Judea. Not all Jewish communities were recognized as communities for the purposes of having their own law,[26] and these groups would have had to make use of local law for their ordinary legal business. If under such circumstances the Jewish law were regarded as a "special," "holy," or "sacred" law, different from ordinary day-to-day law, legal metaphors might well be referred to either law for their detail. However, all this assumes that the Epistles were written to Jews. But one must also recognize that the bulk of the Epistles were not written to homogeneous Jewish communities but to churches consisting of Gentiles and Jews. In that context one should be wary of attributing legal metaphors to the uncertain detail of Jewish law. Further, it is demonstrable in some cases—for example, in adoption and in some of the special incidentals of slavery, notably freedmen[27]—that use is made of metaphors that have no proper basis in Jewish law. These must

be referred to other legal systems for their interpretation. This
by implication lessens the likelihood of Jewish law as a source
of other metaphors.

Be that as it may, the last important point that must be
recognized in relation to Jewish law is that the work of the
scribes and Pharisees in elaborating the concepts of the law,
whether written or oral, was much more akin to the activities of
the Roman jurist and to the academic lawyer of today than to
the activities of present-day theologians. The translation "lawyer," which is found in the Gospels in some versions, is not
inaccurate. The Jews had developed a lawyer class (whose education is considered more fully in appendix 5, "Paul") and a
form of legal science. This legal science was not as coherent and
methodical as that developed by the Roman lawyers, due primarily to the copiousness of the material involved. The Jewish
lawyer dealt with rules covering all of life, encompassing what
we would today consider to be legal matters, moral matters, and
also whole areas of theological understanding. This did not,
however, prevent him from developing legal skills—indeed, it
would have required such development rather than have hin-
dered it.

Greek Law

The remaining major possible source for the legal metaphors and analogies of the New Testament Epistles is often referred to as Greek or Hellenistic law. However, the first thing
that must be said is that there was no such thing as a coherent
body of Greek law that may be described as emanating from the
Greek legal system, for there was no Greek legal system. Greek
law in the sense of a common law or legal system applicable
throughout the area of Greek civilization simply did not exist.
Greek civilization consisted of a number of city-states, each of
which had its own legal system and organization. Although the
common cultural background of these city-states did give rise
to a certain harmony of institutions, this harmony did not amount
to a coherent legal system as such. As the late G. M. Calhoun
put it in his *Introduction to Greek Legal Science*, " . . . the Greek
world was split into many small independent political units.
Each of these had its own particular body of law, based ulti-
mately on what may be termed the common law of the Hellenes,
but differing from others at many points and effective only in

its own territory."[28] In short, the degree of variation among the laws of the various Greek city-states at the time of the New Testament was more akin to that found among the several legal systems of modern Europe than to the degree of variation among the legal systems of the separate states of the United States, which display a fair measure of homogeneity. Many of the legal systems of Europe do have certain superficial similarities in organization and do share certain common sources, notably Roman law. However, the differences between these legal systems are rather great. It follows that it is a question whether under these circumstances the separate "small independent political units" of the Greeks developed a system of law that might afford a satisfactory body of examples for the New Testament writers to use.

A second difficulty is that even within the individual city-states the Greeks, unlike the Romans or even (within their larger field of operation) the Jews, did not develop a legal science. The Greeks did not produce a body of systematic legal doctrine, nor did specialist lawyers emerge in the population. This is, partly at any rate, due to the basic ethos of the communities. For example, in ancient Athens the national assembly, composed of all citizens, dealt with all matters of public policy, governmental functions being exercised by commissions of citizens appointed for the purpose by ballot. There was nothing sacrosanct about legislation, and legislation could be easily impugned and over-set by the general will. In the area of judicial administration and justice there was no concept of precedent having binding force or even being of persuasive authority for the future. It follows that any development of the law by decision, analogy, or example was extremely difficult. The development of a class of professional lawyers was impeded by both a strict rotation of magistrates and regular scrutiny and review of their performance, including an audit when they retired from office. Before the courts there was an absolute prohibition on accepting fees for services in pleading, and the normal situation was for every man to plead his own case in court. Thus it was not really possible for Athenian legal science to develop a system of jurisprudence, and similar difficulties appear to have applied throughout the Greek city states.[29]

It follows that if Paul and the other New Testament writers refer to "Greek law" for metaphors and analogies, the reference

cannot be other than extremely inexact. If one argues that in
any given instance the reference is precise, then one would have
to argue further that Paul, for example, knew in detail the local
variations of Greek law applicable in each of the cities to which
he wrote. This seems somewhat unlikely. Lawyers are interested
in detail, but one would need much study and an excellent
memory to retain all such information to the degree required to
write or argue on such a basis.

The other problem one has in discussing possible references
to Greek law in the Epistles is a lack of available material on
"Greek law." As a consequence of the fragmentary nature of the
Greek civilization of the eastern empire, little information as to
precise legal provisions has come down to us. It is therefore
difficult to assess the extent of such common elements as undoubtedly existed amongst some of the communities and that
might be dubbed "Greek law." A body of information does exist
as to the law of Athens, although this is somewhat fragmentary,
and relates mainly to the classical period of the fourth and fifth
centuries B.C. A fairly extensive body of information is also
available with respect to the Roman province of Egypt, but this
body of data is not purely Greek.[30]

The effect of this lack of information as to precise provisions
of Greek law is that it is difficult to be certain in one's arguments. The law of Athens and the law of Egypt are not evidence
as to the law of Thessalonica, let alone of the Greek cities of
Asia Minor or of the Decapolis. At the same time one cannot
rule out a reference to "Greek law" simply on the grounds of
lack of data. To do that would be to fall into a trap that is already
fairly well filled with critical theologians.

However, when one couples the lack of precise information
on the legal rules of the actual communities to which the Epistles were sent with the knowledge that the rules did vary in
content between these different communities, one may justifi-
ably argue that the possibility of any particular reference being
to "Greek law" is diminished. The chances of Greek law providing a common store of examples for the New Testament writers are rather small. At the same time, where there is a possible
meaning for particular images—for example, in the areas of
slavery and adoption—the content of "Greek law" as we know
it can be outlined in that connection, as I have done in the main
text.

Law in the Provinces

IN APPENDIX 2 we outlined the sources of Roman law and the structure of government in Rome. In appendices 3 and 4 we will consider the extent to which the recipients of the Epistles would know that law. This involves two elements: First, consideration of the penetration of the empire by Roman law, i.e., the extent to which it was known in the provinces, which is the subject of this appendix; second, the actual conditions affecting the different churches addressed in each epistle, which will be taken up in appendix 4.

The question of knowledge of Roman law is not as simple as it might seem. The difficulty lies in the fact that the Romans did not impose their law or extend their citizenship automatically to those territories that came under their control. It is perhaps too easy when talking of the Roman Empire to give the impression that it was a monolithic, regularly organized and regimented structure, but this is totally misleading for the period that concerns us. Until quite late in the empire much of the territory subject to Roman hegemony was not formally incorporated in the sense of being made Roman, nor was the population of these areas given Roman citizenship. Around the time of Jesus ninety-three percent of the population of the empire were peregrines, technically aliens, in Roman law.[1] The usual method of Roman administration was to operate through the use of the existing centers of population and indigenous local government structures. As we shall see, in some cases full Roman colonies were planted or municipia created, while in other instances a local community might have a special treaty arrangement with Rome (civitas foederata) or be technically free (civitas sine foedere immunis et libera). But apart from these, the bulk of the townships and territories (civitates stipendiariae) were without special privileges, though Rome did not interfere much with their internal arrangements.

The Roman Empire in New Testament times therefore cannot and must not be thought of as being a unit or even a complex of provinces created on a basis of nationality or domicile as we know these concepts today. Rather, it was a large number of civic communities and their landward territories, which were grouped into administrative units called provinces. The province was an area of jurisdiction, the sphere of duty (provincia) of a governor, occasionally formed without the necessary regard to history, geography, or ethnic grouping. Within each province there might well not be uniformity, and uniformity was not imposed. In government the Romans were pragmatists, following the line of least resistance, allowing local diversity as far as possible. The continuation of prior constitutional arrangements was allowed and respected so long as it was not inimical to Roman interests. Each provincial unit was therefore given its own set of regulations (the lex provinciae) for its administration, and laws were promulgated for Roman citizens, but the general populace's law was left alone. In the bulk of the area that concerns us the Romans took over ultimate control, but they did not attempt to interfere with native language, native customs, native law, or native religion, unless this proved to be necessary for reasons of state. Indeed, it is possible to trace how the Roman institutions became "Graecised" in some of the areas of Asia Minor, and how in its classical period Roman law itself imported concepts from Greek law. Where interference was deemed necessary it was simply effected by use of the *imperium* of the magistrate or governor, the broad power entrusted to him to govern the area of his jurisdiction, his *provincia*.[2]

But despite this diversity there were certain elements in the constitution and administration of the empire that contributed to the spread of the knowledge of Roman law. First, there was the Roman military presence, particularly in areas such as Asia Minor and Syria (amounting in some ways to martial law), for the purpose of keeping the peace or of ensuring that the local authorities did so. Second, the form of administration of civil law through the existing structures tended to spread knowledge of Roman law as being a different solution to common problems. Third, there was the existence of a generalized Roman law for a province, summed up basically in the governor's edict. And fourth, there was the fact that Roman law was the law of the citizens of the empire, unavailable to the general population.

The Roman emphasis on peace with preservation of the existing governmental structures and local laws is easily illustrated from the history of the Jews and from the New Testament itself.[3] In the case of the Jews, Roman intervention was crucial for the Herodian dynasty. The Jewish state of the time had arisen through the rebellion chronicled in the Books of the Maccabees.

During the rebellion the Jews had made a treaty with the Romans (1 Macc. 8:1–30; 2 Macc. 11:16–38), which was a contributory cause of Roman intervention in Syria.[4] According to the secular historian Josephus, the Romans first actively interfered in Jewish internal affairs in order to suppress the dissensions among the successors of Queen Alexandra. Pompey occupied Jerusalem in 63 B.C., and thereafter the Jewish kingdom was deprived of the Decapolis region, though retaining self-government.

After the battle of Actium, Herod the Great, who had supported Anthony, offered to serve Octavian (Augustus) and was welcomed as an ally by the future emperor. Thereafter the internal control of Palestine was largely in the hands of the Herodian dynasty, and the degree of Roman interference varied over the years. On the death of Herod the Great, the Romans divided the Jewish territory into three parts. Two of his sons held their tetrarchies for many years. The third, Archelaus, the ethnarch of Judea, was a failure, and in A.D. 6 the Romans reluctantly took over his dominions at the request of the Jews. This territory was returned to Herod's grandson, Agrippa, in A.D. 41. In the interim Tiberius appointed only two procurators to Judea during his long tenure of office, Valerius Gratus and Pontius Pilate.[5] During this period the seat of government was at Caesarea Stratonis.[6] Jerusalem was left with only a small garrison to keep the peace and was governed by the high priest and the Sanhedrin (the national council). In all of this there was no attempt to foist the Roman civil law upon the existing national legal system.

When Tiberius died in A.D. 37, two of the three tetrarchies of Palestine were without rulers. Philip had died in A.D. 34 and Pontius Pilate was recalled from Judea about A.D. 36. Agrippa, who had been in prison under Tiberius, was liberated by Caligula and was nominated to the tetrarchy of Philip, and a new procurator of Judea was appointed. By intrigue Agrippa was able to discredit Herod Antipas and that tetrarchy was added to his own. In A.D. 40 Agrippa went back to Italy and was present there when Caligula was murdered. He was thereafter given Judea and Samaria in consideration of his support of the new emperor, Claudius, with the result that he then ruled over practically the whole of the old kingdom of the Jews. Agrippa died in the spring of A.D. 44, under the circumstances narrated in Acts 12:20–23.[7] Thereafter Rome became unwilling to trust the family of the Herods and reverted to its policy of sending governors from Rome to Judea. In A.D. 52 Felix succeeded to the procuratorship and was faced with a deteriorating political relationship between the Jewish population and the Greeks of the Decapolis. His successor, Porcius Festus, the procurator who sent Paul to Rome, did his best to pacify the area, but matters continued to get worse, eventually resulting in the Jewish War and the destruction of the temple in A.D. 70.

The eventual outcome should not blind us to the fact that for one hundred years the Romans were quite content that the Jewish state should continue its old forms of government and intervened only when they felt it necessary. Of course there were limits to Jewish freedom. Despite the degree of local autonomy that was allowed, there was at the same time martial law in the area, and only the Romans could inflict capital punishment (except in case of blasphemy). Thus Christ was crucified by the Romans,[8] and the Jews sought Paul's death by Roman procedure.[9] However, the willingness of the Romans to intervene in local matters where there was disturbance can be better seen elsewhere in the New Testament.

When necessary the Romans were willing to interfere and punish cities of the empire that failed to conduct themselves properly. In Thessalonica the magistrates were bound to follow up the accusation that Paul was guilty of sedition by preaching of "another king, one Jesus" (Acts 17:5–9). For them to have failed to do this might have led to loss of their privileged status as a free city. Similarly, the town clerk of Ephesus, another free city, secured order by reminding the rioters that they might be called to account for the commotion (Acts 19:34–41). Even colonies were not immune. The magistrates of Philippi were troubled by the accusation that Paul was attacking the Roman state religion (Acts 16:21). They were even more troubled when it proved that they had maltreated a Roman citizen (Acts 16:37–39).[10] The Roman presence was therefore in the minds of the people, but may we go beyond this nebulous consciousness to details of Roman law? I would argue that we can, because through the Roman system of administration there would be consciousness of Roman civil law.

As stated above, the Romans did not impose their legal system throughout the empire. The effect of this was that, broadly speaking, in any part of the empire there might be a variety of legal provisions from different legal systems applicable to a given civil problem. If the parties in dispute were Roman citizens,

then Roman law would apply. If they were provincials from the
same area, their local law might apply. If they were from different legal backgrounds, then it would be up to the court to
determine which law to enforce. And just to complicate matters,
it might be that one of the two was a Roman citizen. Under these
circumstances much would depend on the nature of the court,
and in all probability the citizen would seek to have the matter
removed to a court dispensing Roman justice, the court of the
governor administering his edict.

In considering the penetration of the empire by Roman law,
we must therefore consider the different arrangements with
Rome, for these will provide some evidence for us. If a city was
a colony, obviously Roman law would be present. In other circumstances the chances of its presence diminish, unless contrary proof is forthcoming, as in the case of Thessalonica, which
was the capital of the province of Macedonia (cf. Ephesus). As
stated above, the possible arrangements were for a township or
city to be a colony (colonia), to have the rights and privileges of
a colony (municipium), to be a federate city (treaty-based, civitas
foederata), a free city (no treaty, civitas sine foedere immunis ac
libera), or a stipendiary city (civitas stipendiaria). Of these in
their order.

As we shall see in appendix 4 when considering the individual epistles, one Roman practice was to establish in her territories colonies with full Roman citizenship, either by founding
new communities or by taking over older townships. These colonies, therefore, functioned as enclaves of normal Roman jurisdiction within territory that was governed by another law. Indeed,
within the colonial city itself a distinction would be made between the citizen and the noncitizen in the administration of
the law.

Roman colonies were normally created for one of three purposes. The colony might be a fortified outpost of reasonable
importance within the government of an area that required reminding of Roman power. Alternatively, the colony might be
created to function rather like a modern suburb, absorbing the
excess population of the city. Thus the reforms of the brothers
Gracchi were partially intended to provide colonization possibilities for the underprivileged of Rome, and the refoundation
of Corinth as a colony by Julius Caesar allowed the transplanting
of many citizens from Rome. Lastly, colonies were on occasion
created in order to provide settlements for veterans of the army

(e. g., Philippi) by the will of the emperor or by command of successful generals who had been authorized by the Roman people to do so. Augustus's successors also tended to use the grant of status of colony as a reward to cities that had served the emperor in some way or other (e.g., Thessalonica, later than our period). Indeed, the status of being so recognized by the emperor was apparently much sought after and towns vied with one another—for example, by setting up sanctuaries for the cult of the Emperor—to gain additional privileges and recognition. To become a colony was the most successful outcome of these efforts.

The civil and administrative structure of the colony was much like that of Rome. Indeed, the theory of the transaction was that here was "another Rome" settled upon foreign soil and the ceremonies of setting up the colony included the parceling out of the territory into areas corresponding to the voting divisions or wards found in Rome itself. A fixed number of families were settled in the place, and it was constituted as a colony by authority from Rome and confirmed as such by a formal charter, which set out the normal pattern of Roman civic administration.[11]

In the western part of the empire an alternative was that a provincial town might be set up as a municipium. This was not a colony but was given the Roman franchise and a constitution, either by the governor of the province or by a special commissioner. In this way the town was incorporated into the Roman system of provincial administration, and the distinction between the municipium and the colony was a matter of history and official standing rather than a distinction in rights and privileges. Most municipia were organized virtually in the same manner as colonies.

Since there were no municipia in the areas to which the Epistles were sent, it is unnecessary to go into any details about them. But one point may be made about their organization. Usually the decuriones, the superior magistrates of the town—often a municipal Senate of one hundred life members—were given full Roman citizenship. This was a mark of honor and respect given to these individuals in recognition of their responsibilities. It follows that the concept of citizenship was something exalted in the eyes of the noncitizens. In the east, important dignitaries were also honored with Roman citizenship and had access to the Roman courts when these went on circuit.

Some other towns, neither colonies nor municipia, had special relationships with Rome, governed in each individual case by a treaty (civitas foederata). In general this treaty would specify the immunity of the town from interference by the governor of the province and allow the town whatever political structure it wished. Such a town was normally free of imperial taxation and might use its own laws or adopt those of Rome. The sole area of absolute subservience under the treaty was always foreign policy. But from such limited information as we have we may question whether the existence of the treaty was anything more than a bargaining counter in a dispute. When Rome wished she had the power to intervene.

This counter was not available to the free city (civitas sine foedere immunis ac libera), whose freedom was dependent upon the goodwill of Rome. In fact, although it was less satisfactory not to have one's position defined in an agreed document, there was little to choose between the free and federated cities. To be free was deemed a privilege, but that freedom was slightly less secure than the position of the federate town: Rome might change its mind. And in time such towns began to seek that Rome should regulate their internal affairs. This was part of a general move towards more Roman structures, the municipia seeking colonial status, the federate towns seeking to become municipia and the free towns federate, a process that continued for many years. Even the grant of Roman citizenship to all inhabitants of the empire under the Constitutio Antoniniana of A.D. 212 (the Edict of Caracalla) did not end the process of seeking higher status.

But throughout our period the bulk of the communities remained civitates stipendiariae, provincial towns without special status or privilege. The extent to which they were interfered with, taxed, or had troops quartered in them depended on the will of the governor. Some retained their own laws. Some had incursions made upon their legal systems. Again there was a tendency towards incorporation in the Roman structures, stipendiary cities seeking treaty or free status. The tendency of Rome in later years was to intervene, requiring the restructuring of local governments on Roman lines, with power being given to a minority of wealthy families. These alone might vote and govern. Eventually, after the general grant of citizenship by the Constitutio Antoniniana in A.D. 212, an official magistracy, the decuriones, already known in places, was introduced everywhere, though older official positions persisted.

Such was the broad pattern of authority and law in the provinces. As we shall see in the next appendix, most of the Epistles were written to churches in places where we can reasonably and more specifically deduce the presence of Roman law, but there are certain factors arising out of the broad arrangements for provincial administration that argue for a general degree of knowledge of Roman law in the provinces.

Knowledge of the Roman law would come to the readers of the Epistles in a variety of ways. Where the church was situated in a colony, Roman law was obviously at hand, and the chances of a Roman reference are increased when the church is seen to be at least partially gentile in composition. The Gentiles would not know Jewish law in any detail, and in a colony may be presumed to have known the law governing that colony and administered by its authorities. Even in the free and federate cities there might well be Romans present, and hence knowledge of the law of the empire. It is of course possible that readers of the letters would fill any legal allusions with the ideas of their own personal law, but this does not destroy the Roman reference.

One major source of knowledge of Roman law in a province would be the activities of the governor, particularly if, as was usual, he had served as praetor during his prior career in Rome itself. Since the praetor was immersed in the administration of the law, it is obvious that the able mind of such a person (for the Romans in public positions were by and large able, whatever their morality) would collect a vast quantity of general legal data. On proceeding to his provincial post the governor would carry this with him. He also took with him the Roman practice of issuing an edict as to the law his court would administer in the province. Such men as Sergius Paulus (Acts 13:7), Gallio (Acts 18:12), Felix (Acts 23:26), and Festus (Acts 25:1) would each have issued an edict on arriving in their province.[12] The governor's staff also included legal experts of more junior rank as advisers, who would bring with them knowledge of the Roman law and who would advise on any local peculiarities of importance. As a result local law was not totally without effect, suitable concepts being taken over into the edict.[13] Eventually ideas from provincial law might even come to be important in the civil law, but basically Roman law was administered by the governor for the benefit of his Roman subjects. Each governor went on circuit himself or sent deputies throughout his prov-

ince, holding courts at special assize towns where Roman law
was dispensed under scrutiny in terms of the edict.[14]

The provincial edict passed through the same processes of
development as the urban edict. It was altered in the light of
experience. Commentaries were written and propositions of law
were expounded, discussed, amended, approved, and dis-
carded. We know, for example, that the edict for Asia established
by Quintus Mucius Scaevola in 98 B.C. was influential and much
discussed.[15] Through this work and the discussions of governors
and administrators, standardization among the provinces occurred. Eventually the provincial edict was made practically
uniform as part of the work of general revision by Salvius Juli-
anus, and only very special local variations were thereafter
allowed.[16]

The very exclusion of most of the provincial population of
the empire from the full Roman law can be an argument in favor
of its being used metaphorically in the Epistles. The peregrini
(foreigners) were without access to the full Roman procedures.
The status of Roman citizenship was something that was apparently prized by the individual and citizenship was a favor to
be sought. As indicated, towns that were allied to Rome but
were not officially incorporated in the empire in the same way
as a colony or a municipium tended to renounce their favored
position of continuing quasi-independence in order to become
Roman, either as a colony or as a municipium. Roman citizens
were not subject to the same martial administration that applied
to all other provincials (the "second mile" in Matt. 5:41 may
turn on the duty to carry military burdens) and were exempt
from the severities of administration and punishment. Romans
served on provincial juries and were exempt from the normal
taxation of the provincial authorities. Citizenship was a reward
for doing notable service. The individual with Roman citizenship was in a more favorable legal position than the non-Roman.
This did lead to a degree of assimilation between the Roman
and other legal systems. The extent of this assimilation in the
areas covered by the Epistles has not yet been written up in
English, but work on the Egyptian position has produced some
results.[17] The exclusion of the peregrine population from the
law of the ruling classes did lead to some debasement of the
national peregrine laws where the local legal tradition was none
too strong. Legal thinking in the traditional categories ceased or
diminished and Roman concepts or ways of thought were bor-

rowed. Roman law took precedence and for this reason access to Roman law was sought and the models of Roman law would come to be known. Though assimilation was not all one way, the vast bulk of the population might well consider itself to be subjected to a "second class" law, something different from that of their rulers and something that might be erratic in its application especially when confronted with the Roman law itself.[18]

It is not unreasonable therefore to expect that there was great interest in the technicalities of the law of the privileged class. Even the possibility of academic study of Roman law cannot be excluded. There were university centers in the provinces, Tarsus being an example, and it would seem very likely that schools of legal studies developed there. Certainly Tarsus was famous for its philosophy, and it is very unlikely that the more practical study of law was not also present. Paul lectured in the school of Tyrannus in Ephesus (Acts 19:9), the administrative capital of Asia, a province whose edict was the subject of widespread interest, based as it was on the edict of Quintus Mucius Scaevola, governor in 98 B.C. and the founder of a school of jurists.[19] In Rome commentaries on the edicts were published. Were they not read and discussed in the provinces to illuminate the terms of a provincial edict? It is known that some of the most successful jurists were provincial in origin, possibly including Gaius. Did they not come from groups of students of Roman law in the provinces?[20]

The presence of the Roman law in communities in the provinces, particularly in the colonies, and its conspicuousness through the provincial edict and governors' courts make it therefore reasonable to suppose that the principal features of Roman law were known in the provinces to which the New Testament works were addressed. Allusions to the Roman law would not pass over the heads of the readers. As indicated above, a defect in this argument is that not all the probable recipients of the letters were in fact subject to the Roman law. Roman law applied only to citizens. Thus, in any one city there was a possible proliferation of laws applicable to the population. It is therefore arguable that readers of the letters would have filled Paul's legal allusions with their own local import.

Several arguments may be mustered against that point of view. One elementary point is the actual presence of Roman law in some of the centers to which the Epistles were addressed. This will be taken up more particularly in a few pages, when we consider the destination of particular epistles, but it may be observed here that a number of these epistles, and indeed the most important of them, are addressed to churches in areas or towns that were Roman colonies (e. g., Galatians, Philippians, and Corinthians). It is known that there was in other areas a degree of assimilation of Roman ideas into the jurisprudence of the indigenous courts, making their concepts not as unfamiliar as might be thought.[21] Again it is obvious that in the Epistle to the Romans legal allusions can be held to have reference to Roman law.

Another powerful argument for Paul's deliberate use of analogies drawn from Roman law is that Paul himself was a citizen. In appendix 5 I discuss more fully the extent to which it is proper to consider that Paul had knowledge of and used the Roman law analogies in his writings, but anticipating the conclusions of that appendix, certain things may be said. By his citizenship Paul had access to a law that was not available to many of his contemporaries. He himself had undergone a form of legal training through his education in the Jewish faith, and it is not readily conceivable that a person who had been legally trained would not know the law to which he himself was subject. Accustomed as Paul was to thinking in the relatively legal categories of the Jewish Torah, Halakah, and midrash, he would soon have realized how appropriate his "personal" law was for illustrating gospel truths. For him it would appear obvious that Roman law formed a *lingua franca* of examples. It can even be argued that he could have studied some Roman law during his period in Tarsus while awaiting his commission (Acts 9:30). Paul knew that he was to be a witness to Jesus before the Gentiles. What is more likely than that a lawyer would study to some extent that law whose privileges and jurisdiction he was to use in carrying out his mission?

The last general argument we may present before turning to the particular epistles is this. The main text of this book consists of studies of particular concepts used by Paul and other writers in the New Testament to communicate the truths they were preaching, of the images they used to get certain fundamental ideas across to their readers and hearers. Most of these allusions are particularly suitable to the points being made if one does read Roman content into the legal terminology. It does not seem to me to be likely that the Paul whom we meet in Acts and in the Epistles would have used illustrations of whose effect he could not be certain. Apt illustrations are not to be deemed accidental if they are consistently appropriate.[22] It is perfectly true that some of the illustrations would be meaningless to a person who did not know law. It is true that some of the illustrations would have a degree of meaning to a person who had no legal knowledge (e. g., the idea of slavery). Beyond that, some of the legal language used had meaning under legal systems other than the Roman system, and it would be quite possible in these instances for a peregrine to understand the point that Paul was making without referring to Roman law.

But although all these points may be conceded, it is not justifiable to go on from this to argue that Paul was using legal language without really appreciating what he was saying. Roman law provides a more extended meaning for the bulk of the metaphors considered. In many of these instances the Roman law analogy provides a revealing insight into the ways of God with man. In his letters Paul was seeking to speak clearly to all, but he did not assume that he was speaking to ignorance. He takes for granted detailed knowledge of many things, including the Old Testament Scriptures. It is illogical, therefore, arbitrarily to exclude from his store of examples detailed knowledge of the most wide-spread legal system of his time. On the contrary, if what he says has meaning under that system, and particularly if there is a special or enhanced meaning under that system, it is reasonable to suppose that Paul was using such concepts deliberately. Of course, this argument is less tenable in relation to the other writers of the Epistles, but it is not without validity; however, it will be more appropriate to discuss this in relation to their own particular contributions to the New Testament canon.

Appendix 4

The Epistles

IN APPENDIX 3 we were concerned with the broad picture of law and administration in the provinces of the Roman Empire, seeking to show that, although the Romans did not displace the "native" law and administration, there were reasons why the general population could have known Roman law. The presence of Roman citizens and colonies, the governors' courts, and the provincial edicts all would have helped spread knowledge of Roman law, so that its metaphoric use in the Epistles would have been possible. In the main text the various chapters show that some of the legal metaphors in the Epistles have meaning only in Roman law, while others attain their fullest meaning only if interpreted by Roman law. These points are in themselves powerful arguments that a Roman interpretation is proper. But we can also consider the individual churches to which the Epistles were addressed, and it will be found that in most of the General Epistles there is specific reason to suggest a Roman reference.

Some of the Epistles are addressed to churches situated in cities and towns clearly under Roman influence. Corinth and Phillipi were colonies, Ephesus and Colosse administrative centers of great importance. As another strand in this argument I have also sought, where possible, to indicate what is known, or may reasonably be deduced, of the actual composition of the church addressed—whether it was mainly gentile or whether there was a strong Jewish element present. Where there was a preponderance of Gentiles, the likelihood of any legal metaphor being explicable by reference to Jewish law is lessened. It is true that gentile believers were interested in the Old Testament, but it is likely that Gentiles would refer legal metaphors to concepts found in the legal system that governed their own daily affairs rather than the (to them) rather convoluted and abstruse system of rabbinic Judaism.

The Epistle to the Hebrews and 1 and 2 Peter are, perhaps, exceptions to such an argument, but I include them in the net, since they provide instances of legal imagery which it would be misleading to omit. Depending on one's view of the authorship of Hebrews, and certainly in the case of 1 and 2 Peter, the possibility of a conscious reference to a legal device, let alone to a Roman legal device, is somewhat less than in the case of the Pauline Epistles. Even so, the legal images from the non-Pauline corpus are of interest, both to contrast with and to supplement the legal language in Paul's correspondence. James, Jude, and the three Epistles of John do not really contain legal images, while Revelation does have some echoes.

In looking at the other Epistles, there are certain matters I have neither the knowledge nor the skill to deal with properly. The sequence and dating of the Epistles might provide some additional strand of argument, were such data available and agreed on by the scholars. But the major matter is that of the authorship of the Epistles. Apart from the question of the Epistles of Peter and that to the Hebrews, the Pauline Epistles themselves create problems. I find it therefore interesting that most of the legal metaphors and analogies discussed in the main text are found in the Epistles that are more commonly thought to have been written by Paul. That fact in itself strengthens the argument for the deliberate use of legal language, since this corpus is the apparently coherent product of a single mind. Opinion is more divided on the other Epistles, but there does seem to be an increasing willingness to accept their Pauline authorship. It may be that the use of legal illustrations in them is an element of comparability that might help clarify matters. In any event it seems (to an outsider) that on the matter of the disputed authorship of the Epistles there is at present sufficient division and balance within scholarship to permit me to treat the traditional Pauline Epistles as being the work of Paul.[1]

Finally, it should be said that what is being attempted in these pages is not invalidated were it to be shown that other hands had been at work, but the argument is more elegant if the uses of legal images in the different epistles were made by the same person. One may then look, for example, at adoption (the metaphor most clearly drawn from Roman law) and at citizenship and slavery—(which are fairly clearly Roman) and go on to suggest that, if these are instances of a drawing from Roman law, then there is at least a rebuttable presumption that other legal phrases found in the Epistles may also be referred to the same source for their content.

Let us then look at the Epistles generally to see what may

be drawn from them for our discussion. I begin with a negative point.

The Pastoral Epistles

The letters to Timothy and to Titus are of some interest in our enquiry, not because they contain pronounced legal metaphors, but because they do not. Both men are addressed as "son" (1 Tim. 1:2; 2 Tim. 1:2; Titus 1:4), but apart from that the only reference to a legal idea is to slavery. Paul speaks of himself as a "servant of God" in Titus 1:1, and in 1 Timothy there is a passage discussing the proper attitude of slaves towards their masters (1 Tim. 6:1–2). Paul is not teaching theological truths through these uses. This may suggest that when Paul does use a legal metaphor to instruct, there is a conscious reference to the legal content of the idea. If so, it is important to seek the actual legal system from which the metaphor is drawn, since otherwise a correct interpretation of Paul's teaching is made difficult, if not rendered impossible.

Romans

Of all the Epistles in the New Testament, that to the church at Rome is the most likely to contain references to Roman legal concepts. The church being addressed was one Paul had not seen and in whose foundation Paul had played no part (Rom. 1:10–15; 15:20–22), though his close friends Aquila and Priscilla doubtless had told him much about it (Acts 18:1–3; Rom. 16:3–5). Who founded the church at Rome is unknown, but it seems obvious that Christianity soon spread to the capital of the empire, perhaps taken there after Pentecost by some of the "visitors from Rome" mentioned in Acts 2:10 (though cf. Acts 11:19). Sergius Paulus, the proconsul of Cyprus, may also have played a role when he returned home (Acts 13:7, 12).

Clearly the church at Rome contained both Jews and Gentiles. The epistle contains extensive references to the Old Testament and to the general history of the Jews. On occasions Paul addresses the Jewish element in the church directly (e.g., Rom. 2:16–3:20). On the other hand he also speaks to the Gentiles in particular. After all, he was the Apostle to the Gentiles (Rom. 1:13; 11:13; 15:14–16). Apart from these instances it may be noted that the list of salutations in Romans 16 contains mainly Greek or Roman names. Even if this chapter is a separate letter of greeting and does not form part of the main epistle, as some argue, it nonetheless is massive evidence that the bulk of the well-known people in the church were either Gentiles or sufficiently gentile-oriented to have taken gentile names for ordinary use even by a fellow Jew.

The Epistle to the Romans is therefore seen to be addressed to a church in the capital of the empire, where the dominant legal presence was Roman and where the members may be assumed to have known that law. Paul had not met or spoken with most of them, yet found it convenient and meaningful in places to use the language of law. I therefore consider it reasonable to refer such language to Roman law and indeed to suggest that all legal allusions within this epistle are references to the ideas of that legal system.

1 and 2 Corinthians

There is a strong argument that any legal allusions and metaphors in the epistles to the church in Corinth are to be referred to Roman law, for Corinth was a Roman colony in which the full Roman law was in force.

In the period from the fourth to the second century B.C. Corinth was one of the premier city-states in Greece, having her own colonies in the Aegean and even in southern Italy. She led the Achaean League and at one point bid fair to replace Carthage as Rome's main trading rival. As a result she incurred the irrational hatred with which Rome viewed possible competitors. In 146 B.C. Rome intervened in a dispute between the League and Sparta, and following the defeat of the League by Mummius the Romans selected Corinth for special punishment. On the resolution of the Senate the city was razed to the ground and her inhabitants enslaved or put to death.

The mercantile reasons for Corinth's destruction foreshadowed her rebirth. Geographically Corinth was a necessary city. It had risen as a double port on the isthmus of Corinth. Goods could be transported over the isthmus from port to port, thus avoiding the dangerous passage round the Peloponnese—in itself a sufficient justification for the twin ports. In addition it was but a short trip from Corinth across the Aegean to Ephesus, the western terminus of the main trade route from the east across Asia Minor. Corinth therefore had grown as a major port and transshipment point for all seaborne trade between east and west.

In 45 B.C., partially for these mercantile reasons, Julius Caesar refounded the city of Corinth as a Roman colony. In so doing he was also resettling Roman citizens from the congestion of Rome and expiating the former savagery, for by then Rome was thoroughly under Greek influence. After this resuscitation or revival Corinth did not take long to regain her importance; her development was accelerated under Augustus until she was well-nigh supreme in the eastern trade. At the same time she was becoming Grecian in manner of life and habits and attracted all the normal life of a busy seaport. But she remained a Roman colony. Her citizens were Roman citizens with all the privileges of Roman law. It is not surprising therefore that Paul spent eighteen months in this secondary focus of the Empire, in which it was possible to reach people from many parts of the globe (Acts 18:11).

Three points may be made. First, there is a degree of evidence both in the Epistles and in Acts that the proportion of Gentiles in the Corinthian church was quite high (Acts 18:6–10). Indeed, after the Jewish complaint against Paul there seems to have been a counterdemonstration by Greeks in his favour, a very rare occurrence (Acts 18:17). This argues for a significant gentile following in Corinth. Accordingly, legal references in these epistles should naturally be construed by the law these Gentiles would know, that is, Roman law. Reference to special Jewish rules is very much less likely.

Second, the name of "Erastus, the city treasurer," in the list of salutations in Romans 16:23 must be noted. The Epistle to the Romans was written from Corinth, and whatever Erastus's actual status, whether he were an aedile or a lesser functionary, a freeman or a freedman, the fact remains that the position he held was well up the cursus honorum of a Roman colony and that he was therefore administering Roman Law.[2] Even were he the most civilly distinguished member of the church in Corinth, the link between the gentile members of that church and Roman law is made.

Third, the Corinthian Epistles contain commercial references. For example, as is shown in the chapter on slavery (chap. 2), there is a clear reference to a technicality of the Roman law of slavery, and Roman law would be the law of the slave market in this commercially active colony of Rome (indeed, that market would have been under the jurisdiction of Erastus if he was an aedile). Such technical imagery requires technical reference and cannot be understood as the normal language of a layman who speaks without that additional understanding.

Galatians

In Galatians, written to combat the legalizing activities of the Judaizers, Paul appropriately uses legal concepts, freedom, slavery, inheritance, and guardianship. I would not want to press this too far, but there is a higher proportion of possible legal allusions in this letter than in any of the others.

Controversy has persisted for many years over the question of the destination of the Epistle to the Galatians. One view, preeminently presented in English by Bishop J. B. Lightfoot's *Commentary on Galatians,* is that the churches addressed in this epistle were situated in North Galatia, in Ancyra (Ankara), Pessinus, and perhaps Tavium, and were visited by Paul on the occasions referred to in Acts 16:6 and 18:23. The alternative view is that the churches were those in South Galatia, namely Pisidian Antioch, Iconium, Lystra, and Derbe, visited by Paul and Barnabas during the first missionary journey (Acts 13:4–14:26).

The core of the dispute lies in some of the language of the epistle. The population of the north of the province of Galatia was ethnically Gaulish and hence more appropriately addressed as "Galatians" (Gal. 1:2; 3:1). Certainly the population there was Gallic in origin, having forced its way into the region around 280 B.C., but retaining its individuality. Indeed, they resisted Greek and Roman cultural influences for years. St. Jerome found in his time that the language spoken in North Galatia was comprehensible in Gaul (France).[3] Accordingly, it is said, the references to "Galatians" must be to the people in the north of the province, and Acts must be construed to allow for Paul's founding of churches there.

I find the North Galatian theory untenable, its demolition having been satisfactorily accomplished by Sir William Ramsay. Briefly, in his studies on the question he came to the conclusion that the historical and geographical facts of Asia Minor at the time of the Epistles were such that only the South Galatian theory could fit them. The topography, lines of communication,

and centers of population indicate that the churches addressed
lay in the south of the province. It requires the rewriting, or
ignoring, of history to allow a visit to the northern areas to serve
as a basis for the epistle.[4]

Nevertheless, although I do not myself find the North Galatian theory compelling or indeed attractive, its truth would not
seriously affect our present enquiry. Ancyra, Pessinus, and Tavium were the central towns of the principal tribal divisions of
the Gauls and retained their importance under the Romans. Pessinus was the center of worship of the Great Mother of Mount
Ida, the origin of the cult of the Great Mother adopted by the
Romans in 204 B.C. Ancyra was the administrative capital of its
region and one of the most important centers of the imperial
cult. Indeed, the Monumentum Ancyranum is the best authority
for the famous autobiography of Augustus.[5] It is therefore clear
that Rome's interest was present, and it is likely that its law was,
as well, although none of the three cities was formally a colony.
Against this, one point must be mentioned. Gaius (Institutes
1.55) states that the Galatians had in their family law a concept
of paternal power much like that of Rome, which indicates that
the Gallic law was still active in his day. But the persistence of
Gallic law does not require ignorance of Roman law.[6]

If the epistle were written to churches in South Galatia, to
Pisidian Antioch, Iconium, Derbe, and Lystra, there can be little
doubt that the reference to Roman law is possible.[7] Until 25 B.C.
the whole area embracing Galatia, Pisidia, Lycaonia, Isaurian
Cilicia, eastern Phrygia, and Paphlagonia formed a monarchy
that in later years existed by the grace of Rome. On the death of
King Amyntas in that year the area came into the possession of
Rome under the terms of his will and was reorganized. Pisidian
Antioch and Lystra were both made colonies and were connected by road for defensive purposes about 6 B.C. This road,
the Via Sebaste (the "Imperial Road"), was extended to Laranda
in the foothills of the Taurus and passed through Derbe, an important center of population. About the time of Paul, Derbe was
given important privileges by Claudius (A.D. 41–54), as were
Iconium and Lycaonian Laodicea, but it was not raised to colonial status. Iconium was made a colony later by Hadrian, and
Laodicea by Maximinus. These latter two cities were the most
important in the area. Lycaonian Laodicea was on the main road
from Ephesus to the east and was quite affluent. Iconium lay on

the plain between the eastern trade route and the Via Sebaste. Accordingly Iconium, strategically placed, became the administrative center, dwarfing its fellows.[8]

Southern Galatia was therefore permeated by a Roman network with nodes at each important center, two of which, Antioch and Lystra, were actually colonies. Paul knew the area and the towns well, having visited them twice if not three times, well enough to value and trust their opinion in the matter of Timothy (Acts 16:2). Given such familiarity, it seems likely that before using legal analogies in a letter to them, Paul would have known that the language was meaningful to his friends.

The composition of the Galatian churches is another factor that may help us. It seems that although there were some Jews (Timothy's mother was a Jewess, Acts 16:1), the majority of the church were Gentiles. This would be even more obviously the case if the churches were situated in North Galatia, but the gentile character of the churches is clearly to be inferred from the content of the epistle itself. The problem Paul was tackling was that, after he had preached to these Gentiles, others had arrived preaching that before a person could be a Christian he had to become a Jew (see particularly Gal. 5:2–12; cf. Acts 15:1–2). This problem could only arise in the case of the Gentile, the non-Jew. Paul's legal references are therefore unlikely to be to Jewish law. The Judaizers seem to have been busy instructing the people in Judaism. The church did not know it already. Roman law is therefore the obvious alternative source of Paul's many legal illustrations in this epistle, notably the metaphors of slavery (particularly Gal. 4:22–5:1), adoption (Gal. 4:5), and inheritance (Gal. 3:15–4:7), which are dealt with respectively in chapters 2, 4, and 5 of the main text.

Ephesians

Ephesus was the leading city in the province of Asia and a main seat of government, though the capital of the province was Pergamum. Ephesus was also religiously significant as the seat of the worship of Artemis (Acts 19:34). Despite its importance it did not have colonial status but retained its own forms of government throughout our period, as may be seen in the story of the riot in Acts 19:21–41. However, as the seat of administration and of a major governor's court, the probability of Roman law being known there is very high. Added to this we may note that Paul "argued daily in the hall of Tyrannus" (Acts 19:9) during two of his three years' stay in the city and that a library has been found in the ruins of Ephesus. Where there is intellectual argument, law is bound to be studied by some, and the provincial edict for Asia is known to have been of great interest since the days of Quintus Mucius Scaevola, governor in 98 B.C.[9] Under these circumstances such legal illustrations as inheritance (Eph. 1:18; 3:6), alienage and citizenship (Eph. 2:12, 19), and sonship (Eph. 2:2; 4:6–8) can well be explained in Roman terms.

The composition of the church in Ephesus may also help a little. There seems to have been a strong Jewish element, converted by Paul's preaching in the synagogue (Acts 19:8), some of whom had been formerly itinerant exorcists (Acts 19:18–20). But there were Gentiles as well (Acts 19:17). Paul extols his commission to preach to the Gentiles in the epistle (Eph. 3:4–10), and we are told that "all the residents of Asia . . . both Jews and Greeks" heard the gospel through the Ephesian ministry (Acts 19:10). The Jewish opposition to Paul began after only three months, and he stayed a further twenty-one months in the city. It is arguable that battle lines would have hardened, possibly along ethnic lines, and that toward the end Paul spent most of his time preaching to the Gentiles. If so, there would have been a high proportion of gentile members in the Ephesian church, some of whom (the "Asiarchs") may have been active in city government (Acts 19:31). Some would certainly have been Roman citizens in such an important focus of trade and government, and all would have had some knowledge of the law of the real rulers.

Of course, there is the problem that many present-day scholars consider that Ephesians was not written particularly to that church but was rather a circular letter to the several churches in Asia, sent with Tychicus (Eph. 6:21), who was also bearing the letter to the Colossians (Col. 4:7). This is possible, especially because Ephesians, in contrast to Colossians, does not conclude with personal greetings to a named group. However, there are personal touches (e.g., Eph. 1:15; 3:13) that indicate that the letter was intended to go to only a small group of churches, if not just to the Ephesians. Under these circumstances the general proposition that the letter is addressed to an area where Roman law was present and therefore might be known to the church members does not entirely fall. But by way of further riposte we may note that the Epistle to the Colossians, addressed to a smaller church outside Ephesus, does not contain the same measure of legal allusion as Ephesians. It is tempting therefore to argue that Paul used the more technical analogies of Ephesians because he knew his audience. He knew that they would pick up what he was saying and might even catch allusions to his lectures in the hall of Tyrannus. He was therefore speaking to a church with which he was well acquainted—Ephesus.

Colossians and Philemon

Colossae was one of the three churches of the Lycus valley, inland from Ephesus, the others being Hierapolis and Laodicea (Col. 2:1; 4:13–15). In its previous history Colossae had been important, commanding a pass into the interior, but it had declined as the other two cities grew. The three churches seem to have owed their origin to the preaching of Epaphras (Col. 1:7; 4:12; cf. Acts 19:26) who must have learned from Paul in Ephesus, for Paul had not visited the valley (Col. 2:1).

In the Epistle to the Colossians Paul tackles two problems; incipient Gnosticism and a tendency to turn back to the legalism of the Jews. Thus, in opposition to the "wise," he exalts the wisdom of Christ with its practical results (e.g., Col. 2:8–10; 3:12–4:6) and attacks formal rule-keeping (e.g., Col. 2:11–23). That this was necessary argues that the church was basically gentile in its composition, as in the case of the Galatians who were also troubled by Judaizers (see above). It was Gentiles who were seduced by Gnosticism and who might be open to persuasion that they had to convert to Jewish practices before they could be true Christians. The reference to Gentiles in Colossians 1:27 may also support this probability.

But apart from these hints we do not know much about the Colossian church. If Philemon was resident there rather than in Laodicea (Onesimus is described as "one of yourselves," Col. 4:7–9), then the play on the law of slavery and the references to partnership, to paternal power, and to brotherhood in the Epistle to Philemon might argue knowledge of Roman law. However, Colossae was a rather minor town at this time, and if Philemon was not of Colossae we cannot do more than suggest that even in this minor town there would be general knowledge of the law, for there are in the Colossian letter references to such broad concepts as dominion (Col. 1:13), debt (Col. 2:14), and inheritance (Col. 3:24).

Philippians

Like Corinth, Philippi was a Roman colony (Acts 16:12). For many years it was the terminus of the Via Egnatia, the principal road from Dyrrachium on the Adriatic to the ports for Asia; it was the first important community that travelers from the east would enter, as indeed Paul and Luke did (Acts 16:11–12). Through its port of Neapolis passed much of the trade to Troas and Asia Minor, and the city was therefore of commercial importance.

The Roman colony of Philippi was created in 42 B.C. by the Second Triumvirate—Octavian (Augustus), Antony, and Lepidus—as a memorial celebrating their victory over Brutus and Cassius. Roman citizens were settled there from Rome, and their numbers were added to shortly thereafter. Following the campaign, some of Antony's veterans were settled in colonies in the south of Italy, but they were removed to Philippi and some other Macedonian towns after his defeat at Actium, since they might be politically unreliable.

The founding of the church in Philippi is narrated in Acts 16. There is no reference to Paul preaching in the synagogue as was his custom. On the contrary, his party had to go outside the city to find a place of prayer (Acts 16:13). This and the terms of the epistle suggest that the basic membership of the church was Greek. In addition, it is arguable that a fairly large proportion of the church at Philippi came from the Roman element of the population, since it seems to have been a rich church, willing and able to make extensive gifts for the furtherance of Paul's work (Phil. 4:10–20). There were also some Jews. To such a mixed congregation in a Roman colony, the imagery drawn from ideas of citizenship (Phil. 1:27; 3:20) would have much to communicate.

It was in this colony that Paul first came up against the allegation that he was going against the official religion of the Roman State. "These men are Jews and they are disturbing our city. They advocate customs which it is not lawful for us Romans to accept or practice" (Acts 16:20–21). Pride in their Roman status is clear. The magistrates bear the proper Roman titles, and the success of the allegations, as well as the rapid

alteration in attitude of the authorities on discovering that Paul
was a Roman citizen (Acts 16:37–39), illustrates how important
it was for the colonial administration not to offend Rome. Failure
to keep order might invite Roman disfavor; failure to give a
Roman proper treatment was equally hazardous.[10]

1 and 2 Thessalonians

The two Epistles to the Thessalonians do not contain legal
allusions of any importance, apart from the statement that the
readers "are all sons of light and sons of the day" (1 Thess. 5:5),
and even that phrase may not be intended to speak of the legal
position of sons. (The expression is Semitic and is found, for
example, in the Qumran Scrolls.) However, Thessalonica is of
interest as an example of an extremely important city that was
not Roman.

Thessalonica was one of the cities founded by Cassander
around 310 B.C. In Roman times it was an important city on the
Via Egnatia, the principal road from Dyrrachium on the Adriatic
to Philippi and the ports for Asia. In recognition of its importance it was made capital of the province of Macedonia in 164
B.C. It did not become a colony until the third century A.D., but
it was given the status of free city by Augustus after the battle
of Philippi in 42 B.C. It was therefore in the rather peculiar situation of being a free associate of Rome, yet also the seat of the
governor of the province. Under these circumstances one may
question how free the city was. It was the center of bureaucratic
authority and therefore in close touch with the laws of the empire.

Of course a free city, though proud of this distinction in
most cases, was in a less secure position since it was not able
to point to a treaty as the basis of its relationship with Rome. Its
position was dependent upon the goodwill of Rome. It is therefore tempting to trace an echo of these facts in Paul's experiences
at Thessalonica. When the Jews started a commotion with allegations that Paul, Silas, and the infant Thessalonian church
were "all acting against the decrees of Caesar, saying that there
is another king, Jesus," the authorities were bound to be upset
(Acts 17:5–9). Failure to suppress such sedition might have
brought severe punishment and loss of their city's status upon
them, though it is interesting that the civic authorities, although
they were disturbed, contented themselves with taking security

for good behavior from Paul's hosts (Acts 17:8–9). The success of this action is a tribute to their acumen (Acts 17:10).

Since there is only the one possible reference in the Thessalonian Epistles to Roman law, and an unimportant one at that (1 Thess. 5:5), it is not of major consequence to know the composition of the church addressed in these Epistles. But as evidence of the general character of the churches of New Testament times it is interesting to find that there were substantial Jewish and gentile elements, including some of high social status, both in Thessalonica and in Beroea (Acts 17:4, 12). The gentile element seems, however, to have been preponderant, at least in Thessalonica, since no Jew would have been an idol-worshiper (1 Thess. 1:9) and the new Christians had suffered at the hands of their own countrymen (1 Thess. 2:14).

Hebrews

We do not know who wrote the Epistle to the Hebrews, nor to whom it was written, and this necessarily restricts the weight of the evidence of legal phraseology in it. Almost certainly it is not Pauline, though there have been suggestions that it is a Greek translation of a Hebrew letter by Paul. Certainly the author knew Timothy well enough to travel with him (Heb. 13:23), and this might lend support to Tertullian's assertion that the author was Barnabas. Luke has also been suggested as its author, since there are linguistic similarities with Acts. Luther thought that Apollos wrote the epistle, and this is an attractive suggestion, since the knowledge of the Jewish ceremonial and the Old Testament tradition displayed in the epistle would tie in with what we know of Apollos's background (Acts 18:24–28). Others have suggested the Silas (Silvanus) who was Paul's companion on the second journey (Acts 15:22; 1 Thess. 1:1; 2 Thess. 1:1), Aquila and Priscilla, and Philip the Deacon. The main thing is that the author apparently did not have to identify himself and that he knew his audience. He must therefore have been a traveler. All the suggestions made fit these requirements.

The element in Hebrews that is most striking to a lawyer is the causal chain of argument backed up by examples drawn from a wide knowledge. This stands out particularly in the KJV. Many of the verses begin with "For," "Wherefore," "Therefore," "Now," linking the various parts of the book. One is reminded time and again of the Pauline style, but in a rather more taut structure. Here we have a mind trained in law like Paul, possibly Apollos, who may have been a scribe, perhaps even the lawyer Zenas who is otherwise unknown (Titus 3:13).

These are speculations. The important thing for us is the legal "feel" of the epistle. Probably, in view of its stress on the foreshadowing of the New Testament by the figures of the Old, only Jewish law ought to be used to interpret the few legal analogies we find in Hebrews, but some of its analogies make sense also in Roman law (e.g., "inheritance," "heirs," "city," "strangers," and "promises" in Heb. 11: 8–13). Given the primacy and diffusion of Roman law outlined in earlier pages, it may be that Roman influence may be inferred in an epistle written from Italy (Heb. 13:24). Be that as it may, we can certainly consider what the Roman content of such images may be. Some of its readers would certainly have done so.

1 and 2 Peter

I include the General Epistles of Peter in this discussion because Peter writes to the "exiles (strangers, KJV) of the Dispersion" scattered in the provinces of Pontus, Galatia, Cappadocia, Asia, and Bithynia (1 Peter 1:1). Opinion is divided, but these are probably Jews (1 Peter 2:12) who are exhorted on grounds of their alien status in the world to refrain from worldly pursuits (1 Peter 2:11). It seems to me that this is a conscious reference to concepts drawn from the Roman law of citizenship. Peter, the noncitizen, perhaps writing from Rome (1 Peter 4:13), is bound to have come across the distinction between citizens and aliens while traveling in the empire. In addition, his amanuensis, Silvanus (Silas), who may be responsible for the literary style of the epistles (1 Peter 4:12), had traveled with Paul and Timothy (Acts 15:22; 1 Thess. 1:1; 2 Thess. 1:1) and would also have had a grasp of the distinctions involved.

If this argument is correct, then we have in 1 Peter a non-Pauline example of a writer using a legal analogy drawn from Roman law. If Peter, a peregrine, and a not-too-well-educated peregrine at that, could use such imagery, then it seems more likely that Paul, the well-educated citizen deliberately used a Roman legal analogy when we find such in his writings.

James, John, and Jude

The Epistles of James, John, and Jude add nothing significant to the store of legal metaphors in the New Testament. Both

James (1:1) and Jude (v.1) call themselves (lit.) the "slaves" of Jesus, but this is a concept well known in Palestine, from where both epistles seem to have been written. The only point that can be taken from them is the negative one that, in contrast to Peter and Paul, these untraveled men do not use legal illustrations. It would be rash to place any great weight on this point.

Revelation

It may seem odd to include Revelation here, but although it is not strictly an epistle in the Pauline style, it was written to "the seven churches that are in Asia" (Rev. 2–3). These churches were situated in centers of Roman influence, colonies in some instances, and include the church in Pergamum, the capital, and in Ephesus, the independent city that was nonetheless the administrative capital. The book does contain some legal terminology (e.g., sealing, Rev. 7:2–8, and registration, Rev. 20:12, 15).

Revelation is a difficult book. At present I would not wish to draw too much on its legal language. To do so would require a complete exposition of the book, which I cannot do. I hope this does not disappoint. There are riches there, but to try to open up that seam properly would make these present pages into a different study.

So much for the actual Epistles. Certain points may be summarized from the short discussion of each. First, the use of legal analogy is really confined to those writers who had traveled in the empire (cf. per contra James, John, and Jude). Peter makes a very special use of a technical point of citizenship he would have had cause to know about. Second, most of these uses occur in the writings of Paul, the Roman citizen and trained Jewish lawyer. He uses legal metaphors mostly in explanations and in passages teaching doctrine (cf. the Pastoral Epistles). Their didactic and illustrative function is therefore clear. From the previous appendix we know that knowledge of the Roman law was available throughout the provinces, and of course, in Rome itself. The present discussion has shown that in each of the Pauline Epistles the church addressed was situated where Roman law was likely to be known, but Paul makes least use of these analogies where this likelihood is least. Thus there are few legal analogies in the letter to Colossae, which he had not visited and did not know, though there is play made on the law of slavery and other matters in Philemon—but Paul knew Onesimus and

also Philemon, who may have labored with him in Ephesus
(Philem. 1), so that he knew how he could best address his plea
for Onesimus to him. It is difficult therefore to resist the conclusion that there is a presumption to be made that whenever
legal allusions are made in the Epistles one must find reasons
why they should not be referred to Roman law for their explanation. But this assumes that Paul knew Roman law, a question
to which we must now turn.

Paul

WHILE IT WAS POSSIBLE to deal succinctly with the probable legal knowledge of the writers of the Epistles of Peter, James, Jude, and John, we cannot deal similarly with Paul, who makes the most extensive use of legal metaphors in the New Testament Epistles. He draws individual metaphors from a variety of legal contexts in such a way that it is difficult for a lawyer like myself to do other than consider that his use of them is deliberate. Indeed, in such passages as Galatians 3:15–4:11 and Romans 6 he seems to revel in the changing pictures, in the way in which the different illustrations punch home the truths he is expounding. Consider Galatians 3:15–4:11: annulling a will, heirship, minority, and slavery—the last picked up again later in the chapter in a discussion of one of the roots of slave status, being born to a slave mother (Gal. 4:21–31). This is the sort of tumbling invention one might expect from a skilled lawyer, an advocate at the peak of his powers. The different but easily grasped images present the ideas in an attractive way and make doctrine understandable.[1]

The appropriateness and felicity of the metaphors would of themselves suggest that the use of such imagery is deliberate, but to this we may add the evidence of Paul's own life for there are factors in his background and education that support this impression. He was a Jew, a Roman citizen, and, at first, one of the brighter youngsters of the Jewish legal establishment. These factors necessarily have a bearing on how his language should be construed. They are therefore matters that require separate treatment.

Current New Testament scholarship is divided in opinion as to whether Paul spent his formative years in Tarsus or in Jerusalem. However, in either case a strong argument can be based on his education as fitting him to be a skilled user of legal illustrations.

Our knowledge of Paul's background comes from his speech to the mob in Acts 22:3: "I am a Jew, born at Tarsus in Cilicia, but brought up in this city at the feet of Gamaliel, educated according to the strict manner of the law of our fathers." The traditional interpretation of this verse is that Paul was born in

Tarsus and brought up in the Jewish traditions in his home city until he was sent to Jerusalem for his education at the feet of Gamaliel. If so, it may then be argued that Paul would have imbibed much from the cosmopolitan city of his youth. The son of a citizen of Tarsus (Acts 22:28), he could have received in particular some knowledge of the law of that city and of Roman law, the law of his personal citizenship, as part of his childhood education. Much would of course depend upon the age at which Paul went to Jerusalem. This might have been anywhere from the age of eight until the age of approximately fifteen. It is unlikely that he would have been older than fifteen since he speaks of being "brought up ... at the feet of Gamaliel," but we do know that men of quite advanced years also went to Jerusalem to study. For example, Hillel is said to have come to Jerusalem from Babylon at the age of forty.[2] If Paul went to Jerusalem in his teens, he could already have been knowledgeable in law; this would have been basically Jewish law, we may be sure, but one would expect that, as a matter of course he, as a Roman citizen (Acts 22:28) and trainee businessman (Acts 18:3), would learn some commercial law and doubtless also legal aspects of other important matters such as slavery, inheritance, and citizenship.

The traditional picture of Paul's life presents him as proficient in his studies with Gamaliel and becoming an important man of the younger generation of leaders and a leading figure in the suppression of the new deviant sect. He was then converted on the road to Damascus.

The alternative view of Paul's earlier life has been ably advanced by Professor W. C. van Unnik,[3] who suggests that the correct meaning of Acts 22:3 is that Paul was born in Tarsus but taken to Jerusalem at an early age and was "brought up," in the usual sense of the expression, in that city. On this theory Paul's formative years would have been spent in the more claustrophobic atmosphere of the center of the Jewish religion.

If this is the case it has certain important consequences for theological inquiry. Clearly it affects the long-standing debate as to whether the Pauline teaching reflects and was influenced by the traditional rabbinic teaching of Jerusalem or is more akin to the somewhat different attitudes of the Jews of the Dispersion. Dubiety as to the formative influences on Paul can give rise to much discussion,[4] but I believe that it is unimportant for the purposes of this book.

If the traditional view is correct, and Paul did spend his early life in Tarsus before going to Jerusalem as a more mature person to complete his education, then it is possible that he would have received some knowledge of the law of Tarsus and of the Roman law as part of his childhood experience. If he was brought up from an early age in Jerusalem, he would have encountered Roman law at a later stage in his life. However, in both instances it is clear that Paul did receive the traditional legal training of his time in Jerusalem before coming (again?) into contact with the laws of Rome after his conversion. In either event the case for suggesting that Paul made conscious use of legal metaphors is strong. Whatever the location of his upbringing, either set of facts makes it equally likely that he made conscious use of Roman legal metaphors.

The argument can be put quite succinctly here, although it will be necessary to demonstrate it later at greater length. Paul, having been trained in law by Gamaliel in Jerusalem and having been told by God that he was to be the Apostle to the Gentiles (Acts 9:10–19; 26:15–18), spent at least ten years in Cilicia. Some of that time he spent preaching (Gal. 1:22–23). To communicate with the Gentiles of Cilicia and with the Gentiles to whom he was to be sent, Paul would have naturally turned to his and their common law, Roman law, for figures of speech.

But to return to Paul's education, whichever of the alternative views of his childhood is selected, we have to face the fact that both Tarsus and Jerusalem do play a considerable part in the development of the man Paul. The role of each differs slightly, depending upon which one believes to have been the city of his childhood and youth, but on neither view is the other unimportant. We must therefore consider what we know about both places and about the educative possibilities in both cities. I will assume that Paul was brought up in Jerusalem, since this allows us to separate more clearly the discussion of the training available there and in Tarsus. This selection is therefore made primarily for the purposes of discussion, though I also consider it the more likely hypothesis.

The Jewish educational system developed relatively late in history, owing to the frequent instructions in the Bible that fathers ought to teach their children (e.g., Deut. 4:9; 6:7; 11:19), but by the beginning of the Christian Age rabbinic practice had produced what amounted to a system of primary, secondary, and senior schooling.[5] In the Mishnah (*Aboth* 5:21) the stages of life are summarized as follows: At five, one is ready for Scripture; at ten, for mishnah; at thirteen, for keeping the Commandments (i.e., to bear responsibility); at fifteen, for Talmud; at eighteen, for marriage; at twenty, for a trade or profession. Though this outline is somewhat idealistic, it does represent what appears to have happened. Immediately after mastering the alphabet children were directed to the Scriptures. The child was shown how to read, but it was common practice for the child simply to memorize. After thus learning the Hebrew Scriptures, a translation into Aramaic (a Targum) would quite often also have to be committed to memory along with the particular essential thoughts of Jewish liturgy. Writing would also be taught at this point.

In the secondary school the pupils were instructed in the oral law, both in the midrashic commentaries on the Scriptures and in the Mishnah—the systematic treatment of topics under appropriate headings. Instruction in the oral Torah was naturally delivered orally. As we have seen in appendix 2, this branch of the law was not reduced to writing until the Mishnah of Rabbi Judah of A.D. 200.

Only after thus mastering the written and oral law was the student ready to proceed to become one of a group studying under a rabbi. Here instruction was purely verbal and was given by discussion, by commentary, and by parable. The student would also learn by observing the rabbi as he went about his business. All this was naturally an extremely advanced level and form of instruction, and much depended upon the individual's capacity to learn and also to demonstrate his growing mastery of the law. The example of such a mode of teaching that comes naturally to mind is Jesus and His band of disciples.

Unfortunately, we cannot be completely certain as to the precise content of Paul's training, though we may note strong probabilities. His own evidence is that he had considerable reason "for confidence in the flesh." He was "circumcised on the eighth day, of the people of Israel, of the tribe of Benjamin, a Hebrew born of Hebrews; as to the law a Pharisee, as to zeal a persecutor of the church, as to righteousness under the law blameless" (Phil. 3:5–6). The reference to "a Hebrew born of Hebrews" means that he was brought up speaking Hebrew and would indicate that his education was in the rabbinic tradition. In addition we know that, as the Mishnah indicates was normal (*Aboth* 5.21, above), he had learned a trade, tent making (Acts

18:3), and he refers occasionally to working for his living (1 Cor. 4:12; 9:3–18; 1 Thess. 2:9; 2 Thess. 3:8). This does not, however, appear to have interfered with his education, for he says in Galatians 1:14 that he had "advanced in Judaism beyond many of my own age among my people, so extremely zealous was I for the traditions of my fathers." In itself this would argue for his attaining a fairly high position within the educational structure; this is confirmed by his having studied under the Rabbi Gamaliel (Acts 22:3), whose reputation even today is high. To this we may add the willingness of the Jewish authorities to allow the young man Saul to play a large part in the extirpation of the Christian sect (Acts 8:1–3) and to act as their emissary in dealing with the Christians who had fled from Jerusalem (Acts 9:1–2).

From these points I am myself content to conclude that Paul had gone through the traditional education of his time and had been successful in it, carrying it to a high level. Of course, the evidence is drawn from his own account and from Luke, who may be assumed to be sympathetic, but for me this does not invalidate the conclusion.

Getting back to the matter of Paul's training, we can say in summary that it is apparent that the rabbinic method of reasoning was similar to that found in normal present-day legal discussion. This is not to say that they are identical. The Jewish method of elaborating a passage of Scripture, for example, would often proceed by perceiving relationships between different biblical passages and different mishnaic teachings through verbal similarity of words and through elaborations of concepts; probably the closest modern parallel is the extended imagery of some Plymouth Brethren preachers.[6] But apart from these peculiarities, there is no doubt that the methods of reasoning by analogy and induction and the perception of the relevant and the irrelevant were similar to the normal activities of the legal profession today. In addition, the rabbinic education fitted a person for dealing with all of life's problems, not simply with theological problems. The law dealt with the whole of life, not just with what we today confine to "religion." The teaching given by the rabbis was to a large extent practical and down to earth—the kind of theological thinking that is of interest to the ordinary man. Paul's training therefore did fit him to deal with the legal concepts of everyday life within the body of Jewish jurisprudence, and I would argue very strongly that this made him the more likely to have learned the different rules obtaining in Roman law that governed the same facts. It is an elementary truism that a man will only become a good comparative lawyer if he first makes himself thoroughly skilled in the detail of one particular legal system. That done, he is well placed to understand and appreciate the technical differences that he will find in another system. Indeed, the differences between his own system and the new system will be a point of acute interest to the inquiring mind—and such, I would suggest, was that of Paul.

Finally, in connection with his probable Judaic training the question does arise whether Paul would have come across any Roman legal concepts in the course of his studies. This is something we cannot know for certain, but it is clear from various hints here and there that the rabbis were not indifferent to the law of Rome. We know that knowledge of Greek language and literature was common in orthodox circles until A.D. 70, and that the Romans did send legal delegations on occasion to discuss points of difference with the Jewish authorities.[8] In any event, even if there is no evidence of consistent teaching of Roman law in the rabbinic schools, nonetheless, by virtue of the presence of a Roman government and of Roman citizens—both amongst the real rulers of the province and also no doubt among the "God fearers," many of them proselytes to Judaism—there would have been some knowledge of Roman law to whet the appetite of the legal mind. Roman law might also have been of use in teaching the Jewish rules. Didactically it is occasionally useful to say to a class, "We do it this way, but other people do it in that way." The presentation of the alternative formulation helps to drive the point home.

Following his conversion Paul spent three years in Arabia (Gal. 1:17) mulling over the implications of his vision on the Damascus road (Acts 9:1–9). He then returned to Damascus and had to be lowered to safety in a basket through a window in the wall (Acts 9:23–25; 2 Cor. 11:32–33). Professor Bruce suggests that the reason why Paul fell foul of the authorities may have been that he was preaching while in Arabia, but this is uncertain.[9] Paul then went to Jerusalem to visit Peter, where he remained for fifteen days (Gal. 1:18). However, he again fell foul of the authorities, and the church in Jerusalem took him and sent him to Tarsus (Acts 9:26–30; Gal. 1:18–21). He then spent some ten years in the region of Syria and Cilicia, which was at that time an administrative province of the empire (Gal. 1:21).

In sending Paul to Tarsus the brethren in Jerusalem sent

him back to his own country, for Paul was "a Jew, from Tarsus in Cilicia, a citizen of no mean city" (Acts 21:39). He affirmed his origin before the mob (Acts 22:3) and is described as "a man of Tarsus" in Acts 9:11. It is interesting therefore in hindsight to see that Tarsus was an appropriate city from which to draw a man to do Paul's particular work. Within the Tarsian gates lived a heterogeneous community, drawing its population, traditions, and ethos from both the west and east, from Jewish, Roman, and Hellenic sources.

Tarsus was and is situated on the Cilician plain on the banks of the river Cydnus and commands the eastern approach to the principal pass through the Taurus Mountains. As Sir William Ramsay ably shows in *The Cities of St. Paul* (1907), each of these elements played an integral part in the development of the city. First, the plain of Tarsus is rich with the silt of the centuries and hence the area was well able to support a large and busy population. Given such viability for settlement all the rest followed naturally. Second, Tarsus is situated inland on the Cydnus about ten miles from the coast, but the river was navigable to the sea. It was therefore possible to form at Tarsus a harbor safe both from Mediterranean storms and from the activities of pirates. The harbor was a well-known refuge in ancient times and was the scene of many important events—for example, the meeting of Anthony and Cleopatra, which may have changed the entire course of history.

The third and final element that contributed to the development of the city was its position relative to the Taurus Range of mountains, which sprawls around the Cilician plain, cutting it off from the interior of Asia Minor and the west. The range is, therefore, a significant barrier on the east-west trade route. In classical times when transport was fairly primitive this obstacle was of even greater significance. Because it was not feasible to avoid it by sea passage throughout much of the year, the Taurus Range had to be negotiated in order to penetrate into the interior of Asia by land.

Through the Taurus Range runs a river glen that narrows to a gorge in some places. At the eastern end of the declivity the river goes through an underground passage, and further progress had to be made by foot or pack horse over a narrow track. The Tarsians apparently went to work on an alternative route, using the gullies of two small streams and a very narrow river gorge. This gorge is the famous Cilician Gates so narrow that at first the actual streambed was the route for men and beasts through which trade could pass—except in time of flood. This was not satisfactory for the Tarsians, and they formed a wagon route over the previous track and then chiseled a road out of the solid rock on the west side of the Gates. This allowed the progress of wheeled traffic through the Taurus Range all year round, with a consequent increase in the volume of trade and a lessening of the seasonal peaking of commercial traffic.

For these geographical and social reasons the city burgeoned and became one of the most important metropolises. To its gates came the trade, and in its train the culture and learning, of both principal divisions of the world. Not surprisingly, Tarsus was made the capital of its surrounding area in early times, and when the Romans arrived they made it the capital of their province of Cilicia, with status as a free city.[10]

This active, energetic, bustling city was the place of Paul's birth. It was a place of importance and a place to be proud of, as Paul certainly was (Acts 21:39). It was an exciting place to live, its disparate but synthesized elements doubtless providing great stimulus to an eager mind. In all his journeys Paul tended to head for cities and to concentrate his mission in the city environment. I would hazard a guess that this was at least partially because he felt in his element there. In any city he found nuances of his birthplace, Tarsus in Cilicia.

But it was not only economic vibrancy that made Tarsus suitable as the cradle of Paul. It had other claims to fame than its docks and commercial quarters. In the time of Augustus its university was placed by Strabo on a par with those of Athens and Alexandria.[11] Though this was probably an optimistic evaluation, it may be noted that Tarsus was in the heartland of the great philosophy of the day, Stoicism. This led to a certain restraint in the citizens and a quality of morality not found in the other trading cities of the day. Athenodorus, the philosopher and former tutor of Augustus, had lived in the city and taught in the university.[12] He taught a coherent doctrine of conscience as the most important element in man. While the connection is admittedly tenuous, earlier scholars noted that Paul frequently refers to conscience—a non-Judaic concept—in his letters. C. A. Pierce has shown that Paul's concept of conscience was probably not Stoic,[13] but if it were, it is likely that this notion was picked up by Paul in or around the cultured society at Tarsus. For Paul, though a Jew, was a citizen, and did have access to the society of his city.

His duality of citizenship is an important element in Paul. On the face of things the dual citizenship is not really surprising, given the heterogeneous nature of the Tarsian population. There had been Jews in Tarsus for centuries, but there was a significant development in their condition when the city was reconstituted by Antiochus Epiphanes in 171 B.C. Antiochus reorganized the city on the lines of a normal Greek city-state. In these extraterritorial manifestations of Greek life the burgesses, the citizens, were organized into tribes bound together by certain common religious rites. These were the subcommunities of Philippians 3:20.[14] It is extremely unlikely that a Jew would have been a member of a tribe in the ordinary city-state, since this would have involved embroilment with a pagan religion. The only way in which Jews could have avoided contamination with paganism and yet have been citizens of Tarsus was for them to have had control over the rites of one of the tribes—in other words, for there to be a Jewish tribe. There must therefore have been in Tarsus a large number of Jews, forming a tribe for the purposes of citizenship. It follows that this tribe must have been established by Antiochus.

One may go on from this to ask, as Ramsay does in The Cities of St. Paul, whether Antiochus was responsible for the settlement of the Jews in that region.[15] This is quite uncertain. Although we do know that large-scale resettlement of populations was regular practice in the Near-Eastern world of the time (cf. the relocation of the Jews in Babylon), it is equally possible that Antiochus simply added a body of Jews to an existent resident body to form the tribe.

At any rate, it is clear that the Jewish colony in Tarsus had been in existence for at least two centuries before Paul arrived on the scene. For him to have had Roman citizenship by birth as he claims (Acts 22:25–28) he must also have had Tarsian citizenship by birth, indicating that his family would have been well established in the city. Though Dio (Orationes 32.33) says that citizenship in Tarsus might be bought in his day for five hundred drachmas and that dyers, cobblers, and common artisans were therefore citizens, this does not depreciate Paul's own family's standing. We know that they were well enough off to send their son to Jerusalem for his education.[16]

As a Roman citizen, Paul was a member of the governing

community—in many ways occupying a position analogous to that of the British citizen in the hey-day of the raj. Indeed Professor F. F. Bruce quotes a more extreme formulation of this point, which is not inaccurate. Sir William Calder wrote to him ". . . Paul was a great swell—compare recently, mutatis mutandis, a Hindu K. B. E."[17]

Of course, Paul was a provincial Roman. His citizenship depended both on his birth to a Roman citizen father and upon his birth having been duly registered by his father in the Roman provincial archives for Cilicia.[18] An official copy of the register would have been obtained and either kept in the family archives or carried by Paul. Alternatively, he could prove his citizenship by reference to the taxation census archives.[19] However, since these were primarily for provincial tax purposes, it seems more likely that Paul would have had recourse to his "birth certificate." It may be that Paul had two copies—one to remain in Tarsus, and one to take with him. The possession of proof of his citizenship would seem a reasonable precaution for the Apostle to the Gentiles to have taken.

From all this I would suggest that when Paul was sent from Jerusalem back to Tarsus he would have been in a good position to have made use of such facilities as were available for his purposes. He knew that he was to be the Apostle to the Gentiles (Acts 9:10–17; 26:15–18), and that would have two consequences.

First, Paul was a citizen of the empire. He already had had intimation that the rest of his life was to be spent traveling round the empire preaching the gospel, and it would seem only prudent that he should therefore seek to know some of the detail of the law of his citizenship, Roman law.

Second, Paul would at the same time have been thinking through the gospel and how to present it. We know from his own testimony that he was preaching the gospel to the Gentiles in Cilicia during this ten-year period of his life (Gal. 1:21–23). I would suggest therefore that it is likely that he would have been seeking ways to make his message understood by those who were listening to it. He would have sought to familiarize himself with gentile thought and expressions so that he could communicate with them. He was working out of Tarsus, a university city and provincial capital where Roman law was known and expounded, for Roman law was studied in such provincial capitals. Indeed, some of the greatest jurists began their careers as provincials, Gaius being but one.[20] The opportunity for knowledge was at hand, both during his "ten-year silence" and, I would also suggest, during the one year he ministered with Barnabas in Syrian Antioch (Acts 11:26), to say nothing of his later travels. Therefore, for a citizen of the empire and someone of already considerable legal training, albeit in a different legal system, it would have been natural that Paul would see the concepts of the Roman law both as practically useful to an itinerant citizen of the empire and as a kind of *lingua franca* of illustrations for the gospel he was commissioned to preach. Both needs were met by the same body of lore. The confirmatory evidence is his facility with the legal metaphors found in his epistles, which are explored in the main text of this book.

Notes

Note numbers in cross-references may refer either to specific notes ("chap. 2, n. 3") or to the location of the note number in the text ("chap. 2 at n. 3").

Chapter 1

Introduction

1. Herbert M. Gale, *The Use of Analogy in the Letters of Paul* (Philadelphia: Westminster Press, 1965).

2. Cf. app. 1, "Of Metaphors and Analogies."

3. On the separate legal systems, see app. 2, "The Systems of Law."

4. For what follows, see also app. 2.

5. See, for example, the discussion of the concept of the freedman in chap. 2, following n. 12 (pp. 39–46).

6. Cf. app. 3, "Law in the Provinces."

7. Cf. app. 4, "The Epistles."

8. Cf. app. 5, "Paul."

9. See chap. 3, following n. 21 (pp. 62–63) and app. 5 at n. 17 and following n. 19 (pp. 248–49).

10. See Ball; Muntz; and Septimus Buss, *Roman Law and History in the New Testament* (London: Rivingtons, 1901).

11. E.g., Greer M. Taylor, "The Use of Pistis Christou in Galatians," *JBL* 85 (1966):58–76 (see chap. 7); F. W. Danker, "Under Contract" in E. H. Barth and R. E. Cocroft, eds., *Festschrift to Honour F. Wilbur Gingrich* (Leiden: Brill, 1972), 91–114; J. Paul Sampley, " 'Before God I Do not Lie' (Gal. 1:20), Paul's Self-Defense in the Light of Roman Legal Praxis," *New Testament Studies* 23 (1977):477–82; idem, *Pauline Partnership in Christ* (Philadelphia: Fortress, 1980). A major stimulus to the investigation of legal elements in the Epistles has been the work of J. D. M. Derrett. His *Law in the New Testament* (see Abbreviations) is a pioneering work. Later articles are collected in his *Studies in the New Testament*, 3 vols. to date (Leiden: Brill, 1977–).

Chapter 2

The Slave and the Freedman

The literature on the facts and law of slavery is considerable but is said not to be wholly satisfactory. A general survey is William L.

Westermann, *The Slave Systems of Greek and Roman Antiquity* (Philadelphia: American Philosophical Society, 1955); a useful collection of articles is Finley, *Slavery,* which contains a bibliographical essay on pp. 229–35.

On Roman law I have used the standard texts and Buckland, *Slavery.*

On Greek law, see: Beauchet 2:393–545 and index; Jones, *Greek Law,* 277–86; Harrison 1:163–86; McDowell, 79–83 and index.

On Jewish law there are few precise studies for the period; see Moses Mielziner, "Slavery Amongst the Ancient Hebrews," *American Theological Review* (1861):232–60, 423–38, reprinted in Ella M. F. Mielziner, ed., *Moses Mielziner, His Life and Works* (New York: Privately printed, 1931), 64–103; J. P. M. van der Ploeg, "Slavery in the Old Testament," *Vetus Testamentum,* Supplement No. 22 (1971):72–87; E. E. Urbach, "The Law Regarding Slavery," *Papers of the Institute of Jewish Studies* (London, 1964) 1:1–94.

Material is however available from Cohen, vol. 1; Baron; and Horowitz and is cited in the notes. The earlier law is outlined in De Vaux, 80–90, with a bibliography on p. 525. Juster 2:71–77 is a rather concise survey of the whole period from ancient times to Justinian. Cohn, 231–36 ("Slavery"), gives a very compressed account.

1. Arnold H. M. Jones, "Slavery in the Ancient World," *Economic History Review* 9 (1956):185–99 (cf. Finley, *Slavery,* 1–15); Robert C. Grant, "The Economic Background of the New Testament," in William D. Davies and David Daube, eds., *The Background of the New Testament and its Eschatology: In Honour of C. H. Dodd* (Cambridge: Cambridge University Press, 1956); Mikhail Rostovzeff, *The Social and Economic History of the Roman Empire,* 2nd ed., rev. P. M. Fraser et al., 2 vols. (Oxford: Clarendon, 1957). Cf. Moses I. Finley, "Was Greek Civilization Based on Slave Labour?" *Historia* 8 (1959):145–64 (cf. Finley, *Slavery,* 53–73); Jones, *Greek Law,* 57–59.

2. See previous note and Buckland, *Slavery,* 6–9; Reginald H. Barrow, *Slavery in the Roman Empire* (London: Methuen, 1928; London: Barnes and Noble, 1968); Crook, 179–205; Moses I. Finley, "Between Slavery and Freedom," *Comparative Studies in Society and History* (1963–64):232–49; Arnold M. Duff, *Freedmen in the Early Roman Empire* (Oxford: Clarendon, 1928; Cambridge: W. Heffer and Sons, 1958), 1–11; Millar, 69–83 ("Imperial Freedmen").

3. Buckland, *Slavery,* 291–98 covers all the topic; Buckland, *Textbook,* 67–68; Thomas, 391.

4. Buckland, *Slavery,* 304–17. Cf. chap. 3, n. 20 and chap. 9, n. 16.

5. Buckland, *Slavery,* 397–401; Buckland, *Textbook,* 68–69; Thomas, 390.

6. On this passage and the whole question of the "Pauline privilege," see David Daube, "Pauline Contributions to a Pluralistic Culture: Re-creation and Beyond" in Donald G. Miller and Dikran Y. Hadidian, eds., *Jesus and Man's Hope*, 2 vols. (Pittsburgh: Pittsburgh Theological Seminary, 1971) 2:233–45; idem, "Biblical Landmarks in the Struggle for Women's Rights," *Juridical Review* (1978):177-97 at 184–87; idem, "Historical Aspects of Informal Marriage," *RIDA* 25 (1978):95–101 at 101–2.

7. Buckland, *Slavery*, 420–22. The sale of a child was the basis of adoption (Buckland, *Textbook*, 71); cf. chap. 4 at n. 33 (pp. 86-87).

8. Buckland, *Slavery*, 427–33; Buckland, *Textbook*, 71; Thomas, 393; Crook, 58–61.

9. For what follows see Buckland, *Slavery*, 10–396; Buckland, *Textbook*, 61–67; Crook, 55–57; Thomas, 393–96.

   Jewish slavery was somewhat different; the slave was not so free to act, whether on his own account or in his master's business. See Cohen 1:122–58 ("The Law of Persons"), 1:159–78 ("Civil Bondage"), 1:179–278 ("Peculium"); Horowitz, 244–52; Falk, *Hebrew Law*, 117–22; Falk, *Jewish Law*, 2:263–68. In any event, there were not many Jewish slaves: Baron 1:267–71.

   In Greek law there is a greater correspondence with the Roman position, though we do not know if the Greek owner was liable for obligations entered into by his slave. See Jones, *Greek Law*, 277–86; Harrison 1:163–80; Beauchet, 2:393–545 and index; McDowell, 79–82 and index.

10. Buckland, *Slavery*, 187–206; Buckland, *Textbook*, 65, 533–35.

11. Buckland, *Slavery*, 39–72; Buckland, *Textbook*, 63.

12. Buckland, *Slavery*, 437–551; Buckland, *Textbook*, 72–82; Thomas, 397–401; Duff, *Freedmen* (see above, n. 2), 12–35.

13. See the comparison in Cohen 1:146–55.

14. Baron 1:267, 412. Raymond Westbrook, "Jubilee Laws," *Israel Law Review* 6 (1971):209–26.

15. Baron 1:268.

16. Horowitz, 246–51.

17. Conceivably the synagogue of freedmen consisted of Jews who had been slaves in the empire and had returned to Palestine on being manumitted (freed) by their owners. If so, these might import Roman notions. Cf. Smallwood, 132; R. P. L.-H. Vincent, "Découverte de la 'Synagogue des Affranchis' a Jerusalem," *Revue Biblique* 30 (1921):247–77.

18. Harrison 1:181–86 ("Freedmen"); McDowell, 82–83; cf. Raphael Taubenschlag, *The Law of Graeco-Roman Egypt in the Light of the Papyri*, 2nd ed. (Warsaw: Panstwowe Wydawnictwo Naukowe,

1955), 96–101; William L. Westermann, "Slavery and the Elements of Freedom in Ancient Greece," *Quarterly Bulletin of the Polish Institute of Arts and Sciences in America* (1943):1–16 (cf. Finley, *Slavery,* 17–32); Moses I. Finley, "The Servile Statuses of Ancient Greece," *RIDA* 7 (1960):165–89.

19. Jones, *Greek Law,* 212–13; C. Bradford Welles, "Manumission and Adoption," *RIDA* 3 (1949):507–520; William L. Westermann, "The Paramone as a General Service Contract," *Journal of Juristic Papyrology* 2 (1948):9–50.

20. Harrison 1:184–86.

21. See app. 4 on 1 and 2 Corinthians.

22. Cf. chap. 3 at n. 18 (pp. 60-66).

23. Duff, *Freedmen* (see above, n. 2); Susan M. Treggiari, *Roman Freedmen during the Late Republic* (Oxford: Clarendon, 1969); Buckland, *Textbook,* 87–90; Crook, 50–55 and index s.v. "freedmen."

24. Gustav A. Deissman, *Light from the Ancient East,* trans. Lionel R. M. Strachan (London: Hodder and Stoughton, 1910), 326–30; idem, *Paul: A Study in Social and Religious History,* trans. William E. Wilson (London: Hodder and Stoughton, 1926), 172–76. Cf. Charles K. Barrett, *The New Testament Background: Selected Documents* (London: S.P.C.K., 1956, 1971), 52–53.

Chapter 3

Aliens and Citizens

For this chapter the primary source is Adrian N. Sherwin-White, *Citizenship,* 2nd ed., though the first edition of 1939 is not misleading for our purposes. John P. V. D. Balsdon, *Romans and Aliens* (London: Duckworth, 1979) is a fascinating detailed discussion. Juster presents a contrasting exposition of the Jewish point of view.

1. Augustine's *City of God,* recently readably translated by Henry Bettenson (London: Penguin Books, 1972), refers in its opening paragraphs to aliens and strangers. Cf. John N. Figgis, *The Political Aspects of S. Augustine's City of God* (London: Longmans, 1921); Ernest Barker, "St. Augustine's Theory of Society" and "The Community and the Church," Essays 8 and 9 of his *Essays on Government,* 2nd ed. (Oxford: Clarendon, 1951, 1965), 234–98.

2. Jones, *Greek Law,* 47–57, esp. 55. By the time of the Epistles many such treaties would have existed.

3. Cf. Smallwood, index; Juster; Falk, *Jewish Law*, 2:269–75; and general histories of the region and time.

4. Horowitz, 131–32; cf. Falk, *Jewish Law*, 2:272–73.

5. Horowitz, 231–37; Falk, *Hebrew Law*, 115–17.

6. Horowitz, 234–35; cf. Falk, *Jewish Law*, 2:273–74. To be fair, Horowitz does state that the truer spirit of Jewish law was against this (quoting the Babylonian Talmud, *Bava Kamma* 113a), but the practice existed.

7. Babylonian Talmud, *Bava Kamma* 38a; Horowitz, 236. Cf. Cohen 1:24–27; Mishnah, *Baba Kamma* 4.3; Baron 2:300–301 and extensive note on 430–31 (n. 10).

8. Baron 2:59–62; Smallwood, index, s.v. "Messiah"; Michael Grant, *The Jews in the Roman World* (London: Weidenfeld and Nicolson, 1973), index, s.v. "Messiah."

9. See app. 3. Cf. the attitude of Gallio toward the Jews (Acts 18:12–17) and of the town clerk of Ephesus (Acts 19:35–41).

10. Peter Garnsey, *Social Status and Legal Privilege in the Roman Empire* (Oxford: Clarendon, 1970) is an exposition of this feature.

11. Cf. Acts 23:33–35, where the governor wanted to know Paul's province of origin, and Pilate's attempt to refer the question of Jesus to Herod (Luke 23:6–12). Justinian's *Digest* contains examples of this principle working between provinces (e.g., D.5.1.65; 5.1.2.4–5; 5.2.29.4; 2.8.7 pr); cf. *Codex* 3.13.2, and *Codex Theodosianus* 2.1.4, to the effect that a "plaintiff shall follow the forum of the defendant"; Garnsey, *Social Status* (see above, n. 10), 13–15.

12. See app. 2 at n. 7 (pp. 195–196).

13. Sherwin-White, *Society*, 184–85; Smallwood, 225–30 and index; Ramsay, *Letters*, 142–57. Cf. app. 5 at n. 14 (p. 247). Perhaps Paul, or his family, were part of the Jewish *politeuma* in Tarsus. Cf. Paul C. Bottger, "Die eschatologische Existenz der Christen. Erwagungen zu Philipper 3:20," *Zeitschrift für die neutestamentliche Wissenschaft* 60 (1969):244–63; A. T. Lincoln, "A Re-examination of 'The Heavenlies' in Ephesians," *New Testament Studies* 19 (1973):482.

14. Cf. Lacey, 222–24; Harrison 2:205–7; McDowell, 67–75 (citizens), 75–79 (aliens).

15. E.g., Alexandria—see Peter M. Fraser, *Ptolemaic Alexandria* (Oxford: Clarendon, 1972), index, s.v. the various communities, Jews, etc.); Caesarea—see Lee I. Levine, *Caesarea under Roman Rule* (Leiden: Brill, 1975), 61–85.

16. Sherwin-White, *Citizenship*, 251–74, 399–444, though the evidence is later than our time; Garnsey, *Social Status* (see above

n. 10), 268–69; Millar, 394–410 ("Provincial Communities: The Acquisition of City Status"), 410–20 ("The Cities: Diplomacy and the Retention of Privileges"). Cf. app. 3, pp. 216–17.

17. Lidia S. Mazzolani, *The Idea of the City in Roman Thought,* trans. S. O'Donnell (London: Hollis and Carter; Bloomington: Indiana University Press, 1970), 142–200.

18. Cf. chap. 2 at n. 22 (pp. 42-43). Sherwin-White, *Citizenship,* 322–31.

19. Cf. Rev. 3:5; 13:8; 17:8; 20:12, 15; 21:27; 22:19. Registration is first clearly mentioned in the Bible in Dan. 12:1 and Ezek. 13:9. Cf. Sherwin-White, *Citizenship,* 314–16; and materials cited in app. 4, nn. 12, 13. On manumission by census, see Buckland, *Slavery,* 439–441; Buckland, *Textbook,* 72–73. Cf. chap. 4, n. 27 and app. 5 at n. 18 (p. 248).

20. The translation and the note on p. 16 of John Calvin *Institutes of the Christian Religion,* trans. Ford L. Battles, ed. John T. McNeill (London: S.C.M.; Philadelphia: Westminster, 1960) fail to take the legal point. In his *Address to King Francis,* Calvin says that the truth has been recovered and freed in the public law sense of a return from slavery and bondage, not in a private law sense of being brought into the household once more. Calvin was a trained lawyer.

21. Buckland, *Textbook,* 96–98; Jolowicz, *Introduction,* 58–71; Jolowicz, *Introduction 3,* 58–71.

22. Cf. app. 3 at n. 10 (p. 214); Garnsey, *Social Status* (see above, n. 10), 268–69.

23. The appeal against the act of authority was by the Lex Julia. See Sherwin-White, *Society,* 59–70; Millar, 507–16 ("Appeals to the Emperor"); Arnold H. M. Jones, "I Appeal unto Caesar" in G. E. Mylonas, ed., *Studies Presented to David Moore Robinson* (St. Louis: Washington University Press, 1952), reprinted in Arnold H. M. Jones, *Studies in Roman Government and Law* (Oxford: Blackwell, 1960), 51–65; Peter Garnsey, "The Lex Julia and Appeal under the Empire," *JRS* 56 (1966):167–89.

24. Ramsay, *Letters,* 439 n. 8, indicates that Romans might have some citizenship status in certain eastern cities. Cf. Jolowicz, *Introduction,* 542–47; Jolowicz, *Introduction 3,* 71–74; Sherwin-White, *Citizenship,* 291–313.

25. Jolowicz, *Introduction,* 542–47; Jolowicz, *Introduction 3,* 71–74; Sherwin-White, *Citizenship,* 291–313. On an interesting edict of Augustus from Cyrene of 6 B.C., see esp. Sherwin-White, *Citizenship,* 304–6, 334–35; and Millar, 344, 479. The edict is printed in Fontes, 1:408. Cf. the banning of the taking of holy orders to avoid civic responsibility in the later empire (e.g., *Theodosian Code* 16.2.3

and 6; see translation and commentary by Clyde Pharr, *The Theodosian Code* [Princeton: Princeton University Press, 1952]).

Chapter 4

Adoption

The main authorities for this chapter have been the standard texts on Roman and Jewish law (see introductory note to app. 2). On the Jewish position the following have also been used: Leggett; Eryl W. Davies, "Inheritance Rights and the Hebrew Levirate Marriage," *Vetus Testamentum* 31 (1981):138–44, 257–67; David R. Mace, *Hebrew Marriage: a Sociological Study* (London: Epworth, 1953).

Other material not cited includes Hester and J. H. Tigay, "Adoption," *Encyclopedia Judaica*, ed. Cecil Roth and Geoffrey Wigoder, 16 vols. (Jerusalem: Keter, 1971–73) 2:298–301; Marcel-Henri Prevost, "Remarques sur l'Adoption dans la Bible," *RIDA* 14 (1967):67–77.

1. Cf. The Larger Catechism agreed upon by the Westminster Assembly, Qu. 74: "What is adoption?—Adoption is an act of the free grace of God, in and for his only Son Jesus Christ, whereby all those that are justified are received into the number of his children, have his name put upon them, the Spirit of his Son given to them, are under his fatherly care and dispensation, admitted to all the liberties and privileges of the sons of God, made heirs of all the promises, and fellow-heirs with Christ in glory."

The same question is no. 34 of the Shorter Catechism and is answered: "Adoption is the act of God's free grace, whereby we are received into the number, and have right to all the privileges of the Sons of God."

2. Falk, *Hebrew Law*, 162–64.

3. Cf. Daniel J. Theron, "'Adoption' in the Pauline Corpus," *Evangelical Quarterly* 28 (1956):6–14, at n. 14.

4. Ball, 1–13 (*Contemporary Review* 60 [1891]:280–83); Muntz, 111–23. Cf. James S. Candlish, art. "Adoption" in James Hastings, ed., *A Dictionary of the Bible*, 4 vols. (Edinburgh: T. & T. Clark, 1898–1902) 1:40–42. Ramsay, *Commentary*, 338, quotes Anton Halmel, *Das römische Recht im Galaterbrief* (Essen: Baedeker, 1895) as being to the same effect. I have not read that work.

5. Archibald A. Hodge, *A Commentary on the Confession of Faith* (Philadelphia: Presbyterian Board for Publication, 1901; London:

Banner of Truth, 1958), 191–93 at n. 192; cf. Thornton Whaling, "Adoption," *Princeton Theological Review* 21 (1923):223–35.

6. On Roman ideas, cf. chap. 5 at n. 5 (pp. 108-109). For the Greek position, cf. McDowell, 99–101; Lacey, 2–8. For adoption in the interests of a child, cf. *below* at n. 17 (p. 77); the adoption of a female would also fall into such a category.

7. Horowitz, 259–65; Cohn, 440–41. Cohen does not mention adoption.

8. Mace, *Hebrew Marriage* (see introductory note), 201–20.

9. Mace, *Hebrew Marriage*, 205–6, 213; Cohn, 429–32 ("Yuhasin" [i.e., status arising from parentage]).

10. Horowitz, 261–63; Cohn, 435–38 ("Mamzer"). Certain religious offices and rituals were barred to the bastard, without otherwise affecting his membership in the family.

11. Cf. the banishment of Ishmael (Gen. 21:8–13). Cf. Mace, *Hebrew Marriage*, 261; Horowitz 264–65. Samuel Feigin, reading in modern concepts of legitimacy, considers Jepthah a case of adoption: "Some Cases of Adoption in Israel," *JBL* 50 (1931):186–200.

12. Mishnah, *Yebamoth* and index; Mace, *Hebrew Marriage*, 95–118; de Vaux, 11, 21–22, 37–38, 166–67; Leggett, 29–62; Eryl W. Davies, "Inheritance Rights" (see introductory note); Raymond L. Westbrook, "The Law of the Biblical Levirate," *RIDA* 24 (1977):65–87. Cf. chap. 9 at n. 10 (pp. 160-61).

13. Horowitz, 283–85; Cohn, 403–9 ("Levirate Marriage and Halizah").

14. Cf. James G. Frazer, *Folklore in the Old Testament*, 3 vols. (London: MacMillan, 1918) 2:266–341; Godfrey R. Driver and John C. Miles, *The Assyrian Laws* (Oxford: Clarendon, 1935); ibid., with supplementary notes and corrections by Godfrey R. Driver (Aalen, Germany: Scientia Verlag, 1975), 240–50; Leggett, 9–27.

15. Horowitz, 284; Cohn, 407–9 ("Problems of Levirate Marriage: Problems of Halizah"); cf. Mishnah, *Yebamoth*.

16. Leggett, passim, is very interesting on the whole question of Ruth.

17. Godfrey R. Driver and John C. Miles, *The Babylonian Laws*, 2 vols. (Oxford: Clarendon, 1952) 1:383–405.

18. Feigin (see above, n. 11), 196–200.

19. William H. Rossell, "New Testament Adoption—Graeco-Roman or Semitic?" *JBL* 71 (1952):233–34.

20. Dieter Nörr, "Civil Law in the Gospels," *Irish Jurist* 1 (1966):328–40.

21. See later in this chapter; chap. 5, "Inheritance"; chap. 6, "The Father's Household."

22. Sigmund O. P. Mowinckel, *He That Cometh,* trans. George W. Anderson (Oxford: Blackwell, 1956), esp. 37, 78.

23. Ze'ev W. Falk, "Legal Archaeology," *Iura* 17 (1966):167–173.

24. Harry G. Leon, *The Jews of Ancient Rome* (Philadelphia: Jewish Publication Society of America, 1960), 232–33.

25. Reuven Yaron, *Introduction to the Law of the Aramaic Papyri* (Oxford: Clarendon, 1961), 40–41. In *Gifts in Contemplation of Death in Jewish and Roman Law* (Oxford: Clarendon, 1960), 6–7, Professor Yaron notes that there is no satisfactory example of adoption as a succession device, though there may be hints of such in some documents. The special field of his interest is indicated by the title. Such gifts do not require submission to the authority of the donor or entry into the family.

26. Horowitz, 263; Cohn, 438–40 ("Orphan"), 440–41 ("Adoption") discusses this informal proceeding.

27. Cf. Fritz Schulz, "Roman Registers of Births and Birth Certificates," *JRS* 32 (1942):78–91; 33 (1943):55–64; Sherwin-White, *Citizenship,* 314–16; Sherwin-White, *Society,* 146–49; John D. M. Derrett, "Further Light on the Narratives of the Nativity," *Novum Testamentum* 17 (1975):81-108 at 87–94. Cf. also chap. 3 at n. 19 (p. 61); app. 5 at nn. 18–19 (p. 248).

   Appropriate registration of a child or a person was very important in societies of the time. We know of one Roman case where registration in due form changed status. By the *Lex Aelia Sentia* a valid marriage between certain non-Romans contracted before seven witnesses allowed the man to demand Roman citizenship for himself, his wife, and his child when the couple had a child one year old; Gaius, *Institutes* 1.29–32; Percy E. Corbett, *The Roman Law of Marriage* (Oxford: Clarendon, 1930, 1969), 100–101. The *lex* also allowed registration to cure defects caused by mistake of status (Gaius, *Institutes* 1.65–73); cf. Crook, 46–50.

28. Cf. William M. Calder, "Adoption and Inheritance in Galatia," *Journal of Theological Studies* 31 (1930):372–74, suggests a local referent for the Galatian example based on two inscriptions. Cf. also app. 4, n. 4.

29. Cf. chap. 5, "Inheritance"; app. 5, "Paul."

30. Cf. chap. 5 at n. 5 (pp. 108-9).

31. Gaius, *Institutes* 1.97–107; Buckland, *Textbook,* 124–28; Jolowicz, *Introduction,* 119–20; Jolowicz, *Introduction 3,* 120; Thomas, 437–39; Schulz, *Roman Law,* 144–48.

32. Ball, 38–39 (*Contemporary Review* 60 [1891]:283). Exorcism of the person to be baptized used also to be required; cf. Oswald J. Reichel, *A Complete Manual of Canon Law*, 2 vols. (London: Hodges, 1896), vol. 1, *The Sacraments*, 34, 38, 47, 313.

33. Gaius, *Institutes* 1.87–107; Buckland, *Textbook*, 121–24; Jolowicz, *Introduction*, 119; Jolowicz, *Introduction* 3, 119–20; Thomas, 439–41; Schulz, *Roman Law*, 146.

34. Cf. chap. 2, "Slavery"; chap. 5, "Inheritance," particularly the section on heirs; and chap. 6, "The Father's Household."

35. *Isaeus*, trans. Edward S. Forster, Loeb Classical Library (London: Heinemann; Cambridge, Mass.: Harvard University Press, 1927).

36. Peter W. von Martitz and Eduard Schweizer, articles on *huios* and *huiothesia*, in Gerhard Kittel and Gerhard Friedrich, eds., *Theological Wordbook of the New Testament*, trans. Geoffrey W. Bromiley, 10 vols. (Grand Rapids: Eerdmans, 1964–76) 8:334–99.

37. Lacey, 10, 242 n. 41. Cf. McDowell, 103–8, for a discussion of the case of the estate of Hagnias.

38. Harrison 1:82–96; Jones, *Greek Law*, 196–97; Lacey, 145–46; McDowell, 100–1; Beauchet 2:1–72.

39. Harrison 1:89–90; Lacey, 145; McDowell, 100–101.

40. Harrison 1:90–93; Lacey, 145; McDowell, 101.

41. Harrison 1:84–87; Lacey, 145–46; McDowell, 101–2.

42. Lacey, 96–97 and index (s.v. "religion," "family," and "adoption") McDowell, 99.

43. Harrison 1:201–5; Lacey, 23, 33–99; McDowell, 84–86, 133–34; Beauchet, vol. 3, deals with the law of property. Cf. also Lacey, 220–21, on the tenacity of Greek claims to land.

44. The *epikleros* was a daughter who had inherited or would do so, since she had no brothers. There was a duty, though not an absolute one, laid on her next of kin to marry her so that her estate would not pass out of the family. Harrison 1:132–38; Lacey, 139–45; McDowell, 95–98.

45. Cf. McDowell's discussion of the case of Hagnias, which may have dragged on for fifty years (McDowell, 104–8). The Greeks, as that case shows, thought of the estate in actual physical terms—a piece of property—and not in modern terms of a sum of money; cf. McDowell, 108.

46. Cf. the position of the *epikleroi* (see above, n. 44).

47. Harrison 1:88; Lacey, 145; McDowell, 100. Note also the discussion at the beginning of this chapter (p. 70), differentiating succession and membership in the family.

48. Lacey, 145, quoting *Isaeus* 2.10–12.

49. Harrison 1:23–24, 93–94.

50. Harrison 1:74; Lacey, 84–99; McDowell, 69, 84–86, 92.

51. Beauchet 2:74–146; Lacey, 21–22 and index, s.v. "*kyrios*"; Mc-Dowell, 84–86, 91–92; Harrison 1:70–81.

52. On paternal powers over offspring, contrast Harrison, ibid., with Buckland, *Textbook*, 102–4; Jolowicz, *Introduction*, 118–20, 248–49; Jolowicz, *Introduction 3*, 118–20, 238–39; Thomas, 414–16.

53. Harrison 1:85; Lacey, 24–25, 146.

54. Lacey, 25 (quoting Demosthenes 44.36–42, but expressing some doubt as to the reliability of the evidence), 93 (quoting the same passage), 106; but cf. Lacey, 97 at n. 71.

55. Harrison 1:94: Lacey, 146.

56. See above at nn. 35–37 (p. 89).

57. Lacey, 231.

58. Cf. app. 5, "Paul."

59. Cf. app. 4 on Romans, Galatians, and Ephesians (pp. 225–32).

60. Cf. chap. 6, "The Father's Household," p. 121.

Chapter 5

Inheritance

Much of the material on Roman law is in the main discussion in the major texts; these have to be supplemented by use of their indices.

For theology I have used standard biblical encyclopedias and dictionaries as sources and guides. I would mention particularly Hester as a discussion that does attempt to draw on legal sources. Most of the theological writing confines itself to the concept of inheritance as it has been developed within theological discussion. Ball, 13–28, 29–37 (*Contemporary Review* 60 [1891]:284–86, 288–91), outlines the thinking adopted in this chapter.

1. Hester avoids many of these imprecisions but does not always fully press through the Roman notions, although he sees Roman law as the probable source of Paul's images; Hester, 9.

2. Cf. chap. 7 at n. 15 (p. 139); app. 5 at n. 16 (p. 247).

3. See William D. Davies, *The Gospel and the Land: Early Christianity*

and Jewish Territorial Doctrine (Berkeley: University of California Press, 1974).

4. Horowitz, 378–401; Falk, *Jewish Law* 2:335–37. Yet there is the reference to the heir in the parable of the wicked vinedressers (Matt. 21:38; Mark 12:7; Luke 20:14). This I take as colloquial use. It does diminish but does not destroy what has been said. The legal position is as written. On the parable, see Derrett, 286–312. The killing of the heir is rejection of the title of the owner.

5. Reference point for chap. 4, n. 30; cf. discussion at that note and following, with references. On the Roman rules of succession most of the data for the following pages is drawn from the standard texts; see their indices.

6. See preceding note; Oliver W. Holmes, *The Common Law*, ed. Mark D. Howe (London: Macmillan, 1968), 267–68; Carl W. Westrup, *Introduction to Early Roman Law: Comparative Sociological Studies*, trans. Annie L. Fausbøll, 5 vols. (London: Oxford University Press, 1934–50) 3:219–29 (Vols. 1–3 are based on the theme of the patriarchal joint family, which is connected with the question). See also chap. 6 at n. 4 (p. 120) and material cited in chap. 6, n. 1 and chap. 8, n. 1. This line of argument is rejected by Schulz (*Roman Law*, 215).

7. Cf. chap. 2 at n. 10 (p. 38); Derrett, 100–125 ("The Parable of the Prodigal Son").

8. Horowitz, 422–27; Cohn, 441–45 ("Apotropos [Guardian]"). Horowitz discusses the alternate form, *epitropos*. Both words were applied by the Jews to the same concept; it was a matter of pronunciation.

9. The Vulgate translates *epitropos*, "guardian," as *tutor*; the power of the *tutor* was the *tutela*, the tutory of a young child lacking judgment. The powers of such tutory were related to the progress of the child, but abuse was possible. See Buckland, *Textbook*, 142–67; Jolowicz, *Introduction*, 120–22, 249–50 and index; Jolowicz, *Introduction 3*, 121–22, 239–40 and index; Schulz, *Roman Law*, 162–80; Thomas, 453–63.

10. Cf. chap. 4 following n. 30 (pp. 84-88).

11. Horowitz, 398–99; Falk, *Jewish Law* 2:347–49.

12. Gaius, *Institutes* 3.15a (material found in Egypt and included in the De Zulueta version). On the idea of the joint family, see material cited in n. 6, above; chap. 6, n. 1; and chap. 8, n. 1. On coownership, see Thomas 323–26; Buckland, *Textbook*, 318; and John A. Crook, "Patria Potestas," *Classical Quarterly* 17 (1967):113–22.

13. Mishnah, *Baba Bathra* 8.5; Falk, *Jewish Law* 2:340–47; Reuven Yaron, *Gifts in Contemplation of Death in Jewish and Roman Law* (Oxford: Clarendon, 1960), 39.

Chapter 6

The Father's Household

Although this chapter brings together many of the ideas dealt with in earlier chapters, I have considered it better not to attempt full cross referencing, on the assumption that the other chapters have already been read.

1. See Carl W. Westrup, *Introduction to Early Roman Law* (see chap. 5, n. 6), esp. vol. 3; Henry J. S. Maine, *Ancient Law*, 10th ed. with introduction and notes by Fredrick Pollock (London: John Murray, 1920), 123–230. For rejection, see Schulz, *Roman Law*, 215. A summary of views is found in Geoffrey D. MacCormack, "Hausgemeinschaft and Consortium," *Zeitschrift für Vergleichende Rechtswissenschaft* 76 (1977):1–17. Cf. chap. 5 at nn. 6 and 12 (pp. 109, 115); chap. 8, n. 1.

2. *Monumentum Ancyranum*, 35. 6. 24–27 in Ernest G. Hardy, ed., *The Monumentum Ancyranum* (Oxford: Clarendon, 1923) 162–63; Peter A. Brunt and J. M. Moore, eds., *Res Gestae Divi Augusti* (Oxford: Oxford University Press, 1967), 36–37, with commentary and notes on pp. 5, 80.

3. Cf. Horowitz, 259–65; Beauchet 2:73–102.

4. Chap. 4 at n. 30 (p. 84), chap. 5 at n. 5 (p. 108).

5. John P. V. D. Balsdon, *Roman Women* (London: Bodley Head, 1962) and his *Life and Leisure in Ancient Rome* (London: Bodley Head, 1969) have interesting and relevant data.

6. Derrett, 461–71 ("Romans vii, 1–4. The Relationship with the Resurrected Christ").

7. On the status of the wife, see Buckland, *Textbook*, 104–16, 118–20; Jolowicz, *Introduction*, 112–18; Jolowicz, *Introduction 3*, 114–18; Schulz, *Roman Law*, 101–37; Thomas, 419–31; Percy E. Corbett, *The Roman Law of Marriage* (Oxford: Clarendon, 1930, 1969).

8. Tacitus, *Annals* 13.32. On the family council, see also Wolfgang Künkel, "Das Konsilium im Hausgericht," *Zeitschrift der Savigny-Stiftung für Rechtsgeschichte*, Romanistische Abteilung, 88 (1966):219–51 (also in Künkel's *Kleine Schriften* [Weimar: Bohlaus Nachfolger, 1974], 117–49). On the right of punishment, see Reuven Yaron, "Vitae Necisque Potestas," *Tijdschrift voor Rechtsgeschiedenis* 30 (1962):243–51.

9. Yaron, "Vitae Necisque Potestas," 250–51.

10. In 2 Corinthians 4:17 Paul speaks of our "light affliction" that works for us "a far more exceeding and eternal weight of glory." The

Greek word rendered "affliction" is *thlipsis*, which means "tribulation" (Latin, *tribulatio*) rather than "punishment" (*castigatio*). The Vulgate renders this correctly, *momentaneum et leve tribulationis nostrae.*

11. Cf. C. S. Lewis, *The Pilgrim's Regress,* 3rd ed. (London: Geoffrey Bles, 1950; reprint ed. London: Collins, 1977), 180–82 ("The Black Hole"); idem, *The Problem of Pain* (London: Geoffrey Bles, 1940; many reprint editions), 106–16.

Chapter 7

Trust: The Faith of Christ

Apart from the standard texts the main legal sources for this chapter are Erich Genzmer, "La Genèse du Fidéicommis comme Institution Juridique," *Revue Historique de Droit Francais et Étranger* (1962):319–50; Benjamin Beinart, "Fideicommissum and Modus," *Acta Juridica* (1968):157–209, esp. 157–66.

The main theological source is Greer M. Taylor, "The Function of Pistis Christou in Galatians," *JBL* 85 (1966):58–76 (hereafter cited as "Taylor").

1. Taylor, *passim.* Hester, 51 n. 1, considers Taylor's argument interesting, but an unnecessarily complex one. Goodenough (*infra,* n. 5), 46 n. 3, gives a qualified welcome to Taylor's argument, restricting it, as will be done below, to explain Gal. 3:15–4:7.

2. Taylor, 58, 67. On p. 67 the argument becomes unnecessarily complicated by the importing of ideas of adoption. These metaphors work better if there is no attempt to harmonize them.

3. See Johannes Haussleiter, *Der Glaube Jesu Christi und der christliche Glaube* (Leipzig, 1891), as quoted by William Sanday and Arthur C. Headlam, *Romans,* 5th ed., International Critical Commentary (Edinburgh: T. & T. Clark, 1902), 83. Cf. Joseph B. Lightfoot, *St. Paul's Epistle to the Galatians,* 5th ed. (London: Macmillan, 1900), 154–58 ("The Words Denoting Faith").

4. Gabriel Hebert, " 'Faithfulness' and 'Faith,' " *Theology* 58 (1955):373–79 and in *Reformed Theological Review* (Melbourne), June 1955.

5. Ibid.; Thomas F. Torrance, "One Aspect of the Biblical Conception of Faith," *Expository Times* 68 (1957):111–14, and exchange of letters with Charles F. D. Moule, *Expository Times* 68 (1957):157, 221–22; John Murray, "From Faith to Faith" in his *The Epistle to*

the Romans, 2 vols. (Grand Rapids: Eerdmans, 1960, 1975) 1:363–74; James Barr, " 'Faith' and 'Truth'—an Examination of Some Linguistic Arguments" in his *The Semantics of Biblical Language* (London: Oxford University Press, 1961), 161–205; Erwin R. Goodenough with A. T. Kraabel, "Paul and the Hellenization of Christianity" in *Religions in Antiquity: Essays in Memory of E. R. Goodenough: Fourteen Studies in the History of Religions* (Leiden: Brill, 1968):23–68; D. W. B. Robinson, " 'Faith of Jesus Christ'—A New Testament Debate," *Reformed Theological Review* (Melbourne) 29 (1970):71–81; George Howard, "Notes and Observations on the 'Faith of Christ,' " *Harvard Theological Review* 60 (1967):459–65; idem, "Romans 3:21, 31 and the Inclusion of the Gentiles," *Harvard Theological Review* 63 (1970):223–33; idem, "The 'Faith of Christ,' " *Expository Times* 85 (1974):212–15. These seem to be the main contributions to date.

6. Taylor, 66–67.

7. See chap. 3 for other disabilities. Gaius, *Institutes* 2.285, suggests this disability of peregrines as the probable origin of *fidei commissa*.

8. Cf. Antony M. Honoré, *Emperors and Lawyers* (London, Duckworth, 1981), 2–3.

9. Gaius, *Institutes* 2.260–89; Buckland, *Textbook*, 353–60; Jolowicz, *Introduction*, and Jolowicz, *Introduction 3*, see index; Crook, 125–27; Thomas, 511–14.

10. Taylor, 73 at n. 36.

11. Ibid., at n. 35.

12. Gaius, *Institutes* 2.278, states that in the provinces the governor had jurisdiction in matters of trusts.

13. Taylor, 73 at n. 34; Crook, 127; both cite s. 18 of *Der Gnomon des Idios Logos* (available in Fontes 1:469–78).

14. Cf. Taylor, 73–74.

15. Cf. chap. 5 at n. 2 (p. 103); app. 5 at n. 16 (p. 247).

16. In his literal translation in *The Interlinear Greek-English New Testament*, 3rd ed. (London: Bagster, 1974), Alfred Marshall indicates the ambiguities by bracketing, both in Galatians and in Romans.

Chapter 8

Mercantile Images

1. On *societas*, cf. the patriarchal joint family (chap. 5, nn. 6 and 12; chap. 6, n. 1). See also Buckland, *Textbook*, 506–14 and index; Jolo-

wicz, *Introduction*, 309–11; Jolowicz, *Introduction 3*, 295–97 and index of both; Thomas, 300–304 and index; Schulz, *Roman Law*, 549–54; Crook, 229–36. For the developed law, see Charles H. Monro, *Digest 17.2.: Pro Socio* (Cambridge: Cambridge University Press, 1902) and standard works. J. Paul Sampley, *Pauline Partnership in Christ* (Philadelphia: Fortress, 1980) is an extended treatment centering on the concept of *societas*.

2. Horowitz, 557–64; Herzog 1:213–33 on joint property and 2:155–66 on partnership; Cohn, 275–81 ("Partnership"); John D. M. Derrett, "The Footwashing in John 13 and the Alienation of Judas Iscariot," *RIDA* 24 (1977):3–19 at 10–13.

3. Arthur L. Corbin, *Corbin on Contracts* (St. Paul, Minn.: West Publishing, 1950, 1972) 2:662–67.

4. Ball, 45–46, suggests that the giving of a ring in betrothal derives from the giving of an earnest for the possible damages for breach of promise. *Arra sponsalicia* was known in Roman law: Buckland, *Textbook*, 112; Jolowicz, *Introduction*, 535; Thomas, 420; Schulz, *Roman Law*, 109.

5. Gaius, *Institutes* 3.139; Francis de Zulueta, *The Roman Law of Sale* (Oxford: Clarendon, 1945, 1966), 22–24; Buckland, *Textbook*, 481–82; Jolowicz, *Introduction*, 525–26; Jolowicz, *Introduction 3*, 290–91; Crook, 220–21; Thomas, 280–81. Thomas cites the modern discussion, which is of the law later than our period.

6. Fritz Pringsheim, *The Greek Law of Sale* (Weimar: Bohlaus Nachfolger, 1950), 333–439, includes in his discussion of *arra* a comparison with Roman law. Cf. also Jolowicz, *Introduction*, 304; Jones, *Greek Law*, 229–31; Beauchet 4:421–34.

7. James Stark, *Voices and Echoes from the Braes of Bennachie* (Aberdeen: James Smith, 1923), vi; C. S. Lewis, *The Great Divorce* (London: Geoffrey Bles, 1946; Collins, 1972, 1977), 8.

8. Corbin, *Contracts* (*supra*, n. 5) 1A:385–451.

9. Horowitz, 503–4.

10. See app. 5 at nn. 18–19 (p. 248) and references there.

11. Cf. Jolowicz, *Introduction*, 430; Jolowicz, *Introduction 3*, 416.

12. Ibid.

Chapter 9

Redemption

The main working sources for this chapter have been John D. M. Derrett's *Law in the New Testament*, particularly 389–460 ("The Trial of Jesus and the Redemption"); David Daube, *Studies in Biblical Law* (Cambridge: Cambridge University Press, 1947; New York: Ktav, 1969) (hereafter cited as Daube, *Studies*), particularly 1–73 ("Law in the Narratives"); idem, *The New Testament and Rabbinic Judaism* (London: Athlone, 1956) (hereafter cited as Daube, *Judaism*), particularly 268–84 ("Redemption"); idem, *The Exodus Pattern in the Bible* (London: Faber, 1963) (hereafter cited as Daube, *Exodus*). Leggett also illuminates the area.

There are, of course, a great many theological works on redemption. Derrett, 456–60, gives a useful background bibliography. Leggett, 303–11, does likewise, focusing mainly on works relating to the go'el.

1. Cf. Daube, *Studies*, 60–61. Professor Daube is Jewish.

2. Cf. Henri Hubert and Marcel Mauss, *Sacrifice: Its Nature and Function*, trans. W. D. Halls (London: Cohen and West, 1964); Michael F. C. Bourdillon and Meyer Fortes, eds., *Sacrifice* (London and New York: Academic, 1980).

3. James G. Frazer, *The Golden Bough*, 3rd ed., 12 vols. (London: Macmillan, 1911–15), with supplementary volume, *Aftermath* (London: Macmillan, 1936). *The Dying God* forms part 3 of the *Bough* and is vol. 4 of the work. *Aftermath* has additional material. Adonis, Attis, and Osiris form the subject of vols. 5 and 6, while Balder the Beautiful is dealt with in vols. 10 and 11.

4. Daube, *Studies*, 60–61.

5. See introductory note to this chapter.

6. For what follows, see Daube, Derrett, and Leggett as cited in the introductory note.

7. See Daube, Derrett, and Leggett, and Edward Neufield, "Ius Redemptionis in Ancient Hebrew Law," *RIDA* 8 (1961):29–40; Reuven Yaron, "Redemption of Persons in the Ancient Near East," *RIDA* 6 (1959):155–76. On self-sale, see chap. 2 at n. 7 and following (pp. 33-35).

8. Cf. Raymond Westbrook, "Jubilee Laws," *Israel Law Review* 6 (1971):209–26; Cohen 1:159–78 ("Civil Bondage in Jewish and Roman Law").

9. Cf. Raymond Westbrook, "Redemption of Land," *Israel Law Review* 6 (1971):367–75.

10. Cf. chap. 4 at nn. 12–15 (pp. 72-73); Leggett, passim; Horowitz, 283–85; M. Burrows, "The Marriage of Boaz and Ruth," *JBL* 59 (1940):445–54. Westbrook, "Redemption," 371–75, also comments on Ruth.

11. See Hyman E. Goldin, *Hebrew Criminal Law and Procedure* (New York: Twayne, 1952). The work is a commentary on crimes and the provisions of Mishnah, *Sanhedrin* and *Makkot*, that deal with courts

and procedure. See also Cohn, 530–31 ("Blood-Avenger") and 531–32 ("City of Refuge").

12. De Vaux, 10–12; cf. Cohn, n. 11.

13. See also Daube, *Exodus*, passim.

14. Cf. such passages as Rom. 6:18, 22; 7:23; 1 Cor. 15:57; Gal. 4:5; 5:1; Col. 2:14; Eph. 4:8; 1 Peter 1:18–19.

15. Yaron, "Redemption of Persons" (see above, n. 7), 167; Daube, *Judaism*, 272–84; Daube, *Exodus*, 42–46.

16. Buckland, *Slavery*, 307–17. Cf. chap. 2 at n. 4 (pp. 30-31); chap. 3 at n. 20 (p. 61).

17. Cf. chap. 2, "Slavery."

18. Neufeld, "Ius Redemptionis" (see above, n. 7), 32–40. For what follows, see Derrett, 398–401.

19. Derrett, 399–400.

Appendix 1

Of Metaphors and Analogies

The argument'and discussion in this chapter draw, *inter alia*, on the following works: James Bannerman, *Analogy, Considered as a Guide to Truth, and Applied as an Aid to Faith* (Edinburgh: T. & T. Clark, 1864); Edwyn R. Bevan, *Symbolism and Belief* (London: Allen and Unwin, 1938), especially 297–317 ("Pragmatism and Analogy"); Bishop Joseph Butler, *The Analogy of Religion, Natural and Revealed, to the Constitution and Course of Nature* (1736), Introduction (the nature and application of analogical reasoning); George B. Caird, *Language and Imagery of the Bible* (London: Duckworth, 1980); Charles K. Ogden and Ivor A. Richards, *The Meaning of Meaning*, 10th ed. (London: Routledge and Kegan Paul, 1949); Humphrey Palmer, *Analogy* (London: Macmillan, 1971); Paul Ricoeur, *The Rule of Metaphor*, trans. R. Czerny (London: Routledge and Kegan Paul, 1978).

John Bunyan's "Author's Introduction" to *The Pilgrim's Progress* is instructive, as are many of C. S. Lewis's works. Cf. also Brian Barry, "On Analogy," *Political Studies* 23 (1975):208–24; Brenda E. F. Beck, "The Metaphor as Mediator Between Semantic and Analogic Modes of Thought," *Current Anthropology* 19 (1978):83–97; Mary McD. Shideler, "Philosophies and Fairy Tales," *Theology Today* 30 (1973):14–24.

1. For the purpose of this discussion I will use the terms interchangeably.

2. I have seen this happen in discussions that try to synthesize the legal elements of the concept of redemption; cf. chap. 9. Cf. also my friend I. Howard Marshall's chapter in Robert J. Banks, ed., *Reconciliation and Hope* (Exeter, U.K.: Paternoster Press, 1974), 153–69 at 158.

3. A. Square [Edwin A. Abbott], *Flatland. A Romance of Many Dimensions* (London: Seeley, 1884; New York: Dover, 1958).

4. Cf. James Barr, *The Semantics of Biblical Language* (London: Oxford University Press, 1961), 109.

5. This point depends upon one's view of inspiration. I do not believe that the God of love would leave us unprovided with reliable necessary information. Indeed, we are given much more than we need.

6. Cf. C. S. Lewis, "Transposition," in *Screwtape Proposes a Toast and Other Pieces* (London: Collins, 1965) or in *Transposition and other Addresses* (London: Geoffrey Bles, 1949).

7. Cf. C. S. Lewis, *The Pilgrim's Regress* (London: Geoffrey Bles, 1933; reprint ed. London: Collins, 1977).

8. The quoted words are the answer to the first question of the Shorter Catechism agreed upon by the Westminster Assembly, 1647.

Appendix 2

The Systems of Law

My basic sources for this chapter are as follows. For Roman law I have used: Buckland, *Textbook*, 1–55; Crook, 68–97; Jolowicz, *Introduction* and Jolowicz, *Introduction 3*; Schulz, *Roman Law*; Schulz, *History*; Thomas, 13–124; and Adolf Berger, *Encyclopedic Dictionary of Roman Law*, Transactions of the American Philosophical Society, n.s., vol. 43, pt. 2 (Philadelphia: The American Philosophical Society, 1953, 1968). In addition, William A. J. (Alan) Watson, *Law Making in the Later Roman Republic* (Oxford: Clarendon, 1974) (hereafter cited as Watson, *Law Making*) is very useful.

For Jewish law I have used: Baron; De Vaux; Falk, *Hebrew Law*; Falk, *Jewish Law*; Herzog; Horowitz; Juster; Schürer, vol. 2; Smallwood; articles in the *Jewish Encyclopedia* (mostly available in Cohn, 5–146); Danby's introduction to Mishnah; S. E. Loewenstamm, "Law," in *The World History of the Jewish People*, Jewish History Publications (London: Allen, 1963–) 3:231–67 with notes, 334–37; Martin Noth, *The Laws in the Pentateuch and Other Studies*, trans. D. R. Ap-Thomas, 2nd ed. (Edinburgh: Oliver and Boyd, 1966); and Jacob Neusner, *The Rab-*

binic *Traditions about the Pharisees before 70*, 3 vols. (Leiden: Brill, 1971) (hereafter cited as Neusner, *Traditions*); idem, *Early Rabbinic Judaism. Historical Studies in Religion, Literature and Art.* Studies in Judaism in Late Antiquity, vol. 13. (Leiden: Brill, 1975) (hereafter cited as Neusner, *Judaism*).

For Greek law I have used: Beauchet; Harrison; Jones, *Greek Law*; McDowell; Robert J. Bonner, *Lawyers and Litigants in Ancient Athens. The Genesis of the Legal Profession*, Studia Historica no. 66 (Chicago: University of Chicago Press, 1927; Rome: "L'Erma" di Bretschneider, 1970); George M. Calhoun, *Introduction to Greek Legal Science*, ed. Francis de Zulueta (Oxford: Clarendon, 1944) (hereafter cited as Calhoun).

1. Cicero, *De Legibus* 2.23.59.

2. The Twelve Tables, so far as they are known, are printed in Fontes 1:21–75, and are translated in *Ancient Roman Statutes*, trans. Allan C. Johnson, Paul R. Coleman-Norton, and Frank C. Bourne (Austin: University of Texas Press, 1961, 1976), as part of *The Corpus of Roman Law*, ed. Clyde Pharr, vol. 2, doc. 8; *Remains of Old Latin*, trans. Eric H. Warmington, Loeb Classical Library, 4 vols. (London: Heinemann; Cambridge, Mass: Harvard University Press, 1935–40, 1961) 3:424–515.

3. Trajan's response to Pliny (c. A.D. 112) as to how to deal with Christians in Bithynia is a model example: (Pliny, *Letters* 10. 96, 97). See also Antony M. Honoré, *Emperors and Lawyers* (London: Duckworth, 1981), 24–53 ("The Rescript System"). Cf. Millar, 328–41.

4. Jolowicz, *Introduction*, 43–55; Jolowicz, *Introduction 3*, 45–57; Thomas R. S. Broughton, *The Magistrates of the Roman Republic*, 2 vols. (New York: American Philological Association, 1951–52).

5. Buckland, *Textbook*, 8–12.

6. Francis de Zulueta, *The Roman Law of Sale* (Oxford: Clarendon, 1945–1949, 1957); James Mackintosh, *The Roman Law of Sale*, 2nd ed. (Edinburgh: T. & T. Clark, 1907); Watson, *Law Making*, 82–87.

7. Reference point for chap. 3, n. 12.

8. On the praetors, see Jolowicz, *Introduction*, 195–241; Jolowicz, *Introduction 3*, 191–232; Schulz, *Roman Law*, 11–70; Schulz, *History*, index; David Daube, "The Peregrine Praetor," *JRS* 41 (1951):66–70; John M. Kelly, "The Growth-Pattern of the Praetor's Edict," *Irish Jurist* 1 (1966):340–55; idem, *Roman Litigation* (Oxford: Clarendon, 1966), 85–101 ("The Standard of the Praetorship"); William A. J. Watson, "The Development of the Praetor's Edict," *JRS* 60 (1970):105–19; Watson, *Law Making*, 31–100. The examples I have outlined draw from both praetors. The permanent edict of the praetor urbanus is translated as doc. 244 of *Ancient*

Roman Statutes (see above, n. 2), and is available as a Latin text in Fontes 1:335–89.

9. Buckland, *Textbook*, 20–35; Jolowicz, *Introduction*, 384–403; Jolowicz, *Introduction 3*, 374–94; Schulz, *History*, 102–23; Peter G. Stein, *Regulae Iuris* (Edinburgh: Edinburgh University Press, 1966); Watson, *Law Making*, 101–68. Cf. Clyde Pharr, "Roman Legal Education," *Classical Journal* 31 (1938–39):257–70.

10. Antony M. Honoré, *Gaius* (Oxford: Clarendon, 1962).

11. Herzog 1:xix. Cf. Derrett, xxi–xxiv; Schürer 2:464–87.

12. Mishnah, *Aboth* 1.1 (cf. Deut. 30:14); Mishnah, xvii–xxiii; Horowitz, 11–12.

13. Horowitz, 8–39; Baron 1:140–48; Falk, *Hebrew Law*, 15–43; Falk, *Jewish Law*, 2:5–34; Schürer 2:314–87; Neusner, *Traditions* 3:143–79 ("Oral Transmission: Defining the Problem"; "Oral Tradition"); Neusner, *Judaism*, 3–33 ("The Meaning of Oral Torah"); Mishnah, xiii–xxvii; cf. Jacob Neusner, "The Use of the Mishnah for the History of Judaism Prior to the Time of the Mishnah," *Journal for the Study of Judaism*, 2 (1980):177–85.

14. Robert H. Charles, ed., *The Apocrypha and Pseudepigrapha of the Old Testament*, 2 vols. (Oxford: Oxford University Press, 1913) 2:vii–xi (General Introduction to vol. 2), 2:1 (Introduction to the Book of Jubilees; the translation of the book is found in 2:11–82); cf. also 2:94–122 (the Letter to Aristeas), and 2:83–89 (introduction to the Letter to Aristeas by Herbert T. Andrews). On the Essenes, see Schürer 2:555–90, with bibliography on pp. 555–58, and Geza Vermes, *The Dead Sea Scrolls in English*, 2nd. ed. (London: Penguin Books, 1975), and works there cited, esp. Roland De Vaux, *The Archaeology of the Dead Sea Scrolls* (London: Darton, Longman and Todd, 1973).

15. Mishnah, *Sanhedrin* and index, s.v. "court"; Horowitz, 626–29; Schürer 2:199–236; Roy A. Stewart, "Judicial Procedure in New Testament Times," *Evangelical Quarterly*, 47 (1975):94–107; Solomon Zeitlin, "The Political Synedrion and the Religious Synedrion," *Jewish Quarterly Review*, 36 (1945):109–40; idem, "Synedrion in the Judeo-Hellenistic Literature and Sanhedrin in the Tannaitic Literature," *Jewish Quarterly Review* 36 (1945):307–15; (the latter two articles are also included in Solomon Zeitlin, *Studies in the Early History of Judaism*, 2 vols. [New York: Ktav, 1973] 1:275–302 and 1:303–11 respectively); Hugo Mantel, *Studies in the History of the Sanhedrin* (Cambridge, Mass. and London: Harvard University Press, 1965), esp. 54–101. Cf. Falk, *Hebrew Law*, 15–43; Falk, *Jewish Law*, 1:5–34; and Neusner, "The Use of the Mishnah" (see above, n. 13); Winter.

16. Cf. Acts 4:5–22; 5:17–42; 6:12–7:60; 22:30–23:10; 23:14–15.

17. F. F. Bruce, *The Books and the Parchments*, 2nd ed. (London: Pickering and Inglis, 1953), 94–111; Roland K. Harrison, *Introduction to the Old Testament* (Grand Rapids: Eerdmans, 1969; London: Tyndale, 1970), 260–88.

18. Mishnah, xiii–xxxii; Horowitz, 12–17. Rabbi Judah's Mishnah is the one we know, though it refers to others, cf. Mishnah, xxi n. 6.

19. *The Babylonian Talmud* (with English translation), 34 vols. (London and New York: Soncino Press, 1935–48).

20. Horowitz, 52–58.

21. Josephus, *Jewish War* 2.8.2–14, *Jewish Antiquities* 18.1.2.–6; 1.3–6; Schürer 2:404–14, with bibliography on pp. 381–82; Jean Le Moyne, *Les Sadducéens* (Paris: Librairie Lecoffre, J. Gabalda et cie, 1972); Solomon Zeitlin, *Studies in the Early History of Judaism*, 2 vols. (New York: Ktav, 1973) 2:259–91 ("The Sadducees and the Pharisees").

22. Derrett, xxxiii–xxxiv. On the Pharisees, see Louis Finkelstein, *The Pharisees: The Sociological Background of Their Faith*, 3rd ed., 2 vols. (Philadelphia: Jewish Publication Society of America, 1962); Schürer 2:388–403, with bibliography on pp. 381–82; see also n. 23 below. But cf. Sanders, 33–75, esp. 60–62.

23. Derrett, xxxiv–xxxvi; Neusner, *Traditions* 3:239–48 ("The Missing Traditions"); 3:309–19 ("Summary: The Rabbinic Traditions about the Pharisees before 70"); and a chapter with the same title in Neusner, *Judaism*, 73–89 (also in *Journal of Jewish Studies* 22 [1971]:1–18). See also Solomon Zeitlin, "The Pharisees: A Historical Study," *Jewish Quarterly Review* 52 (1961):97–129; idem, "The Pharisees and the Gospel," Israel Davidson, ed., *Essays and Studies in Memory of Linda M. Miller* (New York: The Jewish Theological Seminary of America, 1938), 235–86; idem, "The Origin of the Pharisees Reaffirmed," *Jewish Quarterly Review* 59 (1969):255–67; the last three articles are included in Zeitlin's *Studies in the Early History of Judaism* (supra, n. 15) 2:226–58, 292–343, 344–57.

24. Neusner, *Traditions*, 3:320–68 ("Appendix: Bibliographical Reflections"), contains, particularly in the lists on pp. 364–66, a major warning of the dangers.

25. Davies, 1–16 ("Introduction: Palestine and Diaspora Judaism"); Sanders.

26. Cf. chap. 3 at nn. 12–13 (p. 58).

27. See chap. 2 following n. 12 (pp. 39-43).

28. Calhoun, 2; cf. McDowell, 8.

29. Harrison 2:1–68; Bonner, passim; Calhoun, 30–75.

30. On Athens: Beauchet; Harrison. A growing amount of work on

Greek law is published in the *Revue Pour l'Histoire des Droits d'Antiquité*. On Egypt: Raphael Taubenschlag, *The Law of Graeco-Roman Egypt in the Light of the Papyri*, 2nd ed. (Warsaw: Panstwowe Wydawnictwo Naukowe, 1955).

Appendix 3

Law in the Provinces

My sources have been Jolowicz, *Introduction*, 66–71; Jolowicz, *Introduction 3*, 63–71; Jones, *Greek City*; Jones, *Cities*; Magie; Millar; Ramsay, *Church*; Ramsay, *Cities*; and Ramsay, *Teaching*. Ramsay's *Commentary*, *Letters*, and *St. Paul* also have relevant data. Millar, 363–464 ("Cities, Provincial Councils and Associations") is very useful.

In addition I have used in this chapter: William T. Arnold, *Roman Provincial Administration*, 3rd ed., ed. E. S. Bouchier et al. (Oxford: Blackwell, 1914); Frank F. Abbott and Allan C. Johnson, *Municipal Administration in the Roman Empire* (Princeton: Princeton University Press, 1926); H. T. F. Duckworth, "The Roman Provincial System" in *The Beginnings of Christianity*, ed. Frederick J. Foakes Jackson and Kirsopp Lake (London: Macmillan, 1920) 1:171–217; Arnold H. M. Jones, "Rome and the Provincial Cities," *Tijdschrift voor Rechtsgeschiedenis* 39 (1971):513–51; Andrew Lintott, "What was the 'Imperium Romanum'?" *Greece and Rome* 28 (1981):53–67; Theodore Mommsen, *The History of Rome: The Provinces*, trans. W. P. Dickson, 2 vols. (London: Bentley, 1886); James S. Reid, *The Municipalities of the Roman Empire* (Cambridge: Cambridge University Press, 1913); George H. Stevenson, *Roman Provincial Administration* (Oxford: Blackwell, 1939); John H.W. G. Liebeschuetz, *Antioch: City and Imperial Administration in the Later Roman Empire* (Oxford: Clarendon, 1972) provides some interesting data, though much later than our period.

1. Robert M. Grant, *Augustus to Constantine* (New York: Harper and Row, 1970; London: Collins, 1971), 25–26, quoting Augustus *Res Gestae Divi Augusti* 8.4.10–8.5.3. See also Ernest G. Hardy, ed., *The Monumentum Ancyranum* (Oxford: Clarendon, 1923), 52–60. Cf. *supra* chaps. 2 and 3.

2. For our purposes the classification of provinces as imperial or senatorial, depending on who appointed the governor and to whom he was technically subject (if the distinction truly ever existed), is unimportant; cf. Fergus G. B. Millar, "The Emperor, The Senate and the Provinces," *JRS* 56 (1966):156–66.

3. For what follows, see Schürer 1:125–558; Smallwood, 1–200; Josephus, *Antiquities*, Books 14–22, *Jewish War*, Books 1–4; Michael Grant, *The Jews in the Roman World* (London: Weidenfeld and Nicolson, 1971), 1–205.

4. Schürer 1:171–3; Smallwood, 4–11.

5. The procurator was a provincial governor of equestrian rank. Cf. Arnold H. M. Jones, *Studies in Roman Government and Law* (Oxford: Blackwell, 1960), 117–25 ("Procurators and Prefects in the Early Principate"); R. P. Saller, "Promotion and Patronage in Equestrian Careers," *JRS* 70 (1980):44–59; Millar, 275–361 ("The Equestrian Order and the Senate").

6. Lee I. Levine, *Caesarea under Roman Rule*, Studies in Judaism in Late Antiquity, vol. 7 (Leiden: Brill, 1975).

7. See also Josephus, *Antiquities* 19.8.2.

8. Jesus was crucified under the power of the governor to execute for political reasons (*coercitio*), a general power that did not require the usual formal trial or proof of breach of a specific criminal law. The power was exercised by Pilate as governor, not as judge. As such, this power was closer to powers under martial law, and it is not helpful to analyze the events from the standpoint of modern ideas of criminal law. See Derrett 389–460 ("The Trial of Jesus and the Doctrine of the Redemption"); Sherwin-White, *Society*, 1–23 ("Coercitio, Cognition, and Imperium in the First Century A.D."), 24–47 ("The Trial of Christ in the Synoptic Gospels"). It is this political element that explains the approach of the Jewish authorities (Luke 20:20; 23:1–5, 13–25; Matt. 27:1–2, 11–14; Mark 15:1–5, 14–15). Contra, Winter, esp. 90–130.

9. Acts 24:1–23; 25:1–12, 14–21; 28:17–30. Cf. Sherwin-White, *Society*, 48–70 ("Paul before Felix and Festus"). Ibid., 108–19 ("Paul at Rome"), gives an account of how the trial at Rome would have proceeded. Bruce, *History*, 343–45 reviews current debate; cf. Ramsay, *Teaching*, 346–82.

10. Sherwin-White, *Society*, 71–98 ("Paul and the Cities"). Punishment could be severe; e.g., Cyzicus in Asia lost its freedom for a period after 20 B.C. for allowing the execution of Roman citizens; see Cassius Dio 54. 7.6–23; 57.24.6; Tacitus, *Annals* 4:36.2; Magie, 474; Jones, *Greek City*, 86–88. Cf. chap. 3 at n. 22 (p. 62).

11. Aulus Gellius, 20.16.13. Cf. Sherwin-White, *Citizenship*, 58–95; Abbott and Johnson, *Municipal Administration*, 3–9, 56–83.

12. Thus Cicero, *Letters to Atticus* 6.1.15, speaks of the edict he issued on arriving in Cilicia, saying he had followed that of Quintus Mucius Scaevola (Asia, 96 B.C.) in many details (Cicero, *Letters to Atticus*, trans. E. O. Windstedt, 3 vols., Loeb Classical Library [London: William Heinemann; Cambridge, Mass.: Harvard University

Press, 1912] 1:431). But cf. Peter A. Brunt, "The Administrators of Roman Egypt," *JRS* 65 (1975):132–6 ("Legal Experience and Duties").

13. Cicero, loc. cit., indicates that the Greeks had sought the privilege of using their own procedures amongst themselves (cf. his *Letters to Atticus* 6.2.4.).

14. G. P. Burton, "Proconsuls, Assizes and the Administration of Justice under the Empire," *JRS* 65 (1975):50–63.

15. Cicero, loc. cit., n. 12.

16. Schulz, *History*, 127; William W. Buckland, "L'Edictum provinciale," *Revue Historique de Droit Francais et Étranger* (1934):81–96.

17. Ludwig Mitteis, *Reichsrecht und Volksrecht* (Leipzig: Teubner, 1891; Leiden: Brill, 1963); Raphael Taubenschlag, *The Law of Graeco-Roman Egypt in the Light of the Papyri*, 2nd ed. (Warsaw: Panstwowe Wydawnictwo Naukowe, 1955), 1–55.

18. Taubenschlag, *The Law of Graeco-Roman Egypt*, 46–55.

19. Cicero, loc. cit., n. 12; Magie 173–74; Schulz, *History*, 64–65; Peter G. Stein, *Regulae Iuris* (Edinburgh: Edinburgh University Press, 1966), 26–48.

20. Antony M. Honoré, *Gaius* (Oxford: Clarendon, 1962), 70–96; Schulz, *History*, 123. Other famous but later jurists are known to have been provincials.

21. Cf. n. 18. Professor Derrett has pointed out to me that the Jews in Egypt used non-Jewish forms, and that in Israel in the time of the Epistles they had the choice of using their own courts or the Hellenistic courts that had been brought in by immigrants and conquerors. This choice of law can be generalized further in other provinces, increasing the likelihood of the knowledge of Roman forms.

22. This argument was crystallized for me by Greer M. Taylor, "The Function of Pistis Christou in Galatians," *JBL* 85 (1966):76.

Appendix 4

The Epistles

My sources have been standard commentaries and Bible dictionaries and encyclopedias; Jones, *Greek City* and Jones, *Cities*; Magie; Ramsay, *Cities*; Ramsay, *Church*; Ramsay, *Commentary*; Ramsay, *Letters*; Ramsay, *St. Paul*; and Ramsay, *Teaching*.

Additional works are: Barbara Levick, *Roman Colonies in Southern Asia Minor* (Oxford: Clarendon, 1967); Joseph B. Lightfoot, *Biblical Essays* (1893); *The Epistles of Paul: Galatians* (1900); *Colossians and Ephesians* (1876); *Philippians* (1891) (all London: Macmillan) contain useful background material; William M. Ramsay, *The Cities and Bishoprics of Phrygia*, 2 vols. (Oxford: Clarendon, 1895–97); idem, *The Historical Geography of Asia Minor* (London: John Murray, 1890; Amsterdam: Hakkert, 1962).

1. Cf. John A. T. Robinson, *Redating the New Testament* (London: S.C.M., 1976), 53–85.

2. Cf. Henry J. Cadbury, "Erastus of Corinth," *JBL* 50 (1931):42–58; Percival N. Harrison, *Paulines and Pastorals* (London: Villiers, 1964), 100–105 ("Erastus and His Pavement"). On the aedileship, see Buckland, *Textbook*, 491–92; Jolowicz *Introduction*, 48–49; Jolowicz, *Introduction 3*, 49–50, 293–94.

3. *On Galatians*, 2. pr.

4. Ramsay put the view forward particularly in his *Church in the Roman Empire*, 8–15, 97–111, and in the *Historical Commentary*, 1–234 ("Historical Introduction"). As Bruce (*infra*) says, "The solid evidence . . . is . . . in . . . his [Ramsay's] *Cities and Bishoprics of Phrygia* and his earlier *Historical Geography of Asia Minor* (1890)." For a recent review, see F. F. Bruce, "Galatian Problems. 2. North or South Galatians?" *Bulletin of the John Rylands Library* 52 (1969–70):243–66.

5. Ernest G. Hardy, ed., *The Monumentum Ancyranum* (Oxford: Clarendon, 1923); Peter A. Brunt and J. M. Moore, eds., *Res Gestae Divi Augusti. The Achievements of the Divine Augustus* (Oxford: Oxford University Press, 1967).

6. Ramsay's view was that Greek or even Seleucid law was present (*Historical Commentary*, viii, 337–44; 349–56; 370–75; 381–85; 391–93); on the last page noted, he cites this as favoring the South Galatian theory. Cf. Ramsay, *Cities*, 203 n. 1, and William M. Calder, "Adoption and Inheritance in Galatians," *Journal of Theological Studies* 31 (1930):372–74.

7. See last note.

8. Levick, virtually passim; the works of Ramsay cited in the introductory note; and Magie, 453–67, show the Romanizing effort.

9. App. 3 at nn. 12 and 15 (pp. 218, 219).

10. Chap. 3 at n. 21 and thereafter (p. 62); app. 3 at n. 10 (p. 214) and *infra* re Thessalonica.

Appendix 5

Paul

There are many books about Paul, to say nothing of articles. Of those already cited I would repeat Ramsay, *St. Paul*, Ramsay, *Cities*, and Sherwin-White, *Society*.

To these may be added: F. F. Bruce: "Galatian Problems. 1. Autobiographical Data" *Bulletin of the John Rylands Library* 51 (1968–69):292–309; Bruce, *History*, 234–46 ("Paul: The Early Years"); idem, "Paul and Jerusalem," *Tyndale Bulletin* 17 (1968):3–25; idem, *Paul: Apostle of the Free Spirit*, 2nd ed. (Exeter, U.K.: Paternoster, 1980); published in the U.S. under the title *Paul: Apostle of the Heart Set Free* (Grand Rapids: Eerdmans); William J. Conybeare and John S. Howson, *The Life and Epistles of St. Paul* (London: Longmans, 1880); George Ogg, *The Chronology of the Life of Paul* (London: Epworth, 1968); William C. van Unnik, *Tarsus or Jerusalem. The City of Paul's Youth*, trans. George Ogg (London: Epworth, 1962). I cite from the version in *Sparsa Collecta: Collected Essays of W. C. van Unnik*. Supplement to *Novum Testamentum*, vol. 29 (Leiden: Brill, 1973).

1. Cf. Derrett, 396–98, esp. 397.

2. Van Unnik, 265 n. 8.

3. Van Unnik, op. cit. in introductory note to this chapter.

4. E.g., Davies; Sanders.

5. Nathan Drazin, *History of Jewish Education from 515 B.C.E. to 220 C.E.* (Baltimore: The Johns Hopkins Press, 1940); Eliezer Ebner, *Elementary Education in Ancient Israel* (New York: Bloch, 1956); John T. Townsend, "Ancient Education in the Time of the Early Roman Empire" in *Early Church History*, ed. Stephen Benko and John J. O'Rourke (London: Oliphants, 1972), also published as *The Catacombs and the Colosseum* (Valley Forge: Judson, 1971), 129–63; Schürer 2:415–63 ("School and Synagogue").

6. Cf. Derrett, xxxvi–xli, and his inaugural lecture, "An Oriental Lawyer Looks at the Trial of Jesus and the Doctrine of the Redemption" (London: School of Oriental and African Studies, London University, 1966), 6–9. David Daube, "Rabbinic Methods of Interpretation and Hellenistic Rhetoric," *Hebrew Union College Annual* 22 (1949):239–64.

7. See the discussion of Jewish law in app. 2 (pp. 200–8).

8. Baron 2:298–307 on influences, 430 nn. 10–11; Cohen 1:1–30 ("Jewish and Roman Law"). Cf. S. Lieberman, "Roman Legal Institutions in Early Rabbinics and in the Acta Martyrum," *Jewish Quar-*

terly Review 34 (1944–45):1–57. There is an interesting later work (probably A.D. 400–425), the *Lex Dei* or *Mosaicarum et Romanorum Collatio*, text in Fontes 2:541–89, and trans. Moses Hyamson (London: Oxford University Press, 1913), which shows a comparative interest but without real discussion. For literature, see Cohen 1:3; Schulz, *History*, 311–14, n. LL at 344.

9. Bruce, *History*, 230.

10. Pliny, *Natural History*, 5.91–92; Magie, 470; Jones, *Cities*, 192–96, 199–200, 206–7.

11. Strabo, *Geographia* 14.5.13.

12. Bruce, *History*, 234; Jones, Greek City, 281.

13. Claude A. Pierce, *Conscience in the New Testament* (London: S.C.M., 1955).

14. Cf. chap. 3 at nn. 12–13 (p. 58). Ramsay, *Cities*, 180–86; *Letters*, 142–57.

15. Ramsay, locs. cit.

16. See also chap. 5 at n. 2 on Paul's inheritance (p. 103).

17. Bruce, *History*, 223 n. 3 (i.e. a Hindu [presumably an Indian] and a knight of the Order of the British Empire). It is occasionally said that Paul's citizenship was an invention by Luke, improbable on the facts and unreliable as being only reported by Luke. An example of the weakness of this "case" can be found in Erwin R. Goodenough, "The Perspective of Acts" in *Studies in Luke-Acts*, ed. Leander E. Keck and J. Louis Martyn (Nashville: Abingdon, 1966; London: S.P.C.K., 1976), 55–56.

18. Fritz Schulz, "Roman Registers of Births and Birth Certificates," *JRS* 32 (1942):78–91 and *JRS* 33 (1943):55–64; Sherwin-White, *Citizenship*, 314–16. Cf. chap. 3 at n. 19 (p. 61) and chap. 4 at n. 27 (p. 80).

19. Sherwin-White, *Society*, 147–49; John D. M. Derrett, "Further Light on the Narratives of the Nativity," *Novum Testamentum* 17 (1975):81–108 at 87–95. Cf. discussion on the census of Quirinius and literature cited, Schürer 1:399–427; Sherwin-White, *Society*, 162–71.

20. See app. 2, n. 10, and text following n. 8 (pp. 199–200).

GENERAL INDEX

NEW TESTAMENT SCRIPTURE INDEX